GROWING GIVERS' HEARTS

GROWING GIVERS' HEARTS

Treating Fundraising as Ministry

Thomas H. Jeavons and Rebekah Burch Basinger

Jossey-Bass Publishers
San Francisco

Epigraph in Chapter 4 taken from *God Is Enough* (Daybreak) Copyright © 1995 by The Zondervan Corporation. Used by permission of Zondervan Publishing House.

Epigraph in Chapter 8 from Worship Resource 725, *Hymnal: A Worship Book*, Mennonite Publishing House, Scottdale, PA, 1992.

Epigraph in Chapter 9 from J. Oswald Sanders, *Spiritual Leadership*, Moody Press, Chicago, IL, 1967, p. 20.

Scripture taken from the *HOLY BIBLE, NEW INTERNATIONAL VERSION. NIV.* Copyright 1973, 1978, 1984 by International Bible Society. Used by permission of Zondervan Publishing House. All rights reserved.

Jossey-Bass books and products are available through most bookstores. To contact Jossey-Bass directly, call (888) 378-2537, fax to (800) 605-2665, or visit our website at www.josseybass.com.

Substantial discounts on bulk quantities of Jossey-Bass books are available to corporations, professional associations, and other organizations. For details and discount information, contact the special sales department at Jossey-Bass.

Manufactured in the United States of America on Lyons Falls Turin Book. This paper is acid-free and 100 percent totally chlorine-free.

Library of Congress Cataloging-in-Publication Data

Jeavons, Thomas.
    Growing givers' hearts : treating fundraising as ministry / Thomas H. Jeavons and Rebekah Burch Basinger.— 1st ed.
        p.   cm.
    Includes bibliographical references and index.
    ISBN 0-7879-4829-2 (alk. paper)
    1. Church fundraising. I. Basinger, Rebekah Burch, date. II. Title.
BV722.5.J43   2000
254'.8—dc21   99-006929

FIRST EDITION

HB Printing   10 9 8 7 6 5 4 3 2

CONTENTS

Acknowledgments   ix
Introduction: Fundraising and the Expression of Faith   1

PART ONE
What Is Christian Fundraising?   15

1. Creating Resources for God's Work   17
2. What the Bible Says About Giving and Asking   37
3. A Brief History of Christian Fundraising   55

PART TWO
Six Essential Characteristics of Fundraising as a Ministry   69

4. Confidence in God's Abundance   71
5. A Holistic Perspective on "Kingdom Work"   87
6. Clarity About Core Theological Beliefs   99
7. Giving Donors Opportunities for Participation   114
8. Integrated Organizational Planning   131
9. Spiritually Mature Leadership   145

PART THREE
The Fundraiser's Ministry   163

10. Fundraising as a Calling   165
11. Fundraising as an Invitation to Cooperate with
     God's Grace   178

References   189
The Authors   195
Index   197

ACKNOWLEDGMENTS

A GREAT MANY individuals and organizations contributed to the work that bears our names. We wish first to express our heartfelt thanks to the leaders, staff, and numerous volunteers and donors at the seven organizations that permitted us to study them over the past two years: Compassion International, Union Gospel Mission of Seattle, the Catholic Charities of Cleveland, the Roman Catholic Diocese of Tucson, San Francisco Theological Seminary, Fuller Theological Seminary, and Biola University. Each one exemplifies excellence in its own way. We were deeply enriched by the time we spent in each of these working Christian communities, and we hope that we adequately convey in these pages the fine qualities of their ministries.

In our various roles as researchers, consultants, and volunteers, we have also spent time in and learned from other organizations, some of which will be named in the text of this book. Many fundraisers, program staff, executives, consultants, volunteers, and donors in these organizations have also been generous with their time and insight, for which we are grateful.

At different times, different groups of people, some scholars and some practitioners, came together to critique early drafts of various portions of this manuscript. In particular, we want to thank the development staff at the diocese of Tucson for their helpful comments, and we thank Suzanne Feeney, Margaret Harris, and Francis Van Loo—all fine nonprofit management scholars—for their valuable criticisms and suggestions.

Let it be very clear that any misunderstandings and shortcomings in this volume are our own, but we acknowledge that many of the best insights in it we owe to others.

A special word of gratitude must go to Mark Cesnik, a "fellow traveler" we met in the course of this project who provided much appreciated help in the editing of this volume in its final stages.

We are also deeply grateful to the Lilly Endowment, without whose financial support we could not have done this work. In addition, the personal support and wise advice we received from our program officer, Fred Hofheinz, was of enormous value.

Finally, we would like to express special appreciation to our spouses, Gretchen Jeavons and Randall Basinger, for supporting us in this work, for putting up with the travel schedules it imposed, and for abiding the long hours when we were physically at home but not really there—during long stints at the word processor or when our minds focused on this topic even when we were engaged in other activities. We could not have completed this study or this manuscript without their willingness to tend to domestic responsibilities we had to leave unattended.

T.H.J.
R.B.B.

GROWING GIVERS' HEARTS

INTRODUCTION

FUNDRAISING AND THE EXPRESSION OF FAITH

For where your treasure is, there will your heart be also.

—Matthew 6:21

THIS BOOK IS ABOUT the process of fundraising and the dynamics and values of faith. It is written primarily for Christian fundraisers working in Christian organizations and for other persons responsible for guiding and managing those organizations, such as executive staff and board members. This is not a "how to" guide for fundraising practices so much as a "what might be better" exploration of those practices—an exploration that we feel has significant potential for changing the ways Christian organizations do this work. We will talk in some detail about how Christian fundraising is and should be done, but we also want to look deeply at the assumptions underlying the practices.

Readers seeking "101 tips" on how to run an annual fund, conduct a feasibility study, or launch a capital campaign need to look elsewhere. There is no shortage of books offering good advice on these matters. However, as Robert Payton of The Fund Raising School at Indiana University notes, books that "ask questions that might stir doubts or second thoughts in the minds of those [they] intend to persuade" are in far shorter supply (Payton, 1988, p. 63).

This book intends to raise questions, stir doubts, and also provide insights. Hence it should also be of substantial interest to pastors and

Note: Biblical quotations in this book are from the New International Version or other published sources or were translated by the authors.

I

other church leaders, perhaps to Christian fundraisers working in secular institutions, and we hope to scholars and academics with an interest in fundraising.

The focus of the book, as the title suggests, is on the connections that can—and, we argue, should—be made between the ways Christian organizations cultivate donor relationships and ask for money, the ways and reasons people give, and the possibilities that can be created in all of this to nurture and express the faith of both the donors and the fundraisers themselves.

For Christians interested in these matters, interested in the intersection of faith and giving and fundraising, the teaching of Jesus quoted at the start is vitally important and critically insightful. People often do not take full notice, we suspect, of the order of the clauses in this verse; or if they do, they do not see the implications of that order.

Jesus did not say to his disciples, "Your money will follow your heart." That is the conventional wisdom in fundraising. That may well be the best explanation for why volunteers in many organizations are generous donors themselves, but it is not the essence of this teaching of Jesus.

He told his disciples, "Your heart will follow your money." In this teaching, Jesus points out the very powerful connections between the ways people use their wealth and their emotional and spiritual commitments. His words suggest that if we are unsure of where our hearts are, looking at where our treasure is spent (or hoarded) may give us a vital clue.

This book focuses on those very powerful connections. It looks at the relationships between giving and growing in faith and between fundraising among and by Christians and the encouragement or discouragement of faith. Indeed, the central purpose of this book is to explore how Christian fundraisers can make the process of fundraising one that nurtures and facilitates growth in faith for the donors. The book looks at how the process of fundraising can become a fuller expression of the ideals of faith for fundraisers and institutions, as well as for donors.

Who Should Read This and Why

As we said, this book is written primarily for Christian fundraisers and others working with Christian organizations, but we expect that it will be of interest to others as well.

Note that when we mention "Christian organizations" in this volume, we are referring most often to *parachurch* organizations rather than to congregations. We use the term *parachurch* in a way that stretches the conventional usage to encompass such extraliturgical organizations as service agencies, outreach ministries, schools, and other movements that are clearly Christian in sponsorship, character, and purpose but exist outside the immediate control of congregations and perhaps even denominations. Moreover, we include the broad range of such organizations, in terms of theological traditions as well as types of service. Although the term *parachurch* is typically used to refer only to organizations in the evangelical sphere of American Christianity, there are parallel sets of organizations within the Catholic and, to a lesser extent, the mainline Protestant sphere as well. We have studied organizations across this broad range and discuss them all in this book.

We focus on parachurch organizations in this expanded sense, rather than on congregations, for two reasons. The first is because of their growing importance to the church as a whole and the potential impact of the types of fundraising that these organizations do. The second is that these institutions, agencies, and programs—Christian social service agencies, Christian schools, colleges, and seminaries, and other "specialized ministries"—employ many of the same strategies and techniques for fundraising as secular nonprofits. By contrast, most congregations still depend on weekly collections during worship service for most of their operating income. The result is a profound difference in the context within which connections between giving and faith can be drawn in a parachurch organization, as opposed to a congregation.

That said, however, this book will also be valuable to pastors and other congregational leaders, for several reasons. First, the rich potential for spiritual growth in the practice of giving explored here is just as important in congregational life as it is in the giving church members do to parachurch organizations and the relationships they have with those organizations. Second, more and more congregations are getting involved in fundraising beyond the weekly collection, using other techniques for raising money for building improvements, special projects, or endowments. Third, an increasing proportion of the spiritual experiences and theological perspectives of members of congregations are now being shaped by their participation in parachurch organizations. And fourth, despite this (or perhaps because of it), pastors have a special responsibility to educate their members about the broader vision of stewardship and about matters of faith and finances. For all these reasons, the matters explored in this book are important for pastors to understand.

For readers interested in fundraising as scholars or professionals, whether they are people of faith or not, this volume may be important because it proposes a very different paradigm for fundraising. It is a vision of fundraising as a process that is as much concerned with the effect on people's character and values as with the effect on organizations' incomes. Individuals involved in the education of the leaders of Christian institutions, such as the faculty at seminaries and Christian colleges, may find this book a useful teaching tool.

A Subtle but Vital Distinction

Most fundraisers say that all good fundraising, secular or religious, is about building relationships with donors that allow the donors the greatest opportunities to "do good" in ways they care about deeply. That is undoubtedly true. (For an excellent articulation of this philosophy, see Rosso, 1991, especially pp. 3–7.)

Still, the traditional focus of the fundraising process tends to be utilitarian before it is humane or spiritual. Individuals are sought out with the anticipation that they can be persuaded to make a gift to the organization initiating the contact and only secondarily (if at all) with a concern for giving as an opportunity for their personal, moral, or spiritual development. Furthermore, the code of ethics that attempts to provide a moral framework for professional fundraising represents a minimalist approach in ethicists' terms (see the NSFRE's *Donor's Bill of Rights;* National Society of Fund Raising Executives, 1994). This is generally true of professional codes of ethics: they focus on establishing an ethical baseline that is primarily about doing no harm to the donor.

The model of fundraising proposed here puts the humane and the spiritual first. It rests on the idea that relationships with donors should be built around the desire to spur their spiritual growth. The ethical baseline is more proactive and less minimalistic. It makes doing good for the donor a primary concern rather than either a side benefit or a "selling point" to entice the prospect. It is rooted in the Gospel vision that goes beyond respecting one's neighbor to loving one's neighbor.

The research we have been doing over the past several years has revolved around our desire to find out if it is possible for organizations that do fundraising in this way to succeed financially as well as spiritually.

Some Key Terms and Definitions

Before we can describe this research, we need to provide working definitions for the key terms and concepts we use. In our study, we found during interviews that there are wide variations in the perceived meanings of even commonly used terms. So it is important that we clarify what we mean when we employ specific terms in this book.

Christian Fundraising

Our use of this term is straightforward. When we speak of Christian fundraising, we are simply talking about efforts to raise money for the church and for church-related agencies, programs, or services that are identified as Christian, such efforts generally being undertaken by Christians. We are not trying to set Christian fundraising in opposition to secular (charitable) fundraising, though we will be drawing some distinctions, but merely delineate the focus of the book, which is on fundraising for Christian bodies, done primarily by Christians and (although less exclusively) among Christians.

As noted, our focus is on efforts outside the usual Sunday morning collection in the congregation, conducted by and, ordinarily, among Christians. We examine the special efforts of parachurch groups, which have recently come to look more and more like the actions of other nonprofit organizations, to elicit contributions directly from individuals or groups for special programs of congregations, denominations, or independent Christian agencies. (Recall we are using the term *parachurch* to refer to all such agencies, regardless of their theological orientation within the Christian tradition.)

Ministry

When we talk of fundraising as a ministry, we use the term *ministry* in a broad sense. It does not refer solely to what clergy or ordained people do or solely to a set of formal activities officially sanctioned by some denomination or congregation. For us, any work that is based on Christian spiritual and moral values and tries to embody and give witness to them can be a ministry. Put another way, we consider any activity a ministry if its intent is to make the presence and love of God visible, tangible, or meaningful to others. So to speak of fundraising as a ministry is to hold out the hope that the work of Christian fundraisers can embody and give witness to the teachings of the Gospel and make the presence and love of God real to others.

Stewardship

Stewardship is a complex notion, interpreted in different ways in different settings. The National Conference of Catholic Bishops (of the Roman Catholic Church in the United States) lifted up the concept of stewardship in 1993 by issuing a pastoral letter titled *Stewardship: A Disciple's*

Response. In it, the bishops take a "comprehensive view of stewardship" as a "sharing, generous, accountable way of life" (p. 5). The term thus becomes almost a synonym for *discipleship.*

Among evangelicals, the term *stewardship* is more commonly used with a narrower focus on how persons of faith think about and use their material resources. In that tradition, stewardship is seen more as a distinct facet or practice of discipleship than as a quasi-equivalent for it. It implies a general emphasis on seeing all things as belonging to God, to be held in trust, and to be used or shared to further God's work.

Mainline Protestants do not seem to talk about stewardship nearly as much as evangelicals, although until recently they talked about it more than Catholics did. But they also seem to think about stewardship more in relation to the realm of material resources and especially in terms of the careful use and wise management of those resources. Indeed, the term *stewardship* has probably been overidentified with fundraising in mainline Protestant circles and even used as a euphemism for it (see Lynn, 1998).

In this volume, we use the concept of stewardship less comprehensively than the bishops but more broadly than some evangelicals. By stewardship, we mean careful attention to the care and use of all the gifts God gives us, including our time and talents, as well as material goods.

Vocation or Calling

The meaning of the concept of vocation or calling also varies from one tradition to another. Some traditions equate a calling or vocation with a commitment to a special status in ministry, such as being a priest or a missionary.

We view the concept and experience of calling differently. We believe that any work or role to which persons feels themselves led and in which they feel themselves guided by the Holy Spirit can be a calling or vocation. From this perspective, the work of a teacher, businessperson, parent, or artist can be perceived as a calling, just as much as the work of a priest or pastor, monk or missionary. And this can be just as true for the fundraiser, engaged in work for which one feels empowered, to which one feels drawn, and in which one feels directed by the Spirit of God.

The Origins of This Volume

Several years ago, with the generous support of the Lilly Endowment, we set out in search of Christian organizations whose fundraising programs are successful both in terms of raising needed financial or material resources and in terms of encouraging the spiritual development of their donors. Expressed more simply, we set out asking, Are there any organizations that see fundraising as a ministry? If so, what forms do their efforts take? Are there central principles or common characteristics around which fundraising efforts conceived of in this way might be organized?

We hoped to find a number of organizations that fit this description and persuade them to let us study them. We hoped to look at their literature; talk with their staff, volunteers, and donors; and see what ideals, principles, and practices shaped their fundraising efforts. We thought that if we could find a number of these organizations and study them in this way, we might be able to come up with models for fundraising in a Christian context that conflict less with Gospel values than what we often see.

A Primary Concern

This point raises the concern that motivates our work as Christians, fundraisers, and donors. In our careers, we have studied the fundraising materials and practices of many Christian organizations and have concluded that many such organizations now do fundraising in ways that do not reflect the best ideals of their faith traditions. Indeed, their practices often seem at odds with basic teachings of the Bible and most Christian traditions.

Too often the fundraising strategies and techniques of Christian organizations (for the most part borrowed directly from the secular world) seem geared to manipulate donors rather than to respect or enlighten them. This is certainly true of appeals carefully crafted to have the maximum emotional effect, even when that means giving an unbalanced or less than comprehensive picture of the problem or situation the organization is addressing. It is true of mailings that look like they could have come from the local mall, complete with coupons to return for premiums, making a pitch that sounds more like a deal one cannot refuse than an opportunity to give that one should consider prayerfully.

In addition, many current approaches seem geared more to appeal to donors' self-interest than to encourage altruism or witness to the values of a shared faith. A heavy emphasis on tax benefits or on ways in which the gift will result in prominent public affirmation for the donor are two common and frequent examples. Moreover, looking at the ways some Christian organizations prospect for and identify donors, it is hard not to conclude that some are far more interested in the status of donors' finances than in the substance of the faith that might prompt and guide their giving.

Ultimately, we believe, many Christian organizations need to be more deeply concerned about how they represent the ideals of the Christian faith in the ways they appeal for support from non-Christians as well as Christians. Fundraising by parachurch bodies is now one of the most public activities of Christian organizations. It is one of the endeavors through which non-Christians are most likely to get an impression of what Christians believe and value.

That makes these matters of critical importance for the whole church! Consider one of the saddest and crassest examples in recent memory. What impression of Christian beliefs and values do you suppose non-Christians took away from the spectacle of a preacher saying that "God would call him home" if his supporters did not immediately give him an extraordinarily large amount of money to fund a pet project?

The initiative behind this book began, then, with this concern about how Christian values are captured, embodied, and promoted—or violated or misrepresented—in the fundraising that Christian organizations do. It began with the sense that fundraising can be a process by which Christian organizations actually encourage and strengthen the faith of donors, as well as convey Gospel values to the "unchurched," and so enrich the life of the whole church. We went looking for organizations that are consciously trying to do this, to see what we could learn from them.

The Research Process

We did not undertake a huge, systematic, closely controlled study. But it was thorough (within its range) and conducted carefully. It generated many insightful, wide-ranging, and probing conversations with Christian fundraisers and donors.

Our attempts to do a major survey of a large number of Christian fundraisers, to get their help in identifying organizations that fit our description of fundraising as a ministry, ran into trouble immediately. We wanted to look at organizations from a variety of theological traditions— Catholic, mainline Protestant, and evangelical. We believe strongly that there is much to learn from all these traditions and that all could provide helpful information across theological lines. So we wanted to conduct our survey through the professional associations that bring together fundraisers from all those traditions. However, we discovered very quickly, as noted earlier, that the key concepts around which we had to construct a survey, such as ministry and stewardship, were understood and used so differently in various faith communities that we could not design a questionnaire that was meaningful to all and still obtain the information we needed.

Instead, then, we began interviewing Christian fundraisers by telephone. We started with a small group of them that we knew were knowledgeable about a significant number of Christian organizations, successful in fundraising, and theologically informed and reflective. They also came from a variety of traditions. We described to these people the kinds of fundraising programs we sought, ones with spiritual as well as financial goals. Then we asked two things: Can you recommend any Christian organization as having a fundraising program like this that we should study? And can you suggest other fundraisers for, executives of, or donors to Christian organizations whom we should ask these questions? (Just these two questions often led to long and fascinating conversations.)

Pursuing the suggestions we received and additional leads from those individuals, over the course of four months we interviewed almost one hundred people. We cannot guarantee that this process identified the best organizations to study, but it pointed us to ten organizations that exhibited characteristics very much in line with our concerns and interests. Some organizations had only recently reshaped their fundraising programs; a couple were trying to work in this new way but struggling with external or historical circumstances that undermined their progress.

In the end, seven of these organizations—Compassion International, Union Gospel Mission of Seattle, the Catholic Charities of Cleveland, the Roman Catholic Diocese of Tucson, San Francisco Theological Seminary, Fuller Theological Seminary, and Biola University—agreed to let us study them. All fit the description we started with, in terms of being successful in meeting both spiritual and financial goals with their development programs. All offered us examples of practices and insights worth sharing. All seven, along with some others, are represented in this volume.

Our Aspirations

Our hope is that this volume can help improve the quality of the fundraising efforts of Christian organizations by helping them see—as we have come to see—how fundraising can show at least as much concern for the spiritual health of donors as for the financial health of organizations. These goals and purposes do not have to be at odds; in fact, they can be mutually supportive.

If Christian fundraisers can create opportunities for giving that are at the same time expressions and celebrations of faith, donors are likely to grow spiritually even as they increase their emotional commitment to the cause. Fundraisers can achieve this through the ways they ask for support, the ways their organizations account for that support, and the ways they follow up with individuals who do and don't give. When interactions with the recipient organization lead donors to a deeper faith, making them more vibrant and trustworthy servants of God in the world, a great good has been achieved. Then whatever work has been done can be deemed a success in the most important measure of the core mission of the church universal.

Yet focusing on the spiritual does not preclude being successful in financial terms as well, especially if one takes a wider and longer view. There is some statistical evidence, and a lot of anecdotal evidence, to suggest that as donors grow spiritually and deepen their commitment, they tend to become more generous. This is certainly a conclusion we drew from our extensive interviews with donors. We also saw that as donors grow more generous, they are likely to become better supporters not only of one organization but also of many aspects of the church's work in the world. A story will illustrate the possibilities.

A Paradigmatic Story

We heard eloquent testimony from one donor-volunteer for Compassion International about the changes he and his wife experienced as they became more and more involved with that organization's ministry. They had gone over a period of time from sponsoring (and building a relationship with) one child to doing this with several children. The husband was now also an active volunteer with the organization, helping in the recruitment of other sponsors.

Compassion International had responded in genuine gratitude for his first commitment without pushing him toward more. But it had also worked hard to help him and his wife have a real relationship with the child they were helping and to understand the nature of the ministry of the organization in both spiritual and practical terms. So this man and his wife, as they became more involved with and more understanding of this ministry, wanted to do more.

This was a retired couple working within a limited income, and we asked the man how he felt about committing more and more of their resources to this ministry over time. He responded that at first they did not know how they could do more "but felt the leading of the Lord each time we took on another child. And you know," he said, "ever since we started doing this, we've always had enough [money] for anything we really need, and we've felt our hearts grow bigger."

Their story is the inspiration for the title of this volume, *Growing Givers' Hearts*. We believe that a central goal of a Christian fundraising program should be to help its donors' hearts grow bigger.

This observation should apply, we would add, to our own hearts as Christian fundraisers. As we enter into relationships with donors, rooted in a shared faith, we find donors ministering to us. And as we get more deeply involved, we may also find that service recipients—those who receive the benefits made possible by gifts we solicit (or give ourselves)— are ministering to us and to our donors. Finally, this is also the case because to be effective in this work, we as Christian fundraisers have to "walk the walk"—to participate—as givers too, growing spiritually with our donors.

This is a good spot to make an important point about motives. We are *not* saying that Christian fundraisers should treat donors and potential donors well, and try to make giving a way to encourage their spiritual growth, with a utilitarian mindset—in other words, so they can pry more money out of them. Motives are crucial. We do not offer models for fundraising as ministry to "improve the take." Christian fundraisers should treat donors well and foster their spiritual growth because donors (or potential donors) are brothers and sisters in faith—or, perhaps, people they may hope will find faith—and it is part of their calling and responsibility to care for them. In this sense, we would like Christian fundraisers to see how their work can contribute to building the spiritual and human resources of the church, as well as the financial ones.

The Design of This Book

Many factors shaped this book. It starts with a broad overview of the challenges of Christian fundraising and the context in which it is done. It then examines the wonderful spiritual resources Christian fundraisers can bring to this work as people of faith. Part One is devoted to this.

We begin by looking at the problems, as we see them, with the ways many Christian organization do fundraising now. Too often non-Christians get wrong ideas about the Christian faith because of the ways Christian organizations raise money, and too often Christians are alienated or given misleading understandings about stewardship because of the ways they are solicited. So Chapter One is devoted to looking at what is problematic in conventional approaches to fundraising and also identifies what is promising when Christian fundraisers begin to conceive of and approach this work as a ministry.

Chapters Two and Three are given to exploring the deep and rich spiritual resources that can inform and support the practice of fundraising as a ministry. We look first at what the Bible, especially the New Testament, has to tell us about giving and asking for money. We look next at part of the rather checkered history of Christian fundraising, recognizing that at least as much can be learned from the mistakes as from the successes. We do all this because it is in a deeper understanding of Scripture, and of the spiritual practices of various faith communities over time, that Christian fundraisers will find the resources for reflection needed to be more thoughtful and faithful in creating the conditions and applying the principles to make fundraising a ministry.

Part Two is devoted to exploring the nuances and potential applications of our six elements of fundraising as a ministry. Each chapter is devoted to one of these elements, including discussion of their interrelationships. The six are so intertwined that it feels somewhat strained to tease them apart. We do so, however, to try to gain clarity on how each in its own way contributes to reshaping the work of fundraising so that it can become a ministry.

Part Three moves from the corporate to the individual. People ask us, "If fundraising is a ministry, must I have a 'calling' to it?" What that question means may depend on one's theological tradition, so we cannot provide a universal answer. But we do believe that it can be very useful for Christian fundraisers to explore the meaning of their work in terms of some conception of ministry and vocation. So we offer a chapter that invites individual development officers and fundraisers to reflect on the work they do as a calling. We hope that many fundraisers in Christian organizations will find it empowering to envision the work they do in these terms.

A Continuing Dialogue

This book grew out of a remarkable process of conversation and dialogue with an informal community of caring, thoughtful, and faithful Christian development professionals that began many years ago and has intensified over the past three years. It is a summary of our learning, gleaned from a number of very smart, extraordinarily committed, theologically reflective, and spiritually mature Christian fundraisers and a number of donors who share those qualities. These people were our guides on a research project that became something of a pilgrimage. They were incredibly gracious about sharing their experiences and their wisdom with us. We put this volume forward with a deep sense of gratitude for these generous souls. Our first hope is that this book will stimulate and extend the conversation and dialogue they created with us.

We know that we have not identified all the things needed to make Christian fundraising more fruitful spiritually. Rather, we have raised a number of critical questions, and now we wait for others to join us in a continued examination of the practices of Christian fundraising—and perhaps other philanthropic fundraising—in light of these questions. Furthermore, we are eager to talk with like-minded colleagues about how we can all make Christian fundraising a true ministry, one that grows givers' hearts much as our own have grown during this extraordinary journey. It is with hopes of stimulating, broadening, and enriching that conversation that we offer what follows.

PART ONE

WHAT IS CHRISTIAN FUNDRAISING?

CREATING RESOURCES FOR GOD'S WORK

Preach the Gospel always; and when necessary, use words.

—Saint Francis of Assisi

THESE WORDS FROM Saint Francis remind us that the way we conduct ourselves in our day-to-day lives—whether with families and friends, with colleagues and customers, or with neighbors and strangers—does far more to convey the true extent of our commitment to the ideals of the faith we profess than anything we say or write. This book seeks to apply that insight to the work of Christian fundraising. So we begin with a question to which Saint Francis's words point: "Are we preaching the Gospel in the ways we do our work as Christian fundraisers?"

Is Christian Fundraising Different?

Coming at this question from a slightly different angle, after years of working in this field we found ourselves asking, Can fundraising become a way of preaching the Gospel for Christian organizations? And if it can, how will that differ from other approaches to fundraising?

From the very beginning of the research process behind this book, some fundraisers we spoke with have insisted that the kind of fundraising we were looking for and talking about is simply "good, ethical, donor-centered fundraising." Certainly we would wish that all Christian fundraising could be fairly described in these terms. And the kind of fundraising we envision as "fundraising as a ministry" is that—but we believe it is also more than that.

Whether fundraising becomes a ministry has to do with the motivations that undergird it and the purposes it serves. It has to do with the spiritual experiences and theological perspectives that shape the fundraising process. It has to do—perhaps more than with anything else—with the spiritual and theological values and visions that the process seeks to embody and promote.

In making the claims we will make about how Christian fundraising ought to work, we are not saying that it is necessarily morally superior to every other form in every other context. (The validity of a claim like that would depend on the moral assumptions with which one starts.) Furthermore, in asserting that there should be higher moral purposes and standards for Christian fundraising, we are not asserting that other kinds of fundraising are unacceptable in other settings.

However, we *will* make assertions about how fundraising should be conducted if it is being done for Christian institutions, assuming two things. First, it is assumed there is a desire to incarnate and give witness to the highest spiritual and moral values of the Christian tradition in the work of fundraising—a desire that should be evident, we believe, in all work done by the church. Second, it is assumed that there is a desire to evoke or nurture those same values in the people touched by the process.

Why Fundraising Might Be Thought of as a Ministry

These two assumptions may be crucial, but they are not always evident in the fundraising efforts of Christian organizations. Individuals who are engaged in resource development for Christian institutions and causes are frequently in a position to talk with people about the values and ideals of their faith. It is to be hoped that the works for which they are raising money are expressions of those ideals. When fundraisers for Christian organizations talk about why people should contribute financial support, they have the opportunity explain that these works are concrete manifestations of the values and vision of the faith. This is true whether these are efforts to help the poor, educate the young, care for the elderly, prepare persons for various ministries (as occurs in seminaries and colleges), or implement those and other ministries of service or evangelization.

The activities and institutions for which Christian fundraisers are developing resources may be—and, ideally should be—ways of "preaching the Gospel," sometimes without words. Requests for support, which generally use words, may also create occasions to share the good news of the faith, which shapes these activities and institutions. They may also create occasions when a donor can share with a fundraiser the good news of that donor's experience of faith. These things do not always happen, however. In fact, they seem to happen rarely.

So the question arises, how can Christian fundraisers best invite and nurture relationships with potential, current, and previous donors that embody and express the highest ideals of the Christian faith? And not just in what is said, but in everything that is done?

As fundraisers ourselves, as students of the work of development, and as frequent recipients of the solicitations of other Christian fundraisers, we have come to see that the strategies and techniques for fundraising that Christian organizations employ often do not create occasions for the celebration or discussion of faith; nor do they embody the values and vision we find in the Gospel.

In This Chapter

We begin this chapter by laying out in the briefest terms the findings of our research, in order to make clear that Christian fundraising can be practiced as a ministry and to show how it differs from other approaches to fundraising when this occurs. That permits us to explain why some current fundraising practices of Christian organizations are troubling and why it is so important that Christian fundraising programs do better. In doing so, we convey some of the frequently repeated concerns we heard from other Christian fundraisers during our study—concerns that added to our own. It is important to discuss the theological significance of these criticisms of current fundraising practice.

We also talk about the potential for spiritual growth to be found in the practice of giving and the opportunities fundraisers have to nurture that potential. Then we lay out some critical questions about underlying assumptions that shape modern fundraising, including Christian fundraising, that are problematic. Finally, we suggest how taking a different view of the church naturally leads to and supports a different approach to fundraising.

A Precis of Our Basic Findings

What we heard in many telephone interviews, on-site visits to seven different Christian organizations (with different fields of service and different theological traditions), and in two daylong symposia with Christian fundraisers convinced us that it *is* possible to practice fundraising as a ministry. And where that is happening, a set of common features—required conditions and operating principles—must be present in the development program. We shall simply identify them here, then discuss them in more detail in later chapters.

In organizations attempting to make fundraising a ministry, six key elements are evident. They are not present simultaneously in every organization, but together they constitute three necessary conditions and three operating principles. Together these elements enable fundraising to be carried on in a way that nurtures the spiritual growth of donors as well as generates needed resources.

The necessary conditions are as follows:

1. The organization and fundraising program operate with an assumption of the abundance of God's resources and grace.

2. The organization and program take a holistic view of God's work, recognizing the need for and value of a variety of ministries but also their own limited role in the totality of God's work on earth, allowing relationships with other ministries that are truly cooperative rather than competitive.

3. The organization and program are clear about the essential theological tenets of their own tradition as those factors shape their work.

The essential principles of operation are these:

1. The organization and the development program make a major commitment to giving donors meaningful opportunities for genuine participation in the ministry as much as possible.

2. The organization as a whole, with vigilant leadership from the development program, recognizes the importance of integrated planning that brings together the processes shaping program goals and operations with the processes shaping fundraising goals and operations.

3. The organization seeks out and supports spiritually mature, theologically reflective leadership for its development program.

We do not set these conditions and operating principles out as a formula, nor can we offer a simple recipe for making them work in other organizations. We cannot provide a simple set of rules for the success or transformation of every development program. Instead, in later chapters, we will describe these principles in greater detail, trying to illuminate their nuances by telling stories about how they appear to operate in organizations we observed and suggesting how they might be applied in some different settings. We believe that understanding and incorporating these elements could make many Christian development programs better.

That said, it is also crucial to recognize that every organization is different. We studied Christian organizations across a wide theological spectrum, and we know that differences in theology matter! Thus creating the right conditions or applying the various principles will vary considerably from an evangelical organization in a Calvinist tradition to a Roman Catholic diocese or an Anabaptist service agency. There will be tensions to manage in every case, but the nature of the tensions may differ enormously from one case to another.

We will pose many questions in this volume about how our approach can work, but fundamental to them all is this question: Are fundraisers working for Christian institutions and ministries simply persons who need to apply ethical techniques for meeting bottom-line goals, or should Christian fundraisers be striving to create occasions for growth in faith, both for their donors and themselves, in the process of asking and giving and being a part of God's work on earth?

It is with the vision of the second possibility in mind that we speak of fundraising as a ministry. Table 1.1 differentiates this vision from the more conventional paradigm for fundraising manifest in most Christian institutions.

The Need for Reflection

To move toward this vision of fundraising as a ministry requires a commitment to self-examination, as individuals and as organizations, that some people will find challenging and perhaps even threatening. Nevertheless, creating and sustaining many development programs that really operate as ministries, given the personal and institutional differences in theology and style across many different traditions of the Christian faith, will require specific capacities for and commitments to self-examination and reflection. Chief development officers, chief staff officers, board members, and others will need tools and skills for the reflective examination and application of theological principles and spiritual dynamics in the active work of fundraising, and they need to become "reflective practitioners" (Schön, 1974) of Christian fundraising.

Moreover, this work of reflection and application (and more reflection, and so on) will have to occur at both a corporate level and an individual level. In some instances, the questions will be about how to design or implement a program, and those must be considered corporately. In other

Table 1.1. Differing Visions of Christian Fundraising.

	Conventional Paradigm of Fundraising for Christian Organizations	Alternative Vision: "Fundraising as a Ministry"
Focus and Goals:	To bring people into relationship with our organization and with the work it does in a way that makes them want to support the organization financially.	To bring people into a closer relationship with God through the experiences of giving we help create by offering occasions where giving is consciously evoked as a spiritual act and practice.
Ideal Outcomes:	The donor makes a gift (or series of gifts) to our organization that may be an expression of his or her faith.	The donor comes to a place where he or she is more generous to our organization and/or others because every gift becomes an occasion for and a celebration of growth in faith.
Ethical Framework:	The fundraising process is circumscribed by a professional code based on a minimalist ethic ("do no harm"), which prohibits misrepresentation, self-dealing and deception, or obviously manipulative practices.	The fundraising process is defined by a commitment to embody Gospel values, to serve the truth and care for others—a process in which we make a commitment to listen for, lift up, and (if possible) honor a donor's dreams and visions above our own.
Philosophical and Cultural Underpinning:	The philosophical and cultural root is philanthropy; "private action for public purposes." The intent is to encourage people to feel a commitment to "the common good" and voluntarily give or use their resources—material goods they feel they own—for the benefit of others.	The philosophical and cultural root is stewardship, a commitment to personal and collective behavior that recognizes and honors God's ultimate ownership of and profound generosity in all things. The intent is to encourage people to see all resources as gifts temporarily entrusted to us to be used and shared to promote the welfare of all of God's creation.

Table 1.1. Differing Visions of Christian Fundraising, continued.

	Conventional Paradigm of Fundraising for Christian Organizations	Alternative Vision: "Fundraising as a Ministry"
Ultimate Objective:	To provide financial (and other) support for our organizations, so that they may carry out the godly work to which we believe they are called.	To "build up the household of God" so that there will be more human and spiritual, as well as material, resources to carry on the work of building the kingdom, in whatever form that work may take.

instances, the questions will be about how to respond to a particular donor at a particular point in time, and often a development officer has to discern the correct action individually.

Although these challenges are significant, they must be addressed. They are critical because the absence of theological and spiritual reflection in the design and implementation of Christian fundraising efforts is leading to practices that do not serve the larger and longer-term needs of the church well. In some case, these practices are a source of shame and embarrassment.

Where Christian Fundraising Is Missing the Mark

On a number of occasions over the past several years, we sat with groups of Christian fundraisers who represented many different kinds of institutions and various theological traditions, and we listened to them talk about what made them uncomfortable in the fundraising being done by their own organizations or other Christian organizations. They identified a lengthy list of problems, in which some common themes were evident.

The problems these Christian fundraisers identified included the following:

- Fundraising that is deceptive, misrepresenting programs and finances
- Fundraising that is manipulative, focusing particularly on the donors' emotions
- Fundraising that is arrogant, that "treats donors like ciphers to be solved"

- Approaches and appeals that are "detached from the spiritual basis of the organization"
- Fundraising that fails to capitalize on the potential for joy in giving
- Fundraising that is impersonal, that appears to be unconcerned with who donors are
- The tendency to "treat donors as a means to an end"
- Campaign language: "'targeting donors' and such"
- Strategies and approaches that fail to respect donors' privacy
- Approaches and techniques that emphasize distinctions of class, "treating some gifts and some givers as more worthy than others"

In these conversations and during interviews with other fundraisers and donors who talked about experiences that troubled them in Christian fundraising, four concerns surfaced that seem to be of central importance. These fundraisers and donors suggested that all of us who care about the vitality and integrity of Christian organizations should be especially troubled by any practice in Christian fundraising that does any of the following:

- Falls short of complete honesty and full disclosure in communications with donors
- Fails to give full respect to the dignity, autonomy, and vision of individual donors (usually by attempting to maneuver donors into making a gift that does not express their individual values, passions, or priorities)
- Fails to treat all donors (and potential donors) as being of equal worth in the eyes of God
- Fails to make clear connections between requests for support for work that is motivated and shaped by commitments, values, and ideals of faith and the faith held by the donors so that the act of giving can be felt as an expression of faith

We found these observations compelling. When a Christian fundraising program displays any of these problems, it violates, or at least compromises, central tenets of the teachings of the Gospel. How so? Consider each of these concerns more closely.

The point about truthfulness may seem obvious and not singular to Christian fundraising, and those are valid observations. But why, then, is it so easy to find Christian organizations that do not provide full disclosure of their financial circumstances and dealings to their donors or that supply misleading financial reports? Or to find Christian organizations that paint idealized portraits of the impacts of their programs? Or to find Christian organizations that use "representative images" and synthesize stories to highlight the problems their ministries address and generate more emotional responses in their donors? (Protecting the identity of clients is a legitimate goal, but "enhancing" the stories is quite different.)

How well do these organizations represent the one who said "I am the Light and the Truth and the Way" (John 4:16), and who told us that "the truth will set us free" (John 8:32)? We would ask if Christian organizations do not need to be more scrupulous and hold themselves accountable to a higher standard than that set out by the Federal Accounting Standards Board or the Better Business Bureau.

As for the second point, we would simply ask, When do we ever see Jesus treating a person as a means to an end? His exhortation to us to "love one another" is absolutely central to his teachings (see, among many examples, John 15:9–13). No one treats anyone they truly love as a means, as a tool, to be used or manipulated to accomplish some end of their own. Rather they show a concern for the other's welfare as a whole person and a fellow child of God.

Yet when Christian fundraisers strategize about how to approach potential donors with an interest *solely* in their money—or, more precisely, *solely* with a desire to get the donors to give their money to the fundraiser's organization—they are surely treating these people as objects to serve their own purposes. They do this when they construct appeals that focus more on playing a donor's emotions (tugging on the heartstrings) than on educating the donor about the validity and significance of the mission and then trusting the donor to make a thoughtful decision. They do this when they ask a donor to make a gift that may be problematic to the donor's financial welfare, because their organization "needs" the money. Surely they do this when they fail to make an effort to sustain relationships with those who have given a gift they may not be able to repeat (or improve on) and fail to give those people a chance to have a continuing relationship with the work of faith their gifts support.

Examples of this last problem abound, but we were struck by one incident we encountered recently. A board member of a Christian think tank who is also a significant donor to the organization spoke of her surprise upon coming across a full-page announcement of the center's new name in a national publication. She said, "It's not that I wanted to change anything about the announcement, but it would have been nice if I had seen it before it went into the magazine, if for no other reason than so I could have talked it up to my friends." She added, "I've supported the center since its founding, but I guess that's not enough to warrant occasional communication. I have to admit I'm a little hurt." When the organization next asks for this woman's support, it will find that her heart has followed her treasure elsewhere.

In contrast, a donor to a Christian relief agency talked to us with enthusiasm about regular e-mail updates he receives regarding the agency's work. "What I like best about the communication from this organization is that it includes easy-to-understand information about the situation of the world's poorest people—the people I'm supporting with my gifts. I'm not just a donor, I'm a smarter donor," he said. He is planning on increasing his giving to that organization in the year ahead, and thanks to this communication, he is probably a far more effective agent in interesting others in the work of this organization (and the needs of the poor) as well.

The third concern, the question of how to treat all donors with equal respect, is a tricky one. We are told plainly to "show no favoritism" on the basis of economic status in the conduct of worship or our life as a community (James 2:1–4). We know Jesus was no respecter of people's titles and status. We know too that he gave the highest praise to a very small gift in terms of monetary value, "the widow's mite" (Mark 12:41–44). Yet we also know that to be effective in this work, fundraisers have to approach different people differently, and often the variation in approaches does relate to the potential donor's economic or social status.

Fundraising is not a "one size fits all" kind of activity. So Christian fundraisers (like their secular counterparts) create special venues to cultivate donors with different interests and capacities. Frequently, this has to do with creating better ways to connect with those who have the means to provide more substantial support for their organizations. Typically, they also offer acknowledgments of larger gifts that are not offered for smaller gifts—for instance, in "naming opportunities."

Now there may be nothing *inherently* wrong in any of this. But there is certainly something wrong *if* this leads to a failure to recognize and honor those whose smaller gifts may sometimes represent far greater acts of faith.

The fourth concern involves the need to put the ideals of faith at the center of appeals to and relationships with donors and potential donors. When Christian fundraisers fail to do that, they may deprive these people of opportunities to grow in faith that they may experience in no other way.

Of course, Christian fundraisers need to talk about the good that their organizations do in practical terms, about how significant the problems are that these organizations address, and about how all of our communities would be poorer places if this work was not supported by persons who care about the common good. This is a basic foundation for appealing to donors that Christian organizations share with all philanthropic institutions. Christian fundraisers should be ready to stand on it.

Christian fundraisers and organizations should be able to say more, though. They can appeal to something far more exciting, more transforming, and more beautiful than de Tocqueville's phrase,"enlightened self-interest." They can talk about how the work of their organizations represents efforts to make the values of faith tangible and meaningful, to preach the Gospel (perhaps) without words, and to keep hope alive in a world that often lacks hope. Most important in that context, they can talk about how giving can both be an act of faith and lead to growth in faith.

When they talk in these terms about the work their organizations do and how giving can help, their requests for support become invitations for donors to express their faith. This can often lead to a greater involvement for the donors in the life and work of these faith communities. This is happening at Catholic Charities of Cleveland as a direct result of the ways fundraisers are now connecting with their constituency. As August Napoli, president of the organization, told us, "We are evangelists, too! If [donors] read the stories and see the pictures we present of faith in action and want to get involved in some way beyond writing a check, that is great!"

Giving as the Occasion for Grace and Growth

So if they want to, Christian fundraisers can talk about the meaning of giving in these terms. They can talk about how giving can be an act of trust in the beneficence of God, in the abundance of God's grace, and in the possibilities for making a better world when we cooperate in that grace. They can talk about how taking the risk of making a "stretch gift" (when that is the right thing to do) can become the occasion to learn about how God sustains the faithful. Henri Nouwen once said, "Every time I take a step in the direction of generosity, I know I am moving from fear to love." Christian fundraisers can offer people a chance to take that step and explain its significance.

Our experience in conducting this research brought home to us the spiritual power of the practice of giving, and the power of the witness that may grow from it, in remarkable ways. We were deeply moved by the personal stories of growth in faith we heard from donors who had been truly nurtured—*not* pressured—into making a gift that was a stretch for them or adopting a more regular and more generous pattern of giving. These donors spoke about growing in many ways into a deeper relationship with God, into a richer spiritual life, through their practice of giving.

We are reminded of our encounter with a donor to Fuller Seminary and his testimony to this effect of giving in his life. When starting out in business, he and his brother, who is also his business partner, determined to give 10 percent of the company's profits to charity, splitting the distributions according to their respective priorities. Over the years, this percentage climbed as the company prospered, and it now stands at more than 50 percent of the company's profits. This "hard-nosed" businessman's eyes filled with tears as he talked about what the shared practice of giving had meant for his relationship with his brother and in his own walk with the Lord. "We've never once regretted our decision to make this a giving company," he said. "In fact, it's been a great source of joy for both of us and for our families."

Giving in Faith

Martin Luther, in a particularly striking turn of a phrase, once spoke of the need for a "conversion of the heart, the mind, *and the purse*" in the Christian life (Foster, 1985, p. 19). There are numerous devotional works that speak of giving as a spiritual practice, something intentionally undertaken as a commitment of faith that is expected to lead the giver into a deeper relationship with God. The view that giving of one's material resources is a practice integral to being rooted and growing in faith runs through the writings of the Old Testament, is captured in Jewish traditions of *Tzedakah,* and is surely evident in the teachings of Jesus.

How might giving foster an individual's growth in the life of faith? First of all, in giving, all of us may imitate the gracious God who is always giving us what we need. Attempting to emulate the qualities of the Divine, living "in imitation of Christ," is often a key focus of devotional practice. (See, for example, the devotional classic, *The Imitation of Christ,* by Thomas à Kempis.) In addition, in giving, we may offer concrete expressions of our commitment to the welfare of others and to the justice and mercy we are told God desires to see in all creation and in our individual lives (see Micah 6:6–8). In this we also demonstrate our desire to be "good stewards," as Jesus' teachings tell us we should be. Finally, in our efforts to be more generous givers, reaching beyond our initial comfort level and moving past merely sharing from our excess, we may both demonstrate and deepen our trust in God to provide whatever we really need in the future. In taking these steps, we find the opportunity to recognize the joy of the sufficiency provided by God rather than to continue to buy into the worldly, American tendency to strive for overabundance and luxury.

It has been a profoundly moving experience to talk with people for whom giving is a regular and conscious practice of their life in faith and to hear from them how habits of giving may be transmitted from one generation to the next. We spoke with many people whose earliest understandings of stewardship came from hearing parents or other beloved elders talk about tithing. Most had incorporated the tithe into their own decisions about giving. They all spoke of their commitment to give regularly and generously as an effort to follow the teachings of the Bible more closely and as an expression of their gratitude for and trust in God's grace. Many spoke of going through periods when they struggled to meet their tithe, but in the end they always found they had enough to honor this commitment. And they told of how going through those experiences had greatly deepened their convictions about God's unfailing love for them.

We recall one story of a regular donor in Seattle who, with his wife, practices tithing. He spoke of a time when they were experiencing serious financial pressures and decided to give up all "recreational expenditures"— dining out, movies, and such—to ensure that they could maintain their level of giving. What his family discovered, he noted, was how many ways they could enjoy each other's company without spending money and how this commitment "forced" them to take more time with one another. And in the end, he commented, the deeper appreciation they developed for one another and their family, as well as the satisfaction they derived from their giving, was a blessing far greater than any sacrifice they made to maintain their tithe. It was not that God gave them wealth for being faithful in this commitment to give but rather that being faithful in that commitment led them into other kinds of riches and deepened their sense of God's grace in their lives.

Many questions could be raised about some aspects of tithing and other traditional ways to encourage giving. Setting those aside for a moment, the point is to recognize how, when people are encouraged to give as an act of faith, in gratitude and trust, in keeping with the most profound ideals of their religious traditions, giving can become a vehicle for growth in faith in many ways.

It is because it has this potential, when it is done well, that asking for a gift can become an occasion of ministry. Father Michael Raschko writes that fundraising in a Christian context should be seen as a "pastoral activity" (1997, p. 54). This recognition should stimulate all of us involved in fundraising for Christian organizations to consider more deeply the spiritual implications of the ways in which we approach donors, the assumptions we are working from about how and why people give, and what kind of experience we want them to have in responding to a solicitation.

What Assumptions Have Shaped the Work of Christian Fundraisers?

Earlier we shared a list of concerns raised by Christian fundraisers about the fundraising techniques and strategies of parachurch organizations. We found these concerns widely shared among Christian fundraisers with whom we spoke, who observed troubling practices in many organizations. Why don't the fundraising programs of Christian organizations do better in these matters? Why do many become impersonal and manipulative, treating donors like "ciphers to be solved" and as "means to an end"? Why are many failing to respect the privacy and dignity of the people from whom they would seek support?

These failures occur, at least in part, because the approaches to fundraising many Christian organizations employ are shaped by the basic undergirding assumptions for fundraising more generally, assumptions rooted in sales and commerce, not in service and caring. Fundraising in the wider nonprofit sector of our society has been shaped by the "dominant paradigm" for all human interactions in a market economy. This is an economic behavioral model where everything is seen as an "exchange" in which the parties are expected to seek first to "maximize their own interests."

This is the fundamental worldview of the commercial culture that surrounds us and pervades all aspects of our lives. That this culture of commercialism has invaded and in some cases even distorted both the theological vision and the practices of Christians is plainly evident (see, for example, Curtis, 1991; Moore, 1994). Shaped by this consumer culture, fundraising activities appear more and more often to follow a sales model. In that model, the primary question becomes how the fundraiser can convince a potential donor that he or she will gain something of value by "making a gift."

Now this is not to say that "exchanges" are inherently bad; as always, context is crucial. But we must recognize that "making an exchange" is not the equivalent of the sort of giving Jesus taught his disciples—and us—to be involved in. The good Samaritan never expected to be repaid for his kindness or acclaimed in any way. His only reward was his own satisfaction in having acted in accordance with the ideals of his faith and knowing he had done a good thing.

Nor is the point here that all secular fundraising is crassly manipulative and devoid of concern for a donor's welfare. That is clearly not true. But again we must recognize that the underlying assumptions that shape economic behavior in our culture—especially the elevation and coronation of self-interest—will, if allowed to run their course, push fundraising practice in a direction that is often at odds with Jesus' teachings. Moreover, it is also clear that many Christian organizations have imported fundraising approaches based on this paradigm with little or no critical reflection on the implications of these practices.

When conventional economic and marketing assumptions shape and undergird the work of charitable fundraising, whether for Christian organizations or others, potential donors will often be approached with the expectation that they will be more interested in having their names in the program or on a plaque or in receiving a premium or a tax break than in giving to help others "out of the goodness of their hearts." When this happens, fundraisers often fail to recognize or help donors see the potentially world-changing and life-giving power that may be present in or working through the goodness of the donors' hearts and souls; if only someone would acknowledge it, call it forth, and nurture it! Those Christian fundraisers are missing a special opportunity to lift up the power and beauty of faith.

If Christian fundraisers' approaches to this work are shaped by conventional economic and commercial assumptions, where it is expected that each individual will look first after his or her own interests, then often they will not really make a request for a gift so much as make an offer for a market exchange. The widespread use of "premiums" exemplifies this tendency: "Give us at least $25 and you'll get this special embossed Bible." Somewhat more subtle but still essentially evoking self-interest are the many appeals on the order of "Support this child and you will get a wonderful feeling about yourself." Finally, too many organizations that serve the poor and the homeless or provide overseas relief craft their requests for gifts to appeal not to caring, generosity, or altruism but rather to guilt or pride.

The encroaching commercialization of charitable work makes it vitally important that everyone involved in the work of Christian fundraising step back and think theologically as well as economically and psychologically. To be true to Jesus' teachings in the work of resource development requires that Christian fundraisers help donors see choices they may make about giving in spiritual, as well as practical, terms. If donors are presented with opportunities to give as just one more variety of consumer choice—where what matters most is the packaging of the opportunity, how one feels at the moment, or even what benefit (in this life or the next) one might accrue for making a gift—what will become of thoughtful stewardship, spiritual discernment, and true generosity in the act of giving?

If Christian fundraisers regularly approach donors and potential donors in ways that appeal to their self-interests, what expectations will be created in the donors about what they should get for making a gift? Will such motivations for and expectations about giving foster or hamper their growth as a people of faith in the Christian tradition? Where will such self-interested giving lead the church—as opposed to the giving of self that Jesus taught his disciples would lead to "a life more abundant"? The only plausible answers we can discern to these questions are deeply disturbing.

Fundraising and Our View of the Church: Why This Matters

One Christian fundraiser said to us, "The concerns you are raising are interesting, but this cannot be our problem. It is the pastors' job to do stewardship education and cultivate the faith of their flocks. Our job is to raise the money needed to fund Christian ministries." Another said to us, "As long as a Christian fundraiser's efforts generate the financial resources needed to fund the good works his or her organization does and the fundraiser is honest and trustworthy, these other questions you are raising should not be their worry."

Whether this position holds up depends on one's view of the church. It holds up *only* if one assumes that the church and its ministries are equivalent to its buildings and its programs, so the only resources it needs are material or financial—and maybe a few people. We contend that a different view of the church, a different *ecclesiology,* is called for here, one that is truer to the voice of Scripture.

It is easy for individuals who work in the administrative structures of the church to come to think that buildings and staff *are* the church. That is the way the surrounding secular society thinks about institutions. It is easy for those who work in various Christian agencies and organizations to think that the social service, health care, outreach, educational and pastoral programs they provide with their staff and services and technologies are the church's ministries. But this is at best a limited perspective.

Moving beyond the narrower concept of fundraising to the broader concept of development, we believe that the work of development and fundraising in Christian organizations should be about creating and sustaining *all the resources needed to do God's work in the world;* and the most important resources the church has to do God's work, the only resources that are truly indispensable, are faithful people! By this we mean people whose lives are shaped by that faith and whose deepest desires include continuing and growing in the faith. These people whose lives have been transformed by faith and who, sharing that experience with others, are bound together in communities of faith, are the church, the *ecclesia,* to cite the Greek word we translate as "church," the people who are "called out and called together."

This is not to argue that the entire responsibility for the life of the church belongs to the development function. Rather, it is to say that development and fundraising must be in tune with and always guided by theological principles and commitments true to the individual organization's tradition. The mistakes and missteps alluded to earlier are, perhaps as much as anything else, examples of the development function, however unintentionally, working at cross purposes with the core purposes of the church universal in evangelism and pastoral ministry.

Individuals who raise money for the institutional church, or the parachurch, may believe the work they do is essential, and clearly in some ways it is. But they are deluded if they think God's work cannot go on in this world without the dollars they raise. Faithful people who have no money can give of their time and energy and love to help make at least some of God's work happen! Conversely, where there is money but there are no people of faith spiritually mature enough to use it wisely for the right things, God's work will not be done.

A Case in Point

One situation we encountered in our study was particularly striking in bringing this point home to us. We were visiting in the Roman Catholic Diocese of Tucson, interviewing staff, pastors, and members. This diocese is struggling to get out from under a large debt created by a failed venture into broadcasting about a decade ago. People there told us that at one point they found that they were having trouble getting any new initiatives going, even ones that were obviously needed, because everyone felt so burdened by this debt.

So the bishop asked the development office to run a large focus group with priests and laity to try to discern what work the church there was called to and to envision what tasks it might take on if the debt were *not* a problem. This group generated a list of thirty-seven vitally important things to do as the church in that diocese. All were works of faith and service that would serve the community and the church.

The extraordinary thing the ordained and lay leaders discovered when they studied this list was that they could probably do thirty-four of those things with very little money, or at least no new money. All they needed was the energy and commitment of faithful people who were willing to take on the work.

The point is that the people and communities whose dreams, prayers, and personal commitments of time, energy, and resources create and sustain the buildings, agencies, and programs we are trying to fund—*they* are the church. Simply put, the ministries of the church consist of all the ways that faithful people serve others so that the presence of God becomes visible in the world. Seeing this makes it clear that no matter how much money Christian organizations might raise, they cannot do God's work well if they do not have people of faith to carry on and uphold the ministries that money should support. That is one reason why nurturing people in their faith must be an integral part of the Christian fundraiser's job too.

And Other Reasons

In addition, there is much evidence in the research we have on giving—and in the experience of many religious workers and leaders—to tell us that we cannot expect to raise much of the money we need for the church and its ministries from people whose lives are not rooted in faith. Extensive support for this is reported in *Giving and Volunteering in the United States, 1994* (Hodgkinson and others, 1994). That research shows that members of religious organizations are significantly more likely to make charitable contributions than nonmembers. For example, only 58 percent of individuals who never attended religious services made charitable contributions; whereas 85 percent of those who attend weekly did so. And members of religious congregations were four times as likely as nonmembers to give to both religious and nonreligious groups. The percentage of household income going to charities rises with religious commitment as well, averaging 3.0 percent for those who attend services weekly but only 1.7 percent for all contributors and 0.8 percent for those who never attend services.

Conclusions

It is with this larger view of the needs of the whole church, for both now and the future, that we say the process of fundraising cannot be solely about getting a dollar in the door. It must also be concerned about nurturing the spiritual life and participation in a spiritual community, out of which generosity may grow. At the very least, Christian fundraisers and organizations, in the ways they ask for contributions, need to avoid both sending the wrong messages about Christian ideals and appealing to motives that are at odds with the teachings of their faith. Ideally, they should be creating relationships with donors wherein the act of giving can become for the donors an occasion both to feel and to celebrate their faith, their sense of God at work in their lives.

Moreover, lest our interests seem too parochial, we want to say again that in raising all these questions, we are not just concerned with the effects of Christian fundraising efforts on people already in the church. We are equally concerned with how Christian organizations' efforts to raise money reflect Christian values, ideally Gospel values, to the unchurched.

The work of Robert Wuthnow (1988, 1994b), perhaps the preeminent sociologist of religion in the United States today, documents how much of the activity and vitality of the church has moved outside of congregations and denominations. His research shows that many religious people now identify themselves and define their faith commitments at least as strongly with various Christian agencies and programs—in other words, with parachurch bodies—as with congregations or denominational traditions (Wuthnow, 1988, 1994a). Other research suggests that for the first time ever, the parachurch may be receiving more money in donations than congregations, which were always the primary locus for giving in the past (Barrett, 1996).

Wuthnow's work tells us that parachurch bodies are also becoming the most public face of the church today. It is a fact that these days, unchurched people are more likely to run into (or at least be cognizant of) the activities of parachurch organizations and movements than those of the typical congregation. That is partly because these are often the Christian bodies most visibly active in mission in the wider community, but it is also because these groups are far more likely to be actively raising support from the general public, through direct-mail advertising and special events, than congregations. Some fundraising appeal or another is quite likely to be the first—and may be the only—contact of the unchurched with Christianity today. (This, again, is one reason we decided to focus our studies on parachurch rather than congregational fundraising.)

Thus what parachurch organizations ask for, and *how* they ask, tells potential donors—churched and unchurched—a great deal about what Christians care about, hope for, and believe. They send implicit and explicit messages about what all of us who are Christians value and what we as Christian think other people will value. (Note that most unchurched folks will not distinguish between one kind of Christian and another; we will all be seen as one group.) The ways Christian organizations account to donors and others for how they use the gifts they receive shape others' views of Christian ethics and attitudes. When any of this seems doubtful, just look at the public fallout that has affected almost every Christian organization—and certainly the image of the church as a whole—every time there has been a scandal involving one of these organizations.

In short, the kinds of relationships Christian fundraisers create, or seem to be trying to create, in the development process say a great deal to those who are watching and listening about whether we Christians and Christian organizations really do place commitment to God, the common good, and the best interests of others above our own interests, as the Gospels teach. It is in this context of outreach, as well as in the context of nurturing the faith of those already in the church, that we see the vital importance of treating fundraising as a ministry.

Where We Go Next

The next two chapters explore some of the theological and spiritual resources that can help us all shape and reflect on the work of fundraising as a ministry. In the Christian tradition, the faithful have usually turned to two places for insights in understanding and applying the teachings of Jesus and the values of our faith to daily life. One is the Bible, especially the New Testament and the Gospels. The other is the history of our own faith community, learning from the experiences, reflections, and teachings of our forebears in faith. Accordingly, we give one chapter to examining each of those sources to see what they have to tell us about the processes and implications—spiritual as well as practical—of giving and asking for money for and from members of the church and others.

This is not primarily a book of scriptural interpretation or church history, so our treatment will not be detailed. Still, we hope to go deeply enough into these sources to get a useful picture of the theological foundations on which the work of Christian fundraisers should rest and of the spiritual promise and potential pitfalls this work might open. Obviously, we will continue to look at and wrestle with these matters as we move into Part Two, where we look at the characteristics and experiences of organizations that are trying to practice fundraising as a ministry.

2

WHAT THE BIBLE SAYS ABOUT GIVING AND ASKING

No one can serve two masters. Either that person will hate one and love the other, or he will be devoted to one and despise the other. You cannot serve both God and mammon.

—Matthew 6:24

WHEN CHRISTIANS THINK about Jesus' teachings about money, this quote may be the most familiar—at least the part about God and mammon.

The most simplistic response to this teaching is to decide that any involvement with money will undermine one's faith and be ruinous to one's spiritual life and so one should choose to have nothing to do with money. For the vast majority of people, however, that is not a viable choice. In modern societies, people cannot eschew all involvement with money and survive. They have to acquire and spend a certain amount of money just to exist, to care for themselves and their families, and to do things they need to do.

In fact, most people of faith do many good things with money. In addition to caring for their families, they use it to support a whole host of good causes, including the work of their faith communities. They often use money to meet needs for other persons, members of their own faith and others, who would not otherwise have those needs met.

This same reality applies to the organized church and its various institutions. To exist and carry out their work in a modern society requires that religious institutions have some involvement with money. This cannot be avoided.

The history of the Judeo-Christian tradition demonstrates that people of faith have always felt a tension between, on the one hand, the imperative to keep their attention focused on the moral and spiritual aspects of life and their relationship with God and, on the other hand, their temporal need to obtain and use material resources. Such resources have always been necessary both to care for themselves and to carry out moral and spiritual work in the world. The practice of faith out in the world involves meeting obligations to care "for the poor, the widows, and the orphans" (that is, those most in need), and it requires institutions that train people for religious work. All this means that at least some members of faith communities must find a way of working with mammon.

In any case, a more careful reading of this scripture suggests that avoiding all involvement with money is not what is being demanded. Rather the question being raised is one of control: Do we serve mammon, doing whatever is needed to have more of it? Or do we use mammon to serve God, in ways that demonstrate that our primary interest is in developing and expressing the fullness of a life-enriching relationship with God? What we are being warned against here is the danger that the desire or need for money will come to control our lives and undermine or pervert our relationship with God. That is an important warning for both individuals and the church as a whole.

Still, money by itself is not the problem. Money is not the root of all evil, as another passage is commonly misquoted. Rather it is "the love of money [that] is the root of all evil" (1 Timothy 6:10). The teaching of the Bible on these points suggests that the moral import of money comes not from some inherent characteristic it possesses but from what people make of it, how they feel about it, and what they do with it.

In this context, it is crucial for Christian fundraisers and the institutions they serve to reflect on their work in light of the whole message of the Bible, especially the New Testament, about what constitutes a right relationship with and use of money. The Bible itself and many commentaries on it are replete with instructions and admonitions about the giving and receiving of worldly goods. There are exhortations to graciousness in both giving and receiving, and there are warnings about the myriad ways in which greed can infect, distort, and pervert both those acts.

Christian fundraisers stand in the middle of a process of giving and receiving. Indeed, they are often the people initiating and shaping that process. If that process is going to be an experience filled with grace (and not greed), and so be one that leads to a growth in faith for a donor, it is important that the Christian fundraiser be conscious of the motives being engaged and the rationales being offered to stimulate giving. The Bible has something to say about motives and rationales (and practices) that should be regarded as good and those that cannot be seen that way. That is why we take this chapter to examine how Scripture can illuminate the Christian fundraiser's thinking about fundraising and how the work of development can become a ministry.

We begin by looking at different perspectives on giving that appear in the Bible, examining the motives for giving that are assumed or suggested. We review Old and New Testament texts on the subject. Finally, we examine Paul's work and views as the first fundraiser of note for the social ministries of the church. In all this, the goal is to discern some boundaries for practice and to identify best practices in fundraising so that this work will be expressive of Christian values based in Scripture.

Some Views of the Motivations for Giving

Neither the Old Testament nor the New has a chapter on fundraising. Some sections of Paul's epistles come close to being an exposition of right practices in this realm, but these passages are rather brief and unsystematic. Still, the Bible offers descriptions in a number of places of the circumstances in which and purposes for which funds were sought from members of the Jewish and early Christian communities. For example, funds were solicited for the maintenance of a place of worship and the conduct of religious services (Exodus 30:11–16) and for the care of less fortunate members of the community (Acts 6:1–6). These passages speak to appropriate purposes for gifts. A number of passages in the Bible also expound on the manner and rationale for giving.

The books of the Old and New Testament, the commentaries on the texts, and theological treatises deriving from them suggest that the Judeo-Christian tradition expects giving in the vein of what we now call charity or philanthropy will generally be motivated by one or more of five types of emotions, beliefs, or commitments, which are fear or guilt, a sense of affiliation or obligation to a specific community, a sense of fairness or requirement of justice, the desire for self-aggrandizement, and gratitude or love. In a number of passages, one or more of these motives are often prominent (though in the Bible, as in real life, mixed motives are most often the rule when it comes to human behavior).

Modern psychologists studying "volunteer behavior" have found striking confirmation of the insights of Scripture. Their research generates a very similar list of motivations for volunteering, the giving of time, as a careful exegesis of the biblical texts does for the giving of money. Gil Clary and Mark Snyder examined the motivations of volunteers for giving their time to do various kinds of service work and found that volunteering fulfills one or more of five functions for people: (1) a "values-expressive function," which includes what we would call idealism and altruism; (2) a "socially adjustive function . . . to help one fit in and get along with one's reference group"; (3) an "ego-defensive function . . . to reduce guilt and make one more deserving of desirable [future] outcomes"; (4) a "knowledge function" to gain greater understanding of something one wants to know more about; and (5) an "instrumental function" to help persons gain useful skills for career purposes (1990, p. 81; 1991).

Just writing a check to some cause or person cannot generally fulfill the latter two functions on this list, those that have to do with gaining knowledge and skills (although giving to some organizations does elicit communication that can be quite informative). Still, the first three functions these scholars identify as being fulfilled in volunteering parallel the motivations for giving that the Bible suggests we will see in people's giving.

Fear, guilt, and self-aggrandizement fit very closely to the "ego-defensive function" these psychologists describe. The sense of belonging or obligation to community that is so prominent in many Old Testament passages fits clearly into the "socially adjustive function." And giving out of a commitment to justice or out of love belongs quite clearly to the "values-expressive function."

Of course, the difference between the psychologists' findings and the Bible's perspective is the normative element. That is to say, the psychologists offer us neutral observations on these matters, whereas the Bible suggests that some motivations are more morally desirable than others. So what does the Bible tell us about giving and asking for money?

The Old Testament Perspective

One of the most important things to keep in mind when reading the Old Testament is that it is the story of a people's communal experience, and so the frame of reference for virtually every question or issue is that of the community. This is radically different from our way of looking at things in modern, Western (particularly American) culture. Whereas we look at most behavioral matters in terms of their implications for individuals' lives, rights, and freedoms, most of what the Old Testament has to tell us about behavior and morality simply cannot be understood from that perspective. There the first concern is almost always for the integrity and vitality of the community.

That being said, in the Old Testament we find three models of giving represented, two much more fully than the third. The first explicit incident of religious fundraising appears in Exodus 30:11–16. In this passage, God commands that each adult member of the community "must pay a ransom for his life" (30:12), which is to be appointed and used "for the service of the tent of meeting" (30:16). This payment "for the service of the tent of meeting" is, simply described, money that will support the edifice of worship and religious services for this community. This payment later evolves into the "temple tax," which is a point of controversy in Jesus' time.

This payment is also described (to Moses) as "atonement money," which is a kind of hybrid between a payment of protection money, so "that no plague will come on them when you number them" (30:12), and a debt owed to God for their well-being thus far. (Note that the Israelites feared that God could be angered by their "taking a census," which is also occurring here, and the onset of "a plague" would have been seen as an expression of God's wrath.) This command to give is put forward in plain terms, without moral commentary (although today words like *ransom* and *atonement money* have taken on some negative associations, they were neutral at the time they were written).

In considering the model for fundraising offered here, we should take note of some unique features of these circumstances—in addition to the fact that God is doing the fundraising himself.

First, we need to recognize that the tone and substance of this passage is entirely in keeping with the cosmological and theological views of other Middle Eastern cultures of the time that surrounded and influenced Hebrew culture. Giving for religious purposes in those cultures often took the form of "sacrifices" and was often designed to appease or forestall the wrath of a potentially angry God. That worldview is apparent in some of the language here.

Second, what is sought—actually, commanded—here is not a voluntary contribution but a kind of tax. Members of this religious community were being told what was the minimum financial support expected from them to support its religious infrastructure. This rationale for religious giving never appears in the same way again in the Bible; in fact, it is even ridiculed in some later passages, especially in the Prophets (see, for example, Amos 4:4–5).

Nevertheless, what we have here is one model for a religious community in the Judeo-Christian tradition raising support for itself. It is a model that rests to some degree on motivations of fear and guilt and was accepted in its own time. But this is not the prevalent model, even in the Old Testament.

Rather, the rationale for giving represented in other passages in the Old Testament emphasizes one or both of two motivations: the obligation of each member of "the people of God" to contribute to the common welfare of their covenanted community and the obligation of each member of the community to "act justly and love mercy" (Micah 6:8), not only among themselves but also with respect to others. For the Israelites, in their perception of themselves as a "chosen people" who had promised to obey and "delight in the law of the Lord" (Psalms 1:2), support of the priesthood and the temple was as vital to living in accordance with God's will as acting generously to care for those in need—"the poor, the widows, and the orphans" the Prophets speak of so frequently (see, for example, Psalms 146:9; Isaiah 1:17; Jeremiah 22:3; and Zechariah 7:10). Religious observance and good works were understood to be inseparable!

So on the one hand, there are a variety of passages that emphasize the obligations of members of this community to contribute to the support of the community's religious services and rituals (for example, Leviticus 27:30–32; Numbers 18:21, 25–29), and on the other hand, there are many passages that lift up the importance of contributing to the support of other members of the community who are in need (for example, Exodus 23:10–11; Leviticus 19:9–10; Proverbs 14:31). Finally, there are passages that bring these two themes together, as in Deuteronomy, 14:28–30.

Old Testament Practices

Specific mechanisms or practices facilitated giving for these purposes. These mechanisms can be seen as serving to strengthen the Israelites' faith because they drew on values and ideals that were essential to that faith. So, for example, the practice of leaving some of one's harvest in the field for the poor and the sojourner to glean (Leviticus 19:9–10) does more than just provide some food for the less fortunate; it can also be seen as an act of sharing in thanksgiving, leaving some of the bounty that God has provided where it grew for others to partake as well, and as an act that prompts or requires trust in God's providence, that more will be provided next season.

The practice of tithing can be seen in a similar light. A *tithe* in Hebrew is literally "a tenth." Tithing as described in the Old Testament was the practice of giving a tenth of one's goods or income—typically the "first fruits"(Deuteronomy 26:10–11)—for the support of the community's religious institutions and the religious and charitable works they carried out. The practice was common in non-Hebraic cultures of the time as well.

The practice of tithing serves three important functions in the context of a religious community like the one we find in the Old Testament: it makes a faith statement in acknowledging God's ultimate ownership of "the earth . . . and the fullness thereof" (Psalms 24:1), it provides needed resources for the support of religious institutions central to the life of the community, and it garners resources for charitable work and, to some degree, serves to redistribute resources in a manner more in keeping with the concerns for justice. But note that this practice also requires one to trust God to provide enough for one's own essential needs. It requires one to "act on faith."

Looking at all these commands and practices together, two key assumptions of this community of faith are revealed. First, it is assumed that the quality of the common life of God's people will be undermined by any failure to provide adequate support for the community's worship and liturgy. Second, it is understood that the moral fabric of the community is deeply torn as well by a failure to show compassion and maintain at least a minimum level of economic support and dignity for the most vulnerable members. Falling short in either regard constitutes a breach of the covenant between God and God's people. So giving for these purposes is expected to be motivated by a sense of affiliation and a sense of justice—and perhaps even gratitude—among the people, recognizing that "apart from God," they "have no good thing" (Psalms 16:2).

At the same time, giving for these purposes is supposed to be something that brings blessings to the givers as well, but not in the crass sense of a simple exchange, predicated on the idea that giving one's tithe is a way to bring increased income in the future. (That is a perversion of the scriptural vision too often promulgated in some contemporary churches.) The reward is rather in that giving for these purposes, and the work it supports, creates a faithful and healthy community in which all the members will be blessed. It may well be that those who give most generously to make these things happen will feel these blessings most strongly, but that is not the purpose of the giving.

Still the Israelites are told that when they have been faithful in these practices, they should ask for a blessing. They are told, "When you have finished setting aside a tenth of all your produce . . . you shall give it to the Levite, the alien, the fatherless and the widow. Then say to the Lord, 'I have removed from my house the sacred portion and have given it to the Levite, the alien, the fatherless and the widow, according to all you commanded. . . . [Now] look down from your heaven . . . and bless your people Israel and the land you have given us.'" (Deuteronomy 26:12–15).

What we call charity or philanthropy is in the Old Testament a matter of righteousness and justice. These practices of giving are about maintaining the right order of the community's life in accordance with God's law. Thus, in this view, giving for functions like worship and the care of the poor is simply what one ought to do. Moreover, there is a strong element of reciprocity in this view, in that one can expect to be cared for in such a community and so one has a responsibility to contribute to the support of that community.

There is, however, a last critical element in this picture that takes it one step further, because we often find "the sojourner" or "the alien" added to the Prophet's list of "the poor, the widows, and the orphans" as being among the people one should support with acts of generosity. This addition lifts up the need for members of this community to extend their compassion—the sensibility that should motivate their giving to help others—beyond their own boundaries. In this way, mercy and justice are extended and elevated as a motivation for giving. God tells the Israelites, "When an alien lives with you in your land, do not mistreat him. The alien living among you must be treated as one of your native born. Love him as yourself, for you were aliens in Egypt" (Leviticus 19:33–34).

At its origins, the Judeo-Christian tradition highlights and affirms as motivations for giving a sense of belonging and a feeling of obligation to one's own community, along with a sense of moral obligation to uphold standards of justice, mercy, and decency for other people, even those not of one's own community. The texts of the Old Testament suggest that these are motivations for giving that are morally appropriate and to be drawn on in appealing for contributions. There is one example of an appeal to fear or guilt, but it seems an anomaly, more a text about the reasons for a tax than a rationale for giving.

Some of these texts propose mechanisms for giving that seem very rule-oriented. It is easy to see how people could take the passages about tithing, for instance, and create rigid formulas to decide what every person should give. But this misses something more important, which is the understanding of God at work in the world that undergirds and frames the motivation for giving entirely. In this regard, we must hear the whole voice of Scripture. The Prophets say some very harsh things about those who merely follow the rules in ritual observances, without committing their hearts and minds, and yet believe that this amounts to practicing their faith.

According to the Prophet Isaiah, God has no use for observances of rigid formulas absent a desire to serve God and love one's neighbor, and so "The Lord says, 'These people come near to me with their mouth and honor me with their lips, but their hearts are far from me.'" (Isaiah 29:13). Rather, the Old Testament seems to tell us that God hopes that all people, when confronted by a need for generosity, "will give freely," with "a heart not grudging, because for this God will bless [them] in all [their] work and in all that [they] undertake" (Deuteronomy 15:10).

A New Testament Perspective on Giving

Moving from the Old Testament to the New, there is an important shift in the frame of reference. Just as the Old Testament is primarily the account of a people's collective relationship with God, the New Testament is much more the story, first, of one person and then of other persons whose lives he touched. It focuses far more on people's individual relationships with God. This distinction should not be overemphasized, for at the end of the New Testament, especially in the Book of Acts and the Epistles, more discussion of the life of the community of believers appears. Still, this attention to the community's shared life is preceded almost always in experience and in emphasis by a focus on individual belief, commitment, and practices that lead one into that fellowship.

In this context, little is said in the Gospels about giving out of an obligation to, a sense of reciprocity with, or the need to honor a particular community or tradition. By contrast, such notions seem to be challenged in some places in Jesus' teaching, as in his comments on Sabbath practices (Mark 2:23–27), or even be attacked as hypocritical, as in his challenge to the Pharisees' practice of *Corban* (Mark 7:9–13). So what principles undergird Jesus' teachings about giving?

First, Jesus brings forward from the Old Testament the expectation that people will give out of a commitment to justice and a sense of reciprocity that is more generalized. That is, people will live by the precept "Do unto others as you would have them do unto you." This is still vitally important.

Yet Jesus also extends that idea—and in so doing radically alters it. Jesus asks his disciples, "If you love those that love you, what credit is that to you? And if you do good to those who do good to you, what credit is that to you?" Then he tells them to "love [their] enemies, and do good, and lend expecting nothing in return" (Luke 6:32–36).

Such exhortations move the teaching beyond reciprocity (see also Matthew 5:40–42) and shift the basic rationale for giving from obligation to opportunity. The disciples are not being taught to do good because they need to "give something back" or even to sustain a chain of mutual or communal support that might sustain them in the future. Rather they are being encouraged to "do good" and to give of themselves as an expression of their gratitude for and absolute trust in God's love for them and for all people. The perspective encompassed in Jesus' teachings here assumes that one can induce people to give by appealing to the love and gratitude they will feel and want to express for the grace and love of God, when they have experienced it. In addition, this perspective assumes that one of the best ways to bear witness to the reality of that grace and love—especially among those who have not yet recognized their own experience of it—is through acts of profound generosity.

So Jesus sends his disciples out with simple instructions: "Freely you have received, freely give" (Matthew 10:8). Moreover, he indicates the clear expectation that one of the surest ways to know if someone has been touched by the experience of God's grace and love and has chosen to be in relationship with God is by the evidence of participation in acts of charity and compassion (Matthew 25:31–45). Other voices in the New Testament carry these assumptions forward, as, for example, in questions such as "If anyone has the world's goods and sees his brother in need, yet closes his heart to him, how does God's love abide in him?" (1 John 3:17).

Some interpreters of the Bible discount the emphasis of these teachings by saying that Jesus devalued all material things. They point to passages where the disciples are told to model themselves after "the lilies of the field" and not worry about their material needs (Matthew 6:25–33) or where a rich young man is told he must give all that he has to the poor in order to be perfect (Matthew 19:16–21). But such interpretations miss the focus of these passages, which is not on denigrating material possessions but rather on trusting in God for all our needs, material as well as spiritual. Indeed, some later writings in the New Testament appear to be intended to correct persons in the early church who had misinterpreted the teachings about material goods in ways that led to an irresponsible neglect of their worldly duties or to practices of asceticism that were harmful or brought the Gospel into bad repute (see 1 Timothy, esp. 4–5).

In short, Jesus encouraged his followers to live lives of service and giving rooted in and shaped by their experiences of God's love, understanding of God's faithfulness, and acceptance of God's grace. Nothing in this message suggests that fear or guilt are good or healthy motivations for giving or service. If one central theme of Jesus' message is that "a perfect love casts out fear" (1 John 4:18), then attempts to motivate people to give by playing on their fears—of going to hell, or of the consequences to self or others if they do not give enough to fix some problem in the world—are clearly inconsistent with Jesus' message.

Finally, there are a number of passages in which one prominent motive for giving, self-aggrandizement, is explicitly rejected. When Jesus teaches about charity, he warns against seeking honor or other worldly rewards for one's good works. "When you give alms, sound no trumpet before you, as the hypocrites do in the synagogues and in the streets, that they may be praised by men," Jesus says. "But when you give alms, do not let your right hand know what your left hand is doing" (Matthew 6:2–3). Exhortations to humility and to good works that truly place the welfare of others above our own self-interests are found throughout the Gospels.

It is true that all of the passages we have examined so far focus on giving, not asking. But certainly it is reasonable to assume that the motives Jesus tells us are desirable as underpinnings for giving are also the motives Christian fundraisers should appeal to, and try to reinforce, in asking. This is especially true if we would like the asking and giving to become an occasion for growth in and expression of faith. Even so, we need to see if the New Testament has anything to say more explicitly about asking, and that is our next task.

The New Testament Perspective on Asking

Very few passages in the New Testament speak about asking for money. But a number of them discuss the purposes and circumstances surrounding requests for money, and those passages provide fundamental insights that we should pay attention to as Christian fundraisers, board members, administrators, pastors, and donors.

We are indebted to the exceptional work done by Jouette Bassler in this realm. Her very helpful book, *God and Mammon: Asking for Money in the New Testament* (1991), is the most thorough and thoughtful piece of biblical scholarship on fundraising we have seen. It has shaped our thinking about these topics very powerfully. Her observations inform many of the comments we will make in this discussion.

Bassler argues that to understand the New Testament teachings about fundraising requires examining the attitudes about asking for money—specifically, about begging—in the Greek and Roman cultures that surrounded and influenced the early Christian community. The classical Greek philosophical view, she notes, as embodied in the writings of Plato and Aristotle, encouraged only a cautious generosity. Unbridled generosity was *not* seen as a virtue.

In the classical philosophical framework, some giving was encouraged, but only to "worthy" people, those who were of good moral character. The catch, however, was that in that culture, poverty was seen as an indicator of moral deficiency, which certainly limited the prospects and obligations for virtuous giving. (The parallels here with our own society's ambiguous views of the virtue of charity and our attempts to distinguish the "deserving" from the "undeserving" poor are striking.) In this context, the Greco-Roman culture of New Testament times looked down on begging, and it defined "good philanthropy" in terms of giving for good causes, primarily to public works, in a framework of expected reciprocity.

Prior to New Testament times, the Cynics represented a radical philosophical perspective, wherein material simplicity was seen as virtuous, in contrast to more mainstream philosophers. It was in the Cynics' view a virtuous practice for itinerant teachers to live a frugal life and to seek money and goods to support themselves from those who might be receptive to their teachings. The corruption of their practices, however, along with the widespread presence of mendicant beggars who looked like the Cynics, led to deeper skepticism among the general public about begging of all sorts.

In the Gospels

This is the cultural framework in which the efforts of the early itinerant missionaries—including the first twelve disciples (Mark 6:8–11) and a second set of seventy-two missionaries (Luke 10:1–12)—unfolded and in which they had to operate. And it is in this cultural context that instructions to them about how to support themselves while on the road were given and need to be interpreted.

There are, in fact, no comments in the Gospels about asking for money apart from indirect references in the "mission instructions" given to the early disciples and missionaries. Hence much of what we can learn about Jesus' views on this subject we have to draw out of the limited texts or passages about giving.

Looking at the instructions to "the twelve" for mission (which appear in similar versions in Matthew 10:5–15; Mark 6:8–11; and Luke 9:3–5) and to "the seventy-two" (Luke 10:2–12), it would appear that asking for money is generally discouraged. The missionaries were told not to take any money on their journeys or even a purse (Matthew 10:9–10; Mark 6:8). These first church workers were told to accept hospitality and support, "for the worker deserves his wages" (Luke 10:7), but were not instructed or even encouraged to ask.

These instructions are framed in the assumption that a disciple or missionary needs to model an attitude of radical trust in God by choosing the circumstances of voluntary poverty and dependence on the generosity of those who will accept the Gospel message. Willingness to live and work under such conditions was viewed as a vital testimony to one's faith. In this context, offers of hospitality and support freely made in response to the preaching of the Gospel were to be viewed as indications of receptivity to that message. Also, the temporal context for these instructions is one of expectation that this work would culminate soon with Jesus' return. (Simply put, these folks did not expect to operate under these conditions for a particularly long time.)

In sum, in Jesus' teachings—or at least in these instructions—we find a firm belief that persons in the service of the Lord should trust in God to provide what is needed for their service. The instructions Jesus gives his disciples assume that timely provision of support by others is one way that will happen. The instructions also suggest that the willingness of others to offer support may be an indication of their potential receptivity or commitment to the Gospel message.

In all this, however, there is a striking reticence about the missionaries' actively seeking support. We find no encouragement and some cautions against people seeking funds for themselves. (Again, recall that the disciples and first missionaries were told not to carry a purse. We can presume from this that it was not expected that they would take any money away from the places they visited.) Finally, in these various passages, the Gospels really say little or nothing about how one could or should ask for funds for the work of others.

Paul's Views of Fundraising

In the writing of Paul, many of the same kinds of concerns about the motives for giving appear. We also find much more discussion about the context and manner in which it is deemed appropriate or inappropriate to ask for gifts of support and money.

Paul can be viewed as the biblical prototype of a certified fundraising executive. He worked hard and somewhat systematically to raise funds to support both indigent members of the church and the ministries of the church, especially evangelism. He could be very explicit about the needs to be met. He was clearly (as a modern employment advertisement for a fundraiser might say) "results-oriented." Yet as a Christian, he was also deeply concerned about the motives that were engaged and nurtured in acts of asking and giving.

So it is Paul who writes the church at Corinth to say, "If I give all I possess to the poor . . . but have not love, I gain nothing" (1 Corinthians

13:3). And Paul is the one who later congratulates the Corinthians because "they were not only the first to give, but also [the first] to have the desire to do so" (2 Corinthians 8:10). Clearly, to Paul, motives were as significant as results.

Knowing this, it is worth our while to spend some more time looking a little closer at Paul's observations about fundraising. Following Jouette Bassler's lead, we will consider this material in two sections, with a view to how Paul saw the matter of raising support, first, for himself and his own mission and, second, for others.

Paul deals with questions about seeking support for himself and his own missionary efforts as an apostle spreading the Gospel in 1 Corinthians 9. (He also touches on these issues in other epistles.) The context for his observations in 1 Corinthians is a controversy about who has the right to ask for or expect financial and material support from the church. Paul argues that he has the right to such support—that all apostles do—and that church members should be glad to provide it out of gratitude for his service and for the experience of grace and growth in the Gospel his ministry has brought them (1 Corinthians 9:1–12). However, Paul then goes on to explain why he has not and will not ask for money for himself from those he serves, primarily because he does not want it to appear he is preaching for money rather than the love of Christ (9:15–18).

In fact, looking at all the passages where Paul addresses these matters, we find that he really gives three related reasons for not asking for money for himself: it might appear greedy, it might make it look like he was peddling the Gospel (selling one's teachings was a disreputable practice of some Cynics), and it could have the effect of "hindering the Gospel of Christ" by giving people a reason to reject the message. Paul also appears to be concerned that asking for financial or material support might put too great a burden on the church or members being asked.

In short, Paul believed that "the worker deserves his wages" and that churches had an obligation to support missionaries in order to help others have a chance to receive the spiritual blessings they themselves had received. But he also felt very strongly that asking for money should never be done in such a way as to create obstacles to people's hearing and accepting the Gospel, especially by creating an impression of greed. Putting all these concerns together, Paul seems to feel that asking for money for oneself is problematic but it is acceptable to ask for money for others if done in the right way.

Something of Paul's views of the right way of asking for money for others appears in 2 Corinthians 8–9. There the discussion derives from his efforts to get this church and others to contribute to "the Great Collection"—

funds to support members of the church elsewhere who were in economic distress. Bassler notes that this discussion, and Paul's later commentary (in 2 Corinthians 11:7–11) about why he did not ask for support for himself while in the church at Corinth, shows how easily questions about money and asking for money can become theologically loaded and complex.

Chapters 8 and 9 in 2 Corinthians are worthy of careful study and deep reflection on the part of every Christian fundraiser. The story should seem familiar to any professional fundraiser, for Paul is conducting a campaign "for relief of the saints," for poor Christians in Jerusalem, and is employing a modified lead gift strategy. Here he is telling the brethren in Corinth how much those in Macedonia already gave in order to encourage their generosity.

Yet we need also to notice what is different in Paul's approach, for in this passage Paul focuses not on the amount of the Macedonians' gift but instead on the spirit in which it was made. Paul tells the Corinthians that "out of . . . their overflowing joy and their extreme poverty" the Macedonians gave in "rich generosity . . . even beyond their own ability" and that "they urgently pleaded with us for the privilege of sharing in this service to the saints" (2 Corinthians 8:2–4). Paul then goes on to tell the Corinthians his hope that they will "excel in this grace of giving" (8:7) and he commends them because the year before "they were not only the first to give, but also [the first] to have the desire to do so" (8:10). Paul challenges the Corinthians to respond deeply and truly to their own experience of grace and God's generosity, at least as much as he challenges them to respond to the specific need of the poor or to match the Macedonians' donations.

In this approach, Paul also raises up ideals of community or partnership—the Greek word used is *koinonia*. Drawing on Old Testament ideas, Paul casts his request to the Corinthians (and others) in the framework that assumes that the church is a community of faith and reciprocity, a community where people care for one another out of a commitment to live for one another and for God, whom they trust to care for all of them. In this view, they are all to be partners in God's work and the work of the community. It is against this background that we can understand Paul's explanation to the Corinthians that in asking them to stretch to be generous in their giving, he does "not desire that others might be relieved while you are hard pressed, but that there might be equality. At the present time your plenty will supply their need, so that in turn their plenty will supply what you need" (2 Corinthians 8:13–14).

Paul is appealing here in part to enlightened self-interest but even more to solidarity. The argument he makes is not that by participating in this one will become part of the community but rather that it is because one is already a part of this community, whose members experience both mutual support and God's support, that one is asked to give. In lifting up the example of the Macedonians' giving, Paul is pointing out how the dynamics of grace flow through the extended community that is the church and inviting the Corinthians to participate fully in that dynamic.

Finally, Paul is assuring them that they can count on this grace to continue to flow as they participate in this partnership of faith. So one does not give to get rich; but, Paul assures them, "you will be made rich in every way so that you can be generous on every occasion" (1 Corinthians 9:11).

We can now summarize Paul's views of the spiritual and theological implications of asking for money for others. He was deeply committed to getting church members to provide the resources needed for the good works the church was undertaking, but he was equally committed to the ideal that opportunities to give become occasions for the experience of grace. He clearly hoped that giving would be an act of joy and thanksgiving, one that occurs with a recognition—on the part of those who ask and those who give—of the reality of a special kind of serial reciprocity that exists between believers and God and among the churches and their members.

"Remember this," Paul says, "whoever sows sparingly will also reap sparingly, and whoever sows generously will also reap generously. Each person should give what he has decided to give in his heart, not reluctantly or under compulsion, for God loves a cheerful giver. And God is able to make all grace abound to you, so that in all things and all times, having all that you need, you will abound in every good work" (2 Corinthians 9:6–8). Paul hoped that ultimately giving would become an act of worship, glorifying God and leading to the growth in faith of the donor.

Key Points from a New Testament Viewpoint

What can we conclude from a review of the New Testament texts on asking? Several key points stand out as requiring our attention.

First, the issue of integrity looms large. Jouette Bassler argues that "integrity emerges from these [New Testament] texts as a fundamental issue, not just the moral integrity of the fundraising practices . . . but the integrity of these practices within the whole ministry of the church" (1991, p. 133). We would concur that for Christians involved in fundraising, a crucial question is whether our fundraising practices are fully in line with our ideals and fully expressive of the values we profess.

Second, the spiritual and theological meanings people attach to questions and decision about money are of great importance. Bassler observes that "the texts also make it clear that requests for money can acquire unanticipated theological overtones" that may "change the way the requests are heard and the messages they convey" (1991, pp. 133–134). Anyone who has raised money for the church has had the experience of individuals taking offense at a solicitation message they interpreted in an unanticipated way. We must be particularly attentive to the theological import of our fundraising materials and techniques.

Another crucial message of these texts has to do with the fundamental importance of trust. Trust is a fundamental precondition for all successful fundraising and should be a hallmark in all relationships among Christians. Furthermore, it is vital to see that different kinds of trust have to be evident at many levels for the acts of giving and asking to be fruitful in both spiritual and practical terms. Trust has to be evident for everyone as trust in God's generosity and faithfulness; for donors, as trust in an organization's integrity and reliability; and among fundraisers and organizational leaders, as trust in donors' judgment.

Finally, it is vital to acknowledge that a concept of reciprocity is at work in these discussions of asking and giving, but it is a different view of reciprocity than we commonly encounter. Bassler notes that in the New Testament texts, "requests for money were rooted in a prior exchange of spiritual benefits. They were not made with the promise of *generating* these benefits" (1991, p. 134).

This is the kind of reciprocity (as a joyful response to generosity) that Paul cites and that Jesus highlights in his teachings. It is not a dynamic that can be used to manipulate events to one's own benefit. Rather it is an experience of abundance that comes when one's giving is truly motived by love of God and neighbor.

Conclusions

We started this chapter acknowledging that some involvement with mammon is inevitable for us personally and for the institutional church. Money is a necessity for carrying out many of the good works we are called to do as individuals and as communities of faith. So we cannot avoid being involved in earning, collecting, and spending it, or giving it away, if we want to participate in those good works. But some questions follow from these realizations: For what reasons and in what ways should we give as individual people of faith and members of the church? And for what reasons and in what ways should religious institutions be asking for money?

Beginning with giving, the Bible consistently points to positive, even celebratory motivations as the most spiritually edifying and morally desirable.

The texts suggest that giving out of a desire to affirm and strengthen one's participation in a community of faith, a desire for mercy and justice, or a desire to express one's appreciation for God's love and grace is the kind of giving that "overflows in many thanksgivings to God" (2 Corinthians 9:12). Other texts warn against self-serving motivations for giving, where the intent is to try to ensure some future return benefit or to serve one's own honor or pride. And if we are talking about giving—as opposed to paying some tax or dues—we find no texts that indicate that guilt or fear is ever an appropriate or edifying motivation for giving.

The apostle Paul paid close attention to the spiritual conditions as well as the financial situations of donors and potential donors. He clearly sought to make his fundraising efforts an extension of his ministry in terms of using his appeals as occasions to teach and preach about the Gospel. He sought to engage motivations for giving in the donors that would express and lead to their further growth in faith. Paul sets forth the ideals around which Christian fundraising should be organized in emphasizing that giving should be an act of joy, an expression of one's own experience of and trust in God's love and care, and a reflection of one's sense of being a partner in God's work in the world.

When we help make that kind of experience available to donors by the way we organize and implement our fundraising efforts, we can talk about having a program that reflects Gospel values. At that point, we can talk about having a fundraising program that is a ministry. "It is then," as Jouette Bassler puts it, "that the act of giving can become a joyous celebration of faith, that the givers benefit more than the receivers, and that the requests for money can be seen by all as a link in the operation of God's grace" (1991, p. 135).

Of course, realizing our ideals is never easy. Designing and implementing a fundraising program that reflects biblical ideals so clearly is especially hard given all the social, cultural, and financial pressures that impinge on Christian organizations (as discussed in Chapter One). Moreover, the truth is that our forebears have been involved in Christian fundraising for almost two thousand years, and though many have acted out of the best of motives and purposes, their track record has been spotty. Still, we can learn from their failures as well as their successes. It is in that hope that we devote the next chapter to an examination of the history of Christian fundraising.

3

A BRIEF HISTORY
OF CHRISTIAN FUNDRAISING

There are three conversions necessary [for the Christian life]: the
conversion of the heart, the mind, and the purse.

—Martin Luther

WE OPEN WITH a keen and true observation about the life of faith by a
pivotal figure in the history of the church. Luther understood far better
than many of his contemporaries, and far better than most religious people today, the spiritual effects and significance of our attitudes toward
money. Perhaps this was because he was such a devoted and astute student of the Bible. Certainly, it was because of his own experience as well.

Some church historians have noted that Luther was apparently surprised by the intensity and extent of the reaction to the Ninety-Five Theses he posted on the door of the church in Wittenberg in October 1517.
(That event is generally accepted as the precipitating incident for the
Protestant Reformation.) Why was he surprised? For one thing, two
months earlier, Luther had circulated a more radical document containing ninety-seven theses calling into question some of the central ideas of
the dominant theological movement of his time (Scholasticism), and it had
generated far less controversy.

What is generally not remembered is that these famous Ninety-Five
Theses included a number of propositions contesting the sale of indulgences, a common fundraising practice of the Catholic Church at that
time. The earlier ninety-seven theses disputed theological doctrines in a

way that seemed to have wider implications for the belief system of Christians, but they were really of interest only to some academics and a few clergy. In putting forward theses on the sale of indulgences, however, Luther challenged a fundraising practice of the papacy and the church hierarchy on theological grounds and threatened to jeopardize that practice and the income it generated. This set in motion an ecclesiastical and eventually a political firestorm.

Thus we have a first lesson to be learned from examining the history of fundraising in the church: one of the most significant and dramatic schisms in the history of the church was precipitated by a controversy over the theological implications of fundraising practices! Obviously, the theology and spirituality undergirding our fundraising efforts can have real and lasting impacts on the members and the life of the church. Anyone who thinks there are no significant theological questions associated with fundraising needs to take notice. So must anyone who thinks that the spiritual and theological implications of our choices about fundraising strategies and techniques are unimportant.

This is only the first of many lessons to be learned from church history. We will explore those lessons in this chapter, informed by our examination of Scripture from Chapter Two.

The Bible sets out ideals of the Judeo-Christian tradition for conducting ourselves in all aspects of our lives. If we take our faith seriously, our giving should be guided by those ideals. If we wish to know a deepened sense of God's presence and grace and to grow in faith, giving in these ways should lead to that, for these are the kinds of blessings promised by God to those who are truly generous and faithful in giving.

Surely, all people involved in raising money for Christian organizations must hope that their donors experience these kinds of blessings too. If so, their ways of asking and thanking donors must be shaped by the ideals we found in the Bible. But how does one translate biblical insights about what should motivate giving and appropriate ways of asking into fundraising practice?

With these questions in mind we look at the practices, and commentaries on the practices, of our forebears in Christian fundraising. Those of us working in development for Christian organizations today are not the first generation of people trying to raise money for religious organizations or Christian causes. Unfortunately, if our hope is to find ready-made models for practices that embody the goals and ideals for giving and asking we saw in the Old and New Testaments, we are likely to be disappointed in looking at church history. Reviewing our spiritual predecessors' practices may ultimately show us more about what not to do than anything else. Yet this too can be useful learning.

The Church's Earliest Fundraising Practices

In examining the fundraising work of the apostle Paul, we have already looked at fundraising practices in the earliest stage of the church's existence. There is no need to review that material again, except to recall three quick points. First, the Pauline record reveals that the primary causes for which early Christians asked other early Christians for money were for relief of the poor (especially the poor in their own community, which was a persecuted minority community) and for missionary work. Second, Paul was sensitive to the theological messages and spiritual implications associated with requests for money. Third, Paul tailored his appeals to engage motives for giving in potential donors that he thought were most likely to lead to a growth in grace and faith for the givers.

There are very few documents other than Paul's epistles that tell us more about the fundraising practices in the early church. Only the *Didache,* another important piece of Christian literature of the time, offers any help in this regard. It contains a range of teachings on various subjects relating to the life of faith. Usually dated from the late first century A.D., this document also contains instructions for missionaries seeking material support. It is interesting that in the *Didache,* even at this early date, concerns about abuses and corruption among missionaries seeking support are evident. So the *Didache* offers some suggestions for systematizing support for traveling workers.

Beyond this, we find virtually nothing about fundraising in the church between the apostolic age and about 300 A.D.—that is, between the first generation and formation of the church and the point when Christianity was transformed from the religion of a persecuted minority to the official religion of the Roman Empire.

In reviewing the history of Christian fundraising, it is essential that the political, social, and economic context be kept firmly in mind, because shifts in these contexts surrounding the church's revenue-generating efforts have powerfully shaped and altered the nature of those efforts.

Over the past two millennia, these contexts have been fundamentally altered twice. The first major change occurred when the church went from being a persecuted organization, in which all support had to be voluntary and could even be dangerous to offer, to being an ally (even an arm) of the state, in which all needed support was coerced from taxpayers. The second upheaval came some fifteen centuries later when the institutional church was transformed again—especially in the United States but in some other modern societies as well—into an institution once more separate from the state, in which support again had to be voluntary.

Judeo-Christian Ideals of Charity in the Later Empire and the Middle Ages

When Emperor Constantine decided to make Christianity the officially approved religion of the Roman Empire in 312 A.D., the kind of religious fundraising in which we are interested ceased to be needed or practiced for a very long time, at least in Christian circles. The secular government of the state could employ its power to tax to garner any monetary resources needed to fund the church and its projects, and it did so. (Of course, from that point on, the state could also effectively dictate the content and focus of those ministries and could control the life of the church, and it did that, too.) Some "voluntary giving" to religious institutions still occurred in the later Roman Empire and in medieval Europe, but since these were now also civil or state institutions, the rationale for giving changed.

In fact, not only were church institutions now state institutions, but the melding of the Greco-Roman traditions of philanthropy and Judeo-Christian traditions of charity within the church yielded a very different perspective on giving and asking. The classical cultural heritage carried its own ideas about giving and raising money into the life of the church, and those were ideas not entirely consistent with the Judeo-Christian principles we find in the Bible.

So, for instance, while the classical tradition emphasizes the responsibility to give for purposes of improving the life of the community as a whole (philanthropy), it often conceives of such improvements more in political and cultural than in personal terms. In that context, gifts for public buildings, civic affairs, the arts, and such were (and often still are) the most admired examples of philanthropy. The biblical tradition, by contrast, emphasizes giving for the welfare of individuals (charity) as well as the community and tends to focus more on personal and spiritual ends, on care of the needy and support of activities of worship. In this context, gifts that help individuals in need are often the most worthy of praise.

In addition, as the classical philanthropic tradition derives more from a political and civic context, it also readily accepts and even legitimizes motives for giving, such as pride and self-aggrandizement, that the biblical tradition specifically rejects. In the same vein, another outcome of the blending of the classical and Judeo-Christian traditions and integration of civil and religious functions is that the distinction between giving for religious purposes and spiritual motivations and giving for secular purposes and self-serving motivations becomes less and less meaningful.

This points to another lesson, or at least raises a question, about what underlies views of giving now held by Christian organizations and donors, especially in relation to supporting institutions. Looking at models for raising support (or giving money) for things like buildings and endowments at Christian institutions, it appears that the approaches employed in the church now may derive more from the tradition of the Greeks and the Romans than from the Israelites or the early church. That may explain further the conflicts some people feel between the conventional strategies for such fundraising and the ideals suggested in Scripture for how we should approach donors and how they should approach giving.

In truth, much of the fundraising of the church in medieval times was really a kind of political fundraising, and much of the giving was motivated by a lust for power or by greed or other less than noble urges. Large-scale gifts—particularly to build cathedrals, to support monasteries, and to fund the Crusades—were made in expectation of very concrete returns in terms of public prestige, grants of political or ecclesial offices, and control of income-producing properties.

Furthermore, many smaller and even some larger gifts were motivated by fear, as was the case with the purchase and sale of indulgences, the practice that drew Luther's ire. That practice brought the donors a promise of relief from the punishment of purgatory for themselves or their relatives in exchange for their gifts.

In addition, operating on larger or smaller scales, some elements of the clerical hierarchy were often using such fundraising techniques to add to the tax-funded revenues they received to support a life of self-indulgence, while the poor, the widows, and the orphans starved in their communities. Another lesson? Well, looking at this history tells us that malfeasance and greed in religious fundraising are certainly not the inventions of modern televangelists!

Over the years, involvement in fundraising has proved to be "the occasion of sin" (to use some Catholic terminology) for many in the church—sometimes, it seems, for the church as an organization across many denominations. That obviously does not mean that trying to raise money for Christian causes can or should simply cease. It does mean that all those involved in this work need to understand that abuses or mistakes can become a stumbling block and a scandal to the Gospel, for themselves and for donors.

The approaches to resource development of the medieval church do not for the most part embody biblical ideals in fundraising, nor do they offer examples for contemporary Christian fundraisers to follow. They seem more like cautionary tales. So it is not without some irony that one of the most illuminating and inspiring commentaries on what should motivate and characterize Christian charity derives from this period, the *Summa Theologiae* of Thomas Aquinas, the Dominican friar.

As a theologian, Thomas seemed much interested in what motives inspire and what ideas shape a person's good works, as well as what results come from them. He distinguished between what he calls "corporal works" and "spiritual works of mercy." On the list of corporal works he includes things like feeding and clothing people and rescuing them from danger. On the list of spiritual works he includes things like consoling or teaching people and praying for them. This part of the *Summa* makes it clear that Thomas considered both spiritual concern and useful service necessities.

Both right intention and real action are needed. We are called, he says, to care for the bodies and the souls of the needy; and authentic charity on our part must come from the heart and the hands. He says, "One aspect of neighborly love is that we must not merely will our neighbors good, but actually work to bring it about" (Thomas Aquinas, 1273/1964).

Most important, Thomas's writings on this subject argue that this "neighborly love"—in the Latin, *caritas*—is the best and perhaps the only "right" motive for giving and service. Sharing with one's neighbor the love, the same *caritas,* one experiences coming from God is the essence of the practice of charity in this view.

Whatever the common practice in his time, it seems clear that Thomas would not have seen a desire to buy one's way out of purgatory as a laudable motivation for a gift to the church or any other work of charity. It should be acknowledged that he never questioned and even supported the authority of the pope to offer indulgences (which in Roman Catholic theology are pardons or remissions of sins, reducing the time one would spend in purgatory). But indulgences were originally earned for doing good works and offering service to the church; they were not doled out in exchange for money.

In his commentary on charity in the *Summa,* Thomas pointed his contemporaries back to the Gospel values that should undergird and sustain the practice of Christian charity in all its forms. Unfortunately, his moving and eloquent statement of principles for the practice of Christian service and giving stand in stark contrast to much of the practice of the church and Christian organizations of the time.

In the Aftermath of the Reformation

Even after the Reformation, most churches remained state churches. So most could continue to count on state support and were controlled by the government, if they were of the same denomination as the ruler. Any church that represented a minority perspective or tradition—such as the Anabaptists in Germany, the Huguenots in France, and the Society of Friends in England—was thrown back into the situation of the early church. It became dependent again on voluntary support, often in the face of persecution. But throughout Europe, and then in the European colonies in the New World, the largest and most visible institutional expressions of religious belief and practice continued to be supported primarily by tax dollars.

The situation began to change between the 1600s and 1800s as some minority Christian groups came to be tolerated in certain countries. This allowed for both growth and stability for many of those groups, so that they could, with voluntary support, establish their own church buildings and alternative religious institutions. In the British colonies that were to become the United States, there appeared a similar pattern of voluntary support providing for the creation of alternative churches and religious institutions, which emerge alongside "established" (politically favored and tax-supported) churches. The nature and pattern of that activity depended, of course, on a particular colony's stance on religious toleration.

By the mid-1800s in the United States, with the disestablishment of the last of the state churches in New England, all church bodies and institutions had been thrown back into the financial situation of their earliest forebears, albeit in a more favorable cultural climate. They had to raise all the material resources they required, whether as congregations or as special-purpose institutions carrying out good works in the world, from voluntary contributions. By their responses to this situation, they began to develop the traditions of religious fundraising that Christian fundraisers have inherited today.

A Century and a Half of Christian Fundraising in the United States

The history of Protestant church fundraising in the United States is most helpfully explored by Robert Wood Lynn of Bangor Theological Seminary in *Why Give? Stewardship: A Documentary History of One Strand in American Protestant Teachings About Giving* (1998). An equally useful history of Catholic philanthropy in the United States is *The Catholic*

Philanthropic Tradition in America, by Mary Oates (1995). Understanding the basics of this history will be valuable to any Christian fundraiser because it illuminates the larger context in which he or she is working.

Lynn traces the conversation about money, giving, and support for Christian institutions that has been going on among Protestants in the United States for at least one hundred and fifty years. Oates's book traces the varying dynamics that have shaped Catholics' attitudes toward church funding over the past two centuries and helps us see how history affects their attitudes and behaviors today.

Lynn cites important documents and offers introductory essays that illustrate the key themes, tone, and trends in the Protestant conversation about giving. He makes one fundamental assertion about church fundraising at the beginning of his work, from which the rest of his analysis follows. He says, "Protestants have struggled to locate the authority that would support the appeal of one church member to another to give money to a Christian cause. Any answer to the question 'Why give?' finally involves an appeal to some authority." We generally agree that the need to find and articulate that "authority" has challenged and troubled Christian fundraisers, at least those working in a context where support is supposed to be voluntary, for several hundred years now. This is a claim, however, that we must refine.

It is important to note that for the most part, the authority sought in this context has usually been a kind of moral authority. That is to say, in a social and cultural context where almost all congregations, Protestant and Catholic, have functioned primarily as voluntary associations, the authority that pastors and other Christian fundraisers have looked for to support solicitations of money from other Christians has had to be the authority that derives more from an appeal to common values than from status or office. This, of course, is a dynamic that may play out differently in a Catholic setting than in a Protestant one. Still, both Oates's and Lynn's work generally confirms this view.

In an essentially democratic and highly individualistic society, very few people are going to give simply because the pastor or bishop says so. The vast majority of American Christians are not going to grant to the church, or any of its agents, real authority to dictate personal financial behavior. This lesson is very clear in the recent history of religious fundraising in the United States, and every Christian fundraiser (and pastor) should take heed.

There can be a kind of authority in a community of faith, perhaps exercised through an official, that is more formal and coercive than that. In a few church bodies, expectations about giving as a condition of membership are more formally articulated and enforced by church pastors or officers, and real sanctions are applied to those who do not meet those expectations. That is relatively rare, however. In any case, although it may be possible to exercise that kind of formal authority in a community a person "belongs to," where the person's membership and hence identity as a Christian is rooted, it seems highly unlikely that a parachurch body or agency—or really any group other than the congregation—can successfully claim such authority.

Two Approaches to Asking

The history of the Protestant fundraising efforts over the past hundred and fifty years demonstrates that Christian organizations and agencies (and for the most part even congregations) are most often limited to two choices in how they frame and focus their appeals for money. Either they can attempt to offer a kind of exchange ("make a sale") when they ask, explaining to the potential donor what services and benefits the organization provides to the donor (or others) that the donor ought to be willing to support because of the measurable value of those services. Or they must appeal to a set of possible motives for giving that derive from a sense of affiliation with other Christians or a desire to affirm shared moral and spiritual tenets or values. The latter is more the effort to ground an appeal in the kind of authority that Lynn describes. He says his historical studies reveal that "most Protestants have relied upon the persuasive powers of certain teachings about giving."

The development over the past hundred years of whole vocabularies, disciplines, and regimes designed specifically to increase giving reflects this. Lynn shows us that the terminology and plans for regimens of "proportionate giving," "sacrificial giving," "tithing," and "systematic benevolence" all derived from efforts of Protestant clergy and denominational officials to find and articulate a spiritual and moral authority for asking for money. All these approaches assumed their potential donors' desire to follow biblical or theological precepts; and these Christian fundraisers hoped their appeals for generosity would connect with their potential donors' sense of being "under the authority" of biblical teachings. In fact, Lynn says, the co-option of the biblical concept of stewardship as a virtual synonym for a program of giving is the most visible and lasting result of all these efforts by Protestant denominational leaders and fundraisers. (He argues, and we agree, that this narrowing of the concept is both unfortunate and theologically unsound.)

It should be noted, however, that the two options of talking about the benefits, either for others or oneself, and appealing to shared values and a sense of community are certainly not mutually exclusive. A close examination of the documents Lynn cites indicates that in most cases, Christian leaders and fundraisers have been doing both for the past hundred and fifty years. Typically they have been both explaining the benefits members or others receive for supporting and being part of a particular community of faith or religious organization—whether a mission society, congregation, or denomination—and asking these people to make gifts as an affirmation of their affiliation with that community, its spiritual message, and the good works it does in the world.

The more that a congregation or denomination has been doing to serve others, including those beyond its own membership, the more its leaders have been able to appeal to altruistic motives, being able to tell members their gifts support charity in the sense Thomas Aquinas described, giving concrete expression to love of God and love of neighbor. Whenever that work of service or evangelism (or both) has been seen and explained as something required by or deriving from the tenets or ideals of the faith, the appeal to support it could become, at least in part, an explicit appeal to moral or spiritual authority. Again, however, appeals can be framed at the same time in terms of the practical efficacy as well as the spiritual intent of the service provided—in other words, in terms of the practical good being achieved.

This has surely been the case for the parachurch—for Christian schools, service agencies, and mission organizations of various sorts—as well as congregations. Where practical caring and service for others have been pursued as ways of giving expression to spiritual values, showing potential donors that this is done well, that it truly does benefit others, has been a way of demonstrating that those spiritual values are fully expressed in that work. Many sophisticated Christian donors have long been looking to see both practical and spiritual benefits (for others) from their giving.

The appeals that both Protestant and Catholic leaders have made for support for Christian service agencies and institutions reveal that they have traditionally tried to mix those themes in their efforts to persuade people to give. So not only in the examples of fundraising sermons and tracts that Lynn provides but also in some early appeals for Catholic institutions (such as orphanages and hospitals) we have reviewed, we find this intent to engage both the spiritual and practical interests of the donors. Some of the Protestant tracts and lectures speak of both the spiritual value of practicing the disciplines of "tithing" or "sacrificial giving" and of the admirable impact of the work that could be done with the gifts those practices enable the donor to make. Appeal materials for Catholic institutions speak both of the opportunities to be involved in "works of mercy," which are seen as a key part of practicing one's faith, and of the ways people's lives are touched and changed by those works.

And Now?

In asking for support, our predecessors chose between focusing on the benefits that would derive to the donors or others from the gifts they requested and basing their appeals on the grounds of a shared faith and a set of common values or ideals, or they somehow combined the two.

How are Christian fundraisers and pastors asking now? Is the focus of appeals on giving as an expression of faith, as simply a necessity to support church institutions, particular services and practical needs (to "meet the budget"), or some combination of the two? If appeals combine these elements, how does the balance play out? What message comes through most clearly?

As people who receive many appeals from Christian organizations ourselves and who have sought out even more to study, the trend seems to us to be toward appeals that emphasize the needs that must be met and work that must be done with the gifts sought. This is often to the exclusion of any reference to the faith that should shape charitable work and could be given expression in a gift.

Certainly, the opportunities and needs Christians may see for caring for the needy, for solving human problems, and for sharing the good news of our faith can seem overwhelmingly large and extremely urgent. In that context, Christian fundraisers can end up feeling that they should do whatever is required to get people to give the resources needed for that work. But that is a feeling, when it leads to the sense that working for noble ends might justify ignoble means, to which Christian fundraisers must never acquiesce.

Working in an environment where the wizards of modern marketing—including some who work as "fundraising counsel"—can show Christian fundraisers hundreds of new ways to "motivate" their donors, it is easy to choose techniques and strategies based solely on their potential to generate income in the short term. But we believe that Christian fundraisers have a special responsibility to think about the messages these techniques convey about values, or the ways they may influence the faith perspective of donors, in both the short and the long term. This is not to say we should not learn anything from marketing experts, but we need to reflect with care about how—and sometimes if—it is appropriate to import their techniques. (Note that the sale of indulgences clearly "motivated" donors.)

Again, if history tells us anything, it surely tells us to be very cautious in this regard, for the effects of choosing an expedient solution for our difficulties in raising funds without considering whether or not it is also a faithful solution may be far more serious than we ever thought.

Conclusions

So what should we learn from all this history? First, and most important, we should learn that how and why we ask for funds matters to the larger life of the church. Sound theology and spirituality true to the tradition we represent must shape our efforts in Christian fundraising. This is crucial because when those efforts reflect values other than Gospel values, the result can be destructive to the spiritual life and integrity of donors, organizations, and even the church as a body.

Our examination of the history of Christian fundraising tells us that the institutional church's fundraising efforts have, sadly, often not demonstrated Gospel values—indeed, they have too often betrayed them. For the longest part of that history, the many centuries when the church was co-opted by the state, fundraising that appealed to pride, greed, the lust for power, and fear was commonplace. But many individual Christians also gave out of faith in God's providence, altruism and generosity. Thomas Aquinas wrote in eloquent terms about what should characterize the practice of Christian charity. Yet the record tells us that sometimes donors' actions in providing material support—and often the church's actions in soliciting such support—did not embody or promote the characteristics Thomas so beautifully articulated.

Even if the Protestant Reformation brought an end to some of the most egregious fundraising practices, it did not greatly improve matters beyond that. Fundraising (and large-scale giving) in Protestant and Catholic circles still often seems to be as much about drawing on and reinforcing pride and privilege—serving self-interest—as about nurturing true Christian benevolence.

Over the past two hundred years or so, when the church has not been a state institution, the record shows that Christian fundraising was still fraught with difficulties, both spiritual and practical. The recent history of "entrepreneurial evangelicalism" is especially rife with tales of shameful excesses in fundraising. The search for a persuasive appeal to moral authority that will consistently motivate Christians to give to Christian causes has not been widely successful. The statistics on giving to churches and other Christian organizations make it quite clear that most professed Christians have not been giving their "first fruits," a tithe, or even half a tithe, for that matter, to support the church and the work of the Christian community in the world.

Because of the lack of success in finding and articulating such moral authority in a way that has encouraged Christians to be more generous, the risk is that Christian fundraisers will resort to other approaches for motivating donors. Yet these approaches may not only fail to engage potential donors on the ground of faith but may, even worse, actually encourage attitudes toward giving and patterns of giving that are contrary to the teachings of the Gospel. And sadly, these approaches to fundraising, when taken to the wider public in attempts to solicit funds from them, will give a false impression of the faith and values of most Christians as well.

Combining the Practical and the Spiritual

Ultimately, though, Christian fundraisers and organizations do not have to go the way of high-pressure marketing and sophisticated sales models, pitches to self-interest, and emotional manipulation in order to cultivate and encourage more giving from donors in the Christian community. Indeed, we think most will be far more successful in the long run if they recognize that the "conversion of the purse" Luther says is needed will come most powerfully with the conversion of the heart and mind rooted in a deeper experience of grace and faith. And if Christian fundraisers can approach donors in ways that appeal to the best in the donor, touch the donor at the level of faith, and reinforce the donor's experiences of grace, they can help the donors have that deeper experience of grace and faith in the act of giving.

If Christian fundraisers show as much concern for their donors' spiritual growth as their own organizations' financial needs, these fundraisers will help grow their donors' hearts, resulting in donors who are truly and more consistently generous over a lifetime.

There are Christian organizations that are trying to do this now. They are trying to refocus their development programs so that these programs become ministries in this sense. We have looked at and reflected on Scripture and church history here to consider what Christian fundraisers ought to do (and not do) if they want their fundraising efforts to be a ministry. Part Two looks at our contemporaries in Christian fundraising who are trying to make their development programs work this way. We examine their efforts to learn and reflect, at the most practical as well as spiritual levels, about what fundraising as a ministry might look like here and now.

PART TWO

SIX ESSENTIAL CHARACTERISTICS OF FUNDRAISING AS A MINISTRY

4

CONFIDENCE
IN GOD'S ABUNDANCE

IF GOD OWNS THE CATTLE ON A THOUSAND HILLS

*The greatest lesson a soul has to learn is that God, and
God alone, is enough for all its needs. This is the lesson that all
God's dealings with us are meant to teach, and this is the
crowning discovery of our entire Christian life. God is enough!*

—Hannah Whitall Smith

"URGENT FROM SUDAN." The e-mail message reported that the store-front technical school Peter had equipped with rebuilt computers donated by U.S. corporations was out of money. "The mission organization says we have to shut down. However, they'll give us three months for the transition if we can raise $2,100. That way students currently enrolled in the program can finish their course of study," the message explained.

The mood in the room was tense as the Stewardship Committee presented its recommendation for balancing the church's budget. "We've cut as much as we can from our own programs. The only way we can see to make this work is to reduce our commitment to the denomination by $20,000. We can't count on members giving much more than they already are. We're running 16 percent behind budget as it is," the committee chair stated. Reluctantly, the church council approved the suggested cut.

"I've found myself doubting we'll make the annual fund goal," a seminary fundraiser admitted to his teammates. "Then yesterday, I came across these words from 2 Corinthians 4 in *The Message:* 'Don't throw up your hands; this is God's ministry.' I needed that reminder!" The tone of the meeting brightened considerably as the review of contacts for the coming month continued.

"This debt is an albatross around our necks. We can't move ahead as an organization until we pay it down, but it's tough to raise money to retire debt," the president said in frustration. "I've prayed about our situation— we've all prayed about it—but it just doesn't get easier. I don't see a simple or immediate way out from under this burden."

The four vignettes with which we begin this chapter highlight situations from a single week, and chances are these weren't the only organizations facing a fundraising challenge at the time. After several years of research, more than a hundred extensive interviews with Christian fundraisers, and site visits to seven exemplary organizations, all focused on development as a ministry, we have reached a troubling conclusion: the financial reality of a great many Christian organizations makes it tough to believe that God is enough. In the midst of the bustle and pressure of the fiscal year, it can be hard to imagine a successful conclusion to difficult fundraising situations. However, as one authority reminds us, "there are uninvited billions to be raised out there. [Our] job is to invite them in" (Rosso, 1991, p. 139).

For the most part, individuals drawn to the fundraising programs of Christian organizations are optimistic men and women of faith who are striving to do what they believe is right, both in the sight of God and in the eyes of donors. And on most days, they are confident of God's ability to supply all needs. Yet the tides of institutional life, the influences from the surrounding culture, and economic pressures are all strong. They can combine and pull even the most determined development person away from the sure ground of confidence in divine sufficiency. Fundraising is hard and often lonely work. As our vignettes demonstrated, from time to time the situation seems nearly impossible, at least from a human perspective.

The stakes for the development program are usually high, and the results, good or bad, are out there for all to see. Yet ministry-centered development programs will convey a quiet but sure confidence that God is more than able to supply what is needed, even when things seem especially tough. This kind of confidence was exemplified by Herb Pfiffner, executive director of Union Gospel Mission of Seattle (UGMS), when he observed: "If God is God, he will provide for our work as long as we are doing what he requires. We need to get our egos out of the way. This is not about being bigger. It is about being faithful."

In contrast, when Christian organizations approach the end of one fiscal year after another clawing and scratching toward their stated goals, a very different message is communicated to constituents about God's ability to meet the needs of the church. These organizations say they serve a God who "owns the cattle on a thousand hills," but, plainly stated, many Christian ministries operate in a perpetual state of scarcity and financial panic. The message conveyed to supporters out of this panic is that God is unable to supply even the most basic needs, let alone provide funds for new programs. If this message of panic is a contrived fundraising technique, it is doubly harmful.

Christian fundraisers must think carefully about the image of God they are conveying in the work they do. As Father Michael Raschko points out, "In fundraising, as in any other pastoral activity, we are subtly, yet powerfully, shaping people's images of God, themselves, the Church and their world. If fundraising is done by emphasizing needs in special collection after special collection, or financial drive after financial drive, a certain insidious sense of the Church as an institution of never-ending needs begins to develop" (1997, p. 54). In contrast, this chapter describes a responsible reliance on God's infinite goodness and generosity and explains how fundraising grounded in such reliance can encourage givers' hearts to grow bigger and their souls to turn more toward God. This assumption shapes the first of three necessary conditions identified for a ministry-centered development program: *the organization and the fundraising program operate with an assumption of the abundance of God's resources and grace.*

Turning Toward Abundance

By every global measurement, contemporary or historical, North Americans are among the richest people who have ever lived. Personal income being what it is today, it is staggering to consider what could happen if people of faith would increase their giving by even a percentage point or two. An on-line news release from the Newtithing Group (1999), a San Francisco–based philanthropic research organization, trumpeted the good news that "in 1999 alone, U.S. tax filers can comfortably afford to give nearly a quarter of a trillion additional dollars to charity." The article went on to report, "This figure is up from the $184 billion additional affordable giving that the Group estimated for 1998—and is almost two and one-half times the $100 billion sum estimated for 1994." Nonetheless, an overriding sense of scarcity persists among people of faith, a perception that there is simply not enough of almost anything—natural resources, food, good jobs, education, health care, and wealth. As Robert Wood Lynn (1998), a student of the history of Christian fundraising in the United States, has observed, "In contemporary American society, money has become a potent symbol of security or insecurity about many of our greatest collective anxieties."

The way in which Christian ministries go about raising money can help put an end to this destructive attitude of scarcity. Jesus taught about a God who wishes for humans "to have life and have it more abundantly" (John 10:10)—a desire that extends to the experience of God's people as a whole as well as to the lives of individuals. Unfortunately, too many Christian organizations design their fundraising efforts with a narrow focus just on meeting current needs and ignore the larger vision of development as a means of advancing God's kingdom. "All too often giving has become the occasion for an emotional, high-pressure appeal, largely concerned with the financial response—and lacking in the moral, spiritual, and biblical aspects of a subject clearly set forth in the Scriptures as the God-appointed ministry of every Christian" (Olford, 1972, p. 19).

When fundraisers present opportunities for donors to respond to God's grace in their lives and to celebrate with the organization the good work that God will do with gifts provided, there is a chance for hearts to grow bigger. August Napoli, president of Catholic Charities of Cleveland, said, "We now realize the scope of what the people of God can do by coming together." Or in the words of a donor to Compassion International, "When we give with a happy heart, it's thrilling." How then can Christian fundraisers begin to replace a culture of scarcity with one of abundance? In our experience, it takes a combination of word and deed—of both talking a new talk and walking a new walk.

Communicating an Understanding of God's Abundance in Action and in Words

When talking about fundraising, a lot of newcomers to the profession start with an assumption of limited resources and presume a zero-growth funding environment. It's easy to jump to this conclusion on the basis of prevailing trends in giving. In contrast to what the Newtithing Group has suggested that people *can* give, Independent Sector, a national leader in research on giving and volunteerism, reports that philanthropic contributions overall have largely held steady or declined slightly as a percentage of household income over the past twenty years. Moreover, the share of those dollars going to religious organizations and institutions has begun to shrink, down from 64 percent in 1987 to 58 percent in 1995 (Miller, 1999).

Nonetheless, the fundraisers we met in the course of our research who were guiding exemplary programs went about their work with confidence in the unlimited abundance of God's resources. In their communication with supporters, they emphasize the positive and illustrate through stories the good things being accomplished because God's people have given. They are able to do this consistently because they really do believe that God is enough. As a result, their work reflects a calm assurance that the divine "pie" is so huge that even a small sliver is sufficient to meet any and all organizational needs.

At the same time, ministry-centered fundraisers are quick to recognize that a shallow understanding of God's abundance can encourage waste and carelessness in how funds are allocated. Although it is important to rid the organization of a culture of scarcity, a casual overconfidence in God's sufficiency can be just as destructive. Organizational leaders who wish to nurture the hearts and souls of donors have learned to walk the fine line between rightly appropriate and wrongly presumptuous faith. They do so by paying careful attention to certain issues:

- The importance of appropriate goal setting
- The cumulative negative effect of crisis-centered appeals
- The power of positive thinking and speaking

The Importance of Setting Realistic Goals

If an organization is serious about shaping the development program in ways that nurture the spiritual life of donors, fundraising goals must be realistic. Faith-encouraging goals reflect the organization's understanding of the difference between targets that challenge supporters to stretch themselves on behalf of the ministry and goals that are simply beyond the ability of a constituency to achieve. Though it is good to aim high, overly optimistic expectations almost always lead to frustration, dashed hopes, and failed programs. Spiritually sensitive development staffs understand the subtle but crucial difference between trusting in God's goodness to meet legitimate needs and framing God as a sort of sugar daddy in the sky.

At San Francisco Theological Seminary, the lesson learned from a past fundraising shortfall was that there's little to be gained, and much to be lost, by painting the organization into a financial corner. "Don't get me

wrong," a board member told us. "We're not a timid or overly conserv-
ative bunch of people. However, we've been burned once by overestimat-
ing what the seminary could do in a single fundraising campaign, and
we're not going to make that mistake again." He explained that the
fundraising goals are now set in concert with the board's business and
finance committee and development committee. "We try to avoid an
overly simplistic 'trust in God' philosophy in our goal setting."

There are a number of significant projects the seminary community is
eager to tackle. However, the board is waiting patiently for a go-ahead
nod from Ron Lundeen, the vice president for advancement, before launch-
ing a new fundraising effort. They are willing to go slow because they do
not wish to embarrass the seminary or its donors with a failed fundraising effort.

This doesn't mean Christian organizations should be reluctant to respond to new opportunities. Indeed, too low expectations and too much
acquiescence to the inertia of the status quo do little to build the self-
confidence of organizational staff or the donors who support the work
with their gifts. Acting out of pessimism denies possibilities for both
groups. Still, it takes an honest, clearheaded examination of the organization's capacities, strengths, and weakness, and those of its constituencies, to avoid the trap of fundraising expectations that are too great or
too small. Thoughtful exploration of the following three issues seems especially needed.

First, organizational leaders should assess the potential for increased
giving present within the existing donor base. Organizational leaders who
genuinely care about the people who support the organization financially
understand the difference between challenging supporters to dig a little
deeper for a special reason and setting goals that are left unmet year after
year. It is cruel to approach the people who care most about a work and
set them up for an annual dose of failure. Yet that is precisely what many
religious organizations do on a regular basis. By focusing on what the
organization lacks, fundraisers reinforce in donors a view of God as less
than able to supply the needs of the church, despite our rhetoric to the
contrary. It's no surprise that Christians are anxious about their own
financial futures and little inclined to give away what they may need for
tomorrow. It's not much of a stretch to conclude that if times are tough
for Christian ministries, might not the same be true for individuals?

Pushing toward goals that are beyond the reach of an organization's
historic base of support may impede appreciation of the gifts already
received and those who provided them. Unrealistic expectations pull the
fundraisers' eyes away from the donors at hand and put the focus instead

on elusive, hoped-for donors somewhere beyond the horizon. Income in fundraising doesn't go up suddenly under any circumstances, short of a windfall, and it is unwise to budget expecting the unexpected.

It should be a cause for concern when faithful but stressed donors say (as we heard one remark), "The fundraising program can turn off a generous person." In the rush to expand a donor base, well-meaning but harried fundraisers have been known to discourage and even offend longtime supporters. We saw this again when another faithful giver complained, "My arm still hurts from the last campaign." This longtime supporter of a Christian children's home went on to say, "Someone out there must be coaching presidents and other fundraisers to act as though no doesn't mean no if the word comes from the mouth of a donor. Just once, I'd like a fundraiser to accept what I feel led to give without pushing for what the home wants from me."

Though it is important that Christian organizations constantly seek new sources of gifts, the quest for more and "better" donors should not come at the cost of neglecting or hurting old friends. Note that this hurt can come from two directions, both from pushing donors too hard and from underestimating the capacity of existing supporters to do more. The *Non-Profit Times*'s Web site included the following advice from the president of a national fundraising consulting firm. "Agencies have to maximize their constituency. They have to know who [these people] are and take good care of them. Agencies have to focus on these core support groups because you can't expect the whole community to respond to your needs" (Gardner, 1999). It is usually easier, and certainly more cost effective, to encourage current donors to increase their giving than to seek out new donors.

It was sad to hear a board member for a family services program describe the organization's chances of upping its fundraising goals as "nil, zip, no chance, no way. . . . We simply can't expect much more than what we're presently getting in the way of gifts." Fortunately, others on the board were willing to try a more systematic approach to fundraising, and new dollars followed. More often than not, organizations that believe they are incapable of attracting "real" money fail to do so.

Ann McKusick, the former vice president for advancement at Fuller Theological Seminary, said, "There's a direct correlation between the vision presented through the fundraising program and what donors give. Ask for a dollar, and you get a dollar. Ask with a bigger vision, and donors respond in kind." In the end, it takes honest, thoughtful discussion across the whole of an organization to avoid the trap of expectations for the fundraising program that are too great or too small.

Second, organizational leaders need to be realistic about the number of development staff needed to reach the hoped-for funding goals. After less than ten months on the job, the development officer looked and sounded worn down and discouraged. "There's so much to do, but never enough time to get the whole job done. I'm working as hard as I can, but I don't feel like I'm even close to keeping up. Maybe I'm not cut out for development work," he suggested. He had come into his position with high hopes and a passion for the cause he was to represent. Unfortunately, the demands of a job that could use the efforts of a staff twice the size of the one in place had taken a toll. And to make matters worse, the executive director was oblivious to the mental, physical, and spiritual state of the CDO—a person he had worked long and hard to recruit to the organization.

Even with God's blessing, there is a limit to what a one- or two-person fundraising office can produce. To push staff beyond what is humanly possible—and Christians in development work are, after all, human—is both unfair and unproductive. It is well to heed Peter Drucker's advice that "any job that has defeated two or three [persons] in succession, even though each has performed well in previous assignments, must be assumed unfit for human beings. It must be redesigned" (1966, pp. 78–79).

Nothing saps the enthusiasm and passion of a fundraising team quicker than the struggle of pursuing unrealistic fundraising goals year after year. When goals are missed, it is a matter of organizationwide conversation, yet when goals are met, too often the development staff celebrates alone. Everyone wants to share in the benefits of the fundraiser's work, but in most organizations few others are willing to lend a hand in bringing in the resources necessary to support a ministry or to acknowledge the effort required to meet funding goals.

Moreover, the stress that comes with striving for goals that are beyond the reach of the organization does bad things to good people; and it can cause good people to do bad things. If it is agreed that an organization cannot or should not expand the size of the development staff, then goals must be set accordingly. In these matters, organizational context is critical. For example, a smallish ministry with a local constituency should not try to mimic the staffing patterns of an organization with a national or international service region. Yet the converse is also true. So when an organization has grown from smallish beginnings to have a larger ministry and a wider reach, it needs to enlarge its development office to keep pace with the growth in support needed.

Wise leaders are able to find the right balance between too few and too many fundraisers; less experienced decision makers can have trouble on this point. Because so much of what the development staff does is external to the organization, it is likely that their work is little known or poorly understood by coworkers. When a fundraiser was asked how her program was perceived across the organization, she responded, "They'll tell you we're the people with the credit cards." In the absence of personal exposure to what fundraising staff actually do, it can be hard for others in the organization to appreciate the stresses of the work and the number of staff needed to accomplish stated goals.

Especially instructive are the comments of a trustee who wasn't convinced that staffing up the development office was really necessary. "Given what we've told you about the size and distinctiveness of our parent denomination, wouldn't you agree it would be foolish for us to hire eight or nine fundraisers?" His question was posed as a challenge to this organization's president's recommendation that they increase the size of the development staff from a one-day-a-week position to a full-time spot. The suggestion for compromise fell on deaf ears, and the organization continues to struggle along financially with its very minimal fundraising program.

The positive vision that contrasts with the preceding tale can be seen in another story from a newcomer to fundraising. Over dinner at a gathering of seminary administrators and presidents, a group of development officers talked about the feeling of "otherness" they've experienced in the places where they work. "I came to my assignment with different credentials and a different career path than the faculty and other administrators in the seminary," one of the women stated. "If it weren't for the president's willingness to 'part the waters' for me—to convince the rest of the community that my work is a legitimate and important part of the seminary's mission—it would have been a tough go."

Fortunately, this woman enjoys the support of a president who understands and can interpret the development program to the campus community. As a result, she feels supported in her work and her person. Concurrently, others at the seminary are also learning from and being encouraged by this president and this development officer, and they are getting involved and discovering the joy that comes from connecting with donors for whom giving is a spiritual activity.

Program staff in exemplary programs benefit from an understanding that to participate in the ongoing spiritual nurture of donors, the work of raising funds cannot be seen as the responsibility of the development staff alone. Everyone, or at least a significant group of members of the organization, must feel that they share in a joyous ministry with donors. As Deal and Baluss have noted, "Organizational culture is inextricably intertwined in everything fundraisers do" (1994, p. 7).

Third, organizational leaders must be realistic in assessing the capacity of board members to "give or get" funds for the ministry. It is reasonable and typical for organizational staff to expect all board members to support the organization through personal giving, albeit each according to his or her means. As Henry Rosso observed, "The trustee can be an important moving force for fund raising, its strongest advocate, and its primary volunteer exemplar. The dedication of the trustee can serve as an inducement to others to become involved" (1991, p. 133).

This does not mean, however, that board service is reserved only for the wealthy. Board work is a multifaceted activity, and members should be selected for their talents and their willingness to devote time to the organization, along with generous contributions of treasure. In the case of board members for Christian organizations, an additional consideration—theological fit—should be added to the mix, as the newly appointed chair of a development committee for a denominationally sponsored organization recognized.

This man voiced concern about advice he had received from a friend who served on the board of a larger and more socially prominent organization. "I've been told that the most important consideration in selecting board members is their ability to give or help raise major gifts. That just doesn't feel right when I consider the work of this board. It seems to me our most important role has more to do with faithfulness than funding." Although a relative novice with regard to fundraising, this trustee had intuited the critical importance of matching board member beliefs to the Christian mission of the organization.

Although every board member should give something, too much emphasis on the amount they give to or get for the organization is counterproductive. It is not right when board members who thought they were recruited because of their love for a particular work are made to feel inadequate in their service because they are not able to give or lead the organization to major gifts. It is useless to set fundraising goals that exceed the ability of the board, either through their own gifts or through those of their contacts in the organization's broader constituency. If, in the recruitment process, a strong faith commitment is cited as the most important credential for board service, then it may be that the trustees selected will be less able to give or get significant gifts than is the case in organizations that make it a priority to recruit a majority of board members who also are persons of wealth.

At this point, it is useful to note that most board members, serving in a religious or a secular setting, are not particularly wealthy people. A review of the trustees for a large group of private colleges revealed that fewer than 20 percent of the nearly twenty-four hundred board members were "captains of industry" or significant philanthropists. Moreover, the predominance of the "nonwealthy" is even more pronounced when looking at the boards of community-based organizations of various types. Although every one of the boards reviewed in this study included a few persons with substantial financial resources, the majority of trustees were actually rather average. Thus adding a spiritual component—the fourth 't'—to what we expect from board members really does not represent a disadvantage for Christian organizations.

In fact, the advantage of a deep and heartfelt commitment to a specific mission is always of great value to an organization's fundraising program. There are no more powerful fundraisers than volunteer leaders who define board service as an extension of their faith in God. There are also no wiser counselors in setting appropriate goals for the fundraising program. (See Exhibit 4.1.)

A Determination to Avoid Crisis Appeals

"I don't need a calendar to know it's May," the longtime friend of a Christian ministry stated. "Any day now, I'll get that 'with two months to go in the fiscal year, we still need $300,000 to balance the budget' letter. I'll

---

Exhibit 4.1. What's a Board to Do? A Short Guide to Fundraising.

- Board members must be willing to give as they are able—to the annual fund, to capital projects, and through estate gifts.

- After making their own gifts, board members should be involved in solicitation activities.

- Board members should be involved in writing thank-you notes to donors.

- Board members should insist on a strategic plan for the organization that includes a strategy to ensure that necessary funds will be provided to turn the plan into reality.

- Board members should monitor the development program to maximize fundraising potential.

- Board members should be as informed as possible about the organization's programs, recipients, and initiatives.

give again, but I have to tell you, after more than twenty years, the crisis approach is wearing thin."

As this comment from a faithful donor illustrates, it's hard to feel good about one's giving when it is never enough and every year brings another near-failure. An occasional budget shortfall can be excused, but supporters become frustrated when organizations consistently budget beyond their means. Organizational leaders who wish to model good stewardship must demonstrate careful and wise financial management in the way the development program is shaped.

The annual cliff-hanger experienced by all too many fundraising programs should encourage fundraisers to question the wisdom of pursuing the same programs with the same donors in the same sequence, year after year. It doesn't make sense to expect different results from doing the same thing over and over. Yet this seems to be what many fundraising staffs have been doing, having left their basic structures, processes, and assumptions unexamined and undisturbed for decades.

Most fundraising cycles reflect a strange attachment to old and often failed ways of doing things. Too commonly, fundraisers lead off the annual fund effort with a one-size-fits-all sort of approach to the broadest possible group of donors—usually via direct mail and with very little segmentation. Preparation of the mailing consumes a huge amount of staff energy, and just as the first mailing clears the post office, it's time to begin work on the next. Following that, it's onto a third appeal (or more), and then, despite the best intentions of the staff who said this wouldn't happen again, the chief executive is signing this year's crisis letter: "With just thirty days remaining in the fiscal year, we must raise $00,000 to balance the budget."

In the last few days of the fiscal year, the chief executive turns in panic to the same few wealthy individuals who have rescued the organization in years past. The budget is balanced, but nerves are frayed, confidence is shaken, and an unfortunate message of scarcity is communicated to the supporters of the organization. Pity the donors who mailed their $50 checks early. Once again, they've been made to feel that their support just doesn't cut it. And once again, the organization has called on its "angels" to save the day. As J. David Schmidt has observed, "We have built our Christian organizations on thousands of shallow relationships (which are pressed frequently and hard), and a handful of major supporters (whom we take good care of)" (1989, p. 186).

How can fundraisers break free from the cycle of crisis funding? Organizational leaders can start the change process by brainstorming how things might be done differently. Just because funds have always been raised in a certain way doesn't mean the program has to continue in that mode. At a minimum, this begins by rethinking with whom the fundraising effort should begin.

What would happen if the persons who time after time bail organizations out in the last few days of the fiscal year were challenged to make their commitments early on? What if an organization's perennial "angels" were invited to help present a message of abundance and grace to others in place of the usual communication of scarcity by giving their gifts earlier in the fiscal year? This is not a new idea, of course. Seasoned fundraisers are well aware that lead gifts can set a brisk pace for other donors to follow. Yet we have something more profound than mere modeling in mind. We are as much interested in how the early gifts might communicate God's abundance as in what those gifts encourage others to do.

If we truly believe that God is enough, there is no risk in breaking free from long-pursued fundraising practices. Indeed, if the way fundraising calendars are usually structured reinforces a perception of scarcity, change is the only plausible option open to Christian fundraisers.

This is not to suggest a Pollyannaish view of the world. As the daily news reminds us, legitimate and tragic crisis situations abound. Natural disasters, war, poverty, and unjust governments, singly or more often in combination, make life harsh for many of the world's citizens. It is not surprising that almost half the four hundred organizations listed in the *Chronicle of Philanthropy*'s annual survey—including the Salvation Army, Compassion International, and Catholic Charities USA—spend much of their energy addressing crises of various kinds.

As a case in point, civil war and famine in Rwanda resulted in a crisis situation for children and by extension for Compassion International. In communicating about this crisis to sponsors and other potential donors, Compassion International asked not for the organization's needs but for resources that would allow Compassion workers to reach displaced children. Compassion invited donors to partner with it in extending God's abundance to children for whom life held little hope or opportunity. Through Compassion's fundraising efforts, donors were educated to an international situation and provided with a concrete means to respond. Even in crises that are beyond the control of the organization, fundraisers must think carefully about how the challenge is presented to supporters. Appeals that focus exclusively on crises, whether internal or external to the organization, reinforce donors' perceptions of scarcity and work against joyful giving in response to God's great abundance.

Accentuating the Positive

It is one thing to tell the stories of recipients of a ministry; it is quite another to use those stories to manipulate the emotions of potential donors, tempting and "effective" though it might be. As Robert Wuthnow suggests, "The picture of a starving child paints a more graphic image, but it is also an image that suggests a familiar response: being 'moved by compassion' in the same way the Samaritan was moved by seeing the injured man on the road, and responding by giving help to a specific individual, not by attempting to alleviate some broader economic condition" (1990b, p. 276).

The situation of Rwandan children, for example, is rife with the possibilities to appeal to guilt or pity. Yet Compassion's approach put the emphasis on hope and possibility, which is consistent with the organization's long-standing determination not to show pictures of dirty, sad children, even though those photos "sell" more sponsorships. (We should note that Compassion was, at the same time, reinforcing the bond of trust with donors. When the outbreak of the war in Rwanda made it impossible to complete some projects and to locate certain children for whom donors had already given, Compassion offered to return those gifts if the donors did not want the funds diverted to meet new emergency needs.)

The staff at the Union Gospel Mission of Seattle talked about their struggle to present an accurate portrayal of the population served by their organization. Research has shown that a majority of casual donors to UGMS, those who respond to newspaper ads or direct-mail appeals, are most likely to give if the recipient of services is pictured as an elderly, dejected man—the quintessential hobo. In reality, though, the mission's typical client is now a Hispanic man in his mid-to late twenties, someone who in pictures looks like a person who should be able to earn his own way in the world. Also, increasing numbers of women with young children are turning to the mission for help, and because welfare mothers are currently not viewed as entirely sympathetic figures, theirs is also not an image that garners much support.

The staff wish to be honest in their presentations of the mission's work and client base. However, when they paint a more realistic picture of the public being served, the return on a mailing or an ad is likely to be less than if they had gone with the older-client stereotype. Nonetheless, the newsletter produced by the UGMS is full of "success" stories of lives transformed through an encounter with Jesus Christ, and usually those lives don't match what the donors might have expected.

The effort in Seattle brings up a concern voiced by a number of fundraisers, which is that people will not give if the situation sounds "too hopeful" or if the beneficiaries of the ministry are deemed not truly needy of the service. Many people seem inclined to give only to "deserving persons" in sad or desperate situations. But unless there is at least a glimmer of hope visible at the end of the giving tunnel, it is unlikely that gifts will continue to flow. Christian fundraisers must be careful not to overwhelm sympathetic people by constantly bombarding them with tales of woe. A fundraising strategy dependent on constant plucking at the donors' heartstrings can in fact backfire as hearts are hardened against the seemingly intractable challenges of the day—a phenomenon identified in recent years as "donor fatigue."

Conclusions

The assumption with which this chapter began, that "God is enough," is the underlying theme of the chapters ahead. If you are not open to this assumption, it might seem that there is little point in going further. We hope, however, to encourage continued investigation of what can happen when a development program of a Christian organization is built on the "crowning discovery" of God's abundance.

In this chapter, we have stressed three practices as particularly important to creating and sustaining such a development program: setting appropriate goals, avoiding crisis-centered appeals and the cumulative negative effects they create, and harnessing the power of positive thinking and speaking in shaping the strategies and appeals of a development program.

In the chapters that follow, we will look at five additional principles that shape and guide ministry-centered development programs. Again and again, we stress the importance of a whole organization understanding and embracing this approach to fundraising as a ministry. Indeed, along with the underlying assumption of God's abundance, this is the other crucial component of our overall prescription for what we feel ails too many development programs in Christian organizations.

The following chapters consider the destructive power of a spirit of competition and what fundraisers can do to move beyond it. They discuss the importance of understanding the theological backdrop against which the organization functions and what that means in hiring staff and in the ways fundraisers communicate with and relate to donors. They stress the importance of planning, both for the organization and for donors as well.

As we explore these matters further in these chapters, we will draw on illustrations from the organizations we have encountered through our research and in our professional lives.

We encourage you to move forward into the rest of the book, keeping in mind the basic assumption laid out here: that we must always plan and pursue the work of fundraising as a ministry with a clear recognition of God's abundance. It is that abundance on which we must rely, and in which we can surely trust, whenever we are looking for resources to do God's work.

5

A HOLISTIC PERSPECTIVE ON "KINGDOM WORK"

If you have any encouragement from being united in Christ,
if any comfort from His love, if any fellowship with the
Spirit, if any tenderness and compassion, then make my joy
complete by being like-minded, having the same love,
being one in spirit and purpose.

—Philippians 2:1–2

SIBLING RIVALRY is nothing new among God's children. One of the first stories recorded in the Bible is that of Cain and Abel, in which Cain, jealous about the favor God had bestowed on his brother's offering, kills Abel (Genesis 4:1–14). This theme of rivalry and jostling for God's attention continues throughout the whole of the Old and New Testaments. Despite the biblical admonition to rejoice in the good fortune of others, such a stance does not come easily to most of us. In a world where scarcity is emphasized and competition glorified, it is difficult to rest in the confidence that God has no favorite causes. Trust in God's abundance, as suggested in the preceding chapter, is the only sure antidote to our all-too-human tendencies toward jealousy and competitiveness.

In our site visits, we were impressed by the fact that the fundraising staff and others in the exemplary organizations spoke about the plethora of causes and ministries vying for donors' funds without any distress or angst. The persons we met exuded a quiet confidence in the rightness of the programs they represented and in their organizations' ability to secure sufficient funds to advance their cause. This did not reflect a "head in the sand" attitude on the part of these particular fundraisers. Indeed, we noted a hard-nosed realism when it came to setting fundraising goals and planning for the future.

The development staffs of exemplary organizations were aware of the fundraising activities of other ministries and kept track of them. They were also well versed in the latest fundraising theories and techniques and were wise in applying the best of both to their programs. At the same time, fundraisers in these organizations felt free to partner with, refer donors to, and speak well of other ministries. As Herb Pfiffner, executive director of the Union Gospel Mission of Seattle, told us, "It's important that Christian agencies do things right—produce good results—which means no one organization can do everything." And Pfiffner's beliefs were made manifest in the behavior of his organization, as illustrated in a story about UGMS we were told by others.

Within the nationwide network of Union Gospel Missions there is an agreement not to solicit funds in another mission's "territory." The leadership team in Seattle takes great care to honor the rule. A few years ago, however, an overlap in radio coverage garnered a number of gifts from a neighboring city. Rather than keeping the accidentally solicited support for their own use, the Seattle staff forwarded the gifts to their sister mission. Asked about this decision, a board member for UGMS said, "In the New Testament, we are taught about the diversity of gifts of the Spirit and urged to value and encourage a variety of ministries. That's what we seek to model in this place."

Ministry-centered development programs reflect a confidence that comes from operating within a clearly identified "kingdom niche," and as a result staffs are not threatened by the existence of other good causes or even similar institutions. This is reflected in the words of a staff member at Compassion International who spoke of "a larger call than just the concerns of Compassion. We want to have a part in advancing the broader kingdom work." Exemplary fundraising programs are grounded in the confidence that God's goodness is great enough to encompass the whole of religious activity and that God has no favorite causes.

From this observation comes the second necessary condition for a ministry-centered development program: *the organization and fundraising program must reflect a holistic perspective on God's work, recognizing the value of a variety of ministries.* There is simply too much work to be done in the world for Christian fundraisers to become concerned when other organizations receive major gifts.

Eliminating the Spirit of Competition

Put a group of development professionals together in a room, and eventually the conversation will turn to the increasing competition in the fundraising realm. More and more organizations are hiring development staff, and many of these new fundraisers are knowledgeable and aggressive. For organizations that were once the only fundraisers on their block, the street seems suddenly crowded and far less sympathetic to their cause. "The abundance of ministries produces a competition for donors' funds. This results in a sense of urgency—we must get these funds before someone else does" (Alcorn, 1989, p. 278). Development officers are tempted to hunker down, clutching "their" donors close to their sides while casting an envious eye at other organizations that seem to do better at raising money. Longtime fundraisers speak wistfully of the good old days when people were more generous or less caught up in materialism or when giving was still the "Christian thing to do." Newcomers to the profession simply wonder about their choice of work. However, there is nothing like the historical record to put the current situation in perspective. (We encourage readers to look at the work of Bob Lynn, the Ronsvalles, and others.) In short, in times like these, it is helpful to remember that there have always been times like these. It has always been tough to convince people, even "the righteous," to part with their funds.

David Tiede, president of Luther Theological Seminary, asked in a letter to the readers of *In Trust* magazine, "Can we learn together to discipline our conflicts with the expectation of good faith and not mere winning and losing? This is a subject significant beyond matters of institutional survival, vital as those are" (1992, p. 2). In response to this question, fundraisers who approach their work as a ministry can answer with a loud and sure yes. Despite an overwhelming perception on the part of many observers that the financial needs of religious organizations are outpacing the ability or inclination of people to give, the fact is that organizations do prosper, funding goals are met, and God's work is advanced on earth.

In Seattle, staff from the UGMS assist local congregations in establishing their own ministries to the homeless. In Tucson, diocesan development officers serve as consultants to parish stewardship committees. At Compassion International, child sponsors are encouraged to become involved in child advocacy activities in their home communities. In these and countless other ways, development programs characterized by a holistic perspective on God's work seek, in the words of Richard Mouw, president of Fuller Theological Seminary, to educate donors to "kingdom consciousness" by emphasizing the need for and value of a variety of ministries.

Implications of a Holistic Perspective on God's Work

Development offices are often the scenes of frenetic activity, with harried staff members rushing in frantic pursuit of equally harried donors. However, the mood of the programs we visited was generally just the opposite. These ministry-centered development efforts were characterized by calm and a quiet assurance in the rightness of their plans and approaches. A member of the diocesan development team in Tucson said, "We don't feel quota driven, and we don't want to create that sort of climate." Although the staffs of ministry-centered fundraising programs are deeply committed to meeting the funding goals of the organizations they serve, their work is characterized by the following freedoms:

- To let donors follow their hearts
- To confront problematic motives for and conditions on a gift
- To share resources and wisdom with other organizations and fundraisers
- To rejoice in the triumphs of other ministries

Fundraisers working in a ministry-centered environment are free to let donors follow their hearts. Mike, a major gifts officer for a Christian organization, appeared downcast and a bit embarrassed upon returning from lunch with a longtime donor. He had gone off that morning confidently anticipating an affirmative reply to his outstanding request for a significant gift to the organization's capital campaign. Instead, he learned that the donor had committed a million dollars to the campaign of a Christian high school on the other side of town. Mike was prepared for a disappointed response from the vice president for development and so was surprised by his supervisor's response.

"No problem, Mike," the vice president responded. "Jake's been a good friend to us for a long time, but we know he has other interests. He'll give again when he's ready. For now, just send a note thanking him for his continued generosity in support of God's work here in our community, and let him know how much we value his friendship and his giving spirit." The vice president was as disappointed as Mike that a much-hoped-for gift had followed a donor's heart to another organization. Still, he wisely chose not to take his frustration out on the staff member. He recognized the situation as a teachable moment and used it to stress the importance of valuing the donor's passion and of rejoicing in an individual's generosity, even when a solicitation didn't go as hoped.

When the success of a fundraising program is measured solely by its financial results, it is counterintuitive for staff to "allow" donors to take the lead in identifying what it is they wish to support and when it will be best for them to make their gifts. Development officers are hired to raise money *now* and for a specific cause. A young fundraiser eager to advance in the profession assumes, and probably rightly so, that future employers are more likely to evaluate his or her performance on the basis of dollars raised than on contributions to building up the generous spirit of God's people. By most standards, it is professionally risky to put the dreams and needs of the donor ahead of the organization by which one is employed. As a result, many donors are frustrated by the kinds of requests that come to them.

The high-pressure tactics and arm-twisting common to organizations intent on beating out the competition have no place for fundraisers who seek to replace donor stress with joyful satisfaction and who claim an affiliation with the Gospel. In the words of a stewardship committee member of a local parish, "The journey we've started on will take years, because we are trying to build a faith community." Fundraisers who desire to contribute to the building of a faith community cannot let the forces of competition lead them into pressuring or manipulating donors. Rather they must be committed to serving their donors, as surely as they are to serving the organizations for which they work.

The discerning development officer knows when to back off from a particular solicitation and even refer the person to another good cause. Rick Bee, director of development at Biola University, states that "it's nearly impossible to change the heart of a donor. Time is best spent with those persons who have a heart for the cause we represent." Still, before moving on, fundraisers must make a true and genuine effort to connect with individuals—not to push donors, but to understand their passions and values.

An experienced donor said to us, "When organizations don't ask appropriately, they're robbing people of the joy of giving." Sometimes donors are unsure themselves about what it is they most want to support. This is especially true for persons who are new to giving or who have only recently "come into money" and who are for the first time able to consider making a major gift.

Ministry-oriented development programs show genuine respect for the wide range of interests, dreams, and priorities of potential donors, as well as for the seeming unsettledness some donors may feel as they sort through a whole host of issues. It is crucial that fundraisers take care to match requests for a gift to what is known of individual interests and that they give donors time to make a reasoned decision. In some cases, it means passing over a "good" name during a prospect review session, recognizing that the project under consideration isn't likely to touch the individual's heart.

We saw this happen recently as a campaign steering committee reviewed prospects for inclusion on a "top ten gifts" list. The names of a very capable and generous couple were removed from consideration in recognition of their significant and long-term commitment to the city's new children's museum. There was no doubting that this couple's treasure and heart were already committed elsewhere. The steering committee for this campaign wisely showed respect for that decision.

There are also times when staff must be free to direct an individual's giving to another organization if it simply isn't possible to match organizational priorities to the interests of the individual. Fundraisers who approach their work as a ministry are free to let gifts flow from the donors' hearts. A development staff member at Catholic Charities of Cleveland told us, "Most people in the agencies, parishes, and schools ask how they can help [us raise the funds needed]. And I say, keep doing what you're doing, and we'll tell the story, letting people know this is the work of the church. Getting donors involved on their [own] terms is bringing them back to the church."

Fundraisers working in a ministry-centered environment are free to confront wrong motives for giving. There's a tongue-in-cheek adage in development circles that says the only thing wrong with tainted money is "t'ain't enough of it." Ministry-centered development programs, however, recognize that it is wrong to accept tainted money or to accept a gift given out of tainted motives. The literature on donor motivation tells us there are many answers to the question of why people give, but not all those reasons, or the gifts they generate, contribute to spiritual and personal growth. It is difficult, but sometimes necessary, to confront wrong motives for a gift—and perhaps to challenge the donor to reconsider before God what to do with his or her money.

Two development officers described this challenge. In the first situation, a longtime contributor offered a significant gift in support of a new program, but on the condition that she could have a part in shaping the program and deciding who should be served by it. This was an initiative that the organization very much wanted to make happen. Still, the development officer with whom she was dealing declined the gift and instead recommended that the woman "prayerfully and earnestly seek the leading of the Spirit in how she should give." Even though turning away this gift delayed the start of an important project, the development officer continued to trust that in doing what he and his colleagues believed was right, an important work of God would be done in this woman's life.

In the second setting, a Christian college in the early stages of a capital campaign, a potential major funder who also happened to be a builder stepped forward with the offer of a lead gift on the condition that his company would be awarded the construction contract. The fundraising staff gently explained that the institution did not accept gifts with conditions and continued the quest for other gifts in other places. Some five years later, the same potential funder returned to the institution with an offer of funding, this time without strings and with the accompanying testimony of how God had worked in his life because of the faithfulness on the part of the college's staff to the principles they knew were right.

Although only one of these stories has a "happy" ending from a purely financial perspective, both situations can be deemed a success. Or perhaps we are meant to wonder about the unfinished story, as with the biblical narrative of the rich young man whom Jesus told to sell all he had (Mark 10:17–22). We never learn if he found his way to discipleship or not. In some cases, the rest of the story remains between God and the donor. Nonetheless, in each instance cited, the development staff knew that turning away the offered gift would delay the start of a much-needed project. There was also the very real possibility that the offered gift would go instead to another organization. However, as the fundraisers acted on their confidence in God's abundant ability to provide a replacement gift, they were free to minister to a donor by saying no to a gift that was wrongly motivated and eventually could have caused much larger problems for the work of the organization.

Fundraisers working in a ministry-centered environment are free to share resources and wisdom with other ministries. One member of a parish stewardship committee spoke of his congregation's struggle to raise the funds necessary to keep open the only remaining Catholic grade school in their city. When asked what kind of assistance might be available from the diocesan development office, the man laughed. "We won't get any help there," he said. "All they care about is meeting their own budget needs and funding their programs. Maybe if we were a wealthy suburban parish, they'd give us a listen. But they look at a poor congregation like ours as having little to offer the diocese's interests." If this man's observation is true, it says something profoundly saddening about the relationship between that diocese's development office and the larger church it should have served.

Consider as another example the problems encountered in a church-sponsored, multiagency charitable organization's attempt to establish a corporationwide development function. The individual agencies, after many years without an effective central development office or any mechanism to coordinate their many individual efforts, would not even trust the new development director with their mailing lists, to be used solely for the purpose of assessing each agency's potential for growth. All were mission-driven and vital organizations in their service to the region's poorest citizens. Yet there was no common vision of fundraising as a ministry. Each agency saw the others, and the parent corporation, as competitors.

In today's world, where knowledge is synonymous with power, it can seem foolhardy to share one's expertise or program strengths with a "competitor." Commonly, the rule of the day is not to give away too much of what we know unless there is something to be gained in return. Indeed, considerable money can be made by charging less able organizations for access to the secrets of another organization's success. But such is not the stance of fundraisers working in a ministry-centered environment where development is seen as a real partner in ministry rather than as a necessary but somewhat distasteful part of the "money game."

Despite very significant pressures on their time and energy, the fundraisers we have met from exemplary programs seem to take considerable pride in the teaching aspect of their work. There is no evidence of concern that a "hot tip" imparted today will result in a lost gift tomorrow. Acting on the confidence that God has no favorite causes, these ministry-centered fundraisers feel free to spread around the lessons they've learned from many years on the job.

For example, Wesley Willmer, Biola University's vice president for advancement, is known throughout the community of religious fundraising for his willingness to pass along what he has learned about fundraising as a ministry. We were deeply impressed with his work as an educator among his own staff. He extends that work to his university's board of trustees and out across the country through organizations such as the Christian Stewardship Association and the Council of Christian Colleges and Universities and through his many books and articles.

On a more local level, the members of the development team at the Roman Catholic Diocese of Tucson define themselves both as fundraisers and as development educators to local parishes. The office is organized to be of greatest service to pastors and parish councils. As a result, there have been marked changes at the diocesan level. "There's much less competition between the central office and parishes," said Bob Heslinga, director of development for the diocese. His assessment was echoed by a parish priest, who described the diocesan development staff as "there to help make this a better parish."

Fundraisers working in a ministry-centered environment are free to rejoice in the triumphs of other ministries. At the conclusion of a prospect management review meeting, the CEO of a Christian organization urged the development staff to "get out there and get those gifts before someone else beats you to the punch." And apparently he is not alone in seeking to beat out the competition. As Joseph Mixer's sad observation suggests, "Many organizations are engaged in continuing philosophical conflict, attempting to weaken or to destroy the cases being made by other organizations. Some organizations deny the social and moral legitimacy of the very mission that other organizations exist to serve" (1993, p. 275).

If, however, fundraisers truly accept the promise of God's great abundance, it is no threat when the Christian organization down the street receives a magnificent gift. The fundraisers can relax in the confidence that comes with knowing that there is plenty more where the other gift came from. They can rejoice that God has touched someone's heart to evoke such generosity for a good cause. In fact, if the ultimate end for which a development team strives is the building up of God's people and the advancement of God's many ministries, fundraisers can and will see gifts that come to other Christian organizations as a triumph for all who view their work in development as a ministry.

This freedom can be seen in action at Compassion International. There the staff has worked hard to develop a strong, cause-oriented army of advocates who speak on behalf of children's interests. If the volunteers choose to support other organizations in addition to or even in place of Compassion, the staff are not concerned. The goal of the organization is to take the love of Jesus to all children, and the staff know that their one organization is not able to do this alone. Compassion International reflects an appreciation for the truth that it takes many ministries to meet the needs of the world's children.

We saw a number of similar examples of the power to be found in liberation from unhealthy competition. In Tucson, we were told that the development staff have "learned the importance of collaboration among all aspects of the work of the diocese." Richard Mouw, president of Fuller Theological Seminary, talked about aligning the school with "other missions and integrating the understanding of our mission with that of other ministries." At San Francisco Theological Seminary, the director of seminary relations spoke of wishing to "encourage covenant relationships between the school and specific congregations—relationships that are mutually beneficial and two-way." When development programs embody these goals and values, they reveal the possibilities for making the kingdom of God visible here and now.

A Kingdom Without Walls

It is important that organizational leaders take every opportunity to break down the artificial walls that all too often separate one ministry from another. Unfortunately, nowhere are the walls of separation more difficult to overcome than between parachurch organizations and local congregations, especially where money is concerned. The idea of ministries that exist outside the confines of congregational or denominational lines is not new—there have always been adventurous men and women who have dared to take the Gospel where no church had gone before. What may be new is the huge increase in the numbers, size, and scope of these ministries (Schmidt and Willmer, 1998). And as parachurch organizations have grown in complexity and sophistication, so have their fundraising programs, and this is a cause of concern for denominational and congregation leaders.

Today, total giving to parachurch ministries exceeds that provided to individual churches and to denominationally sponsored programs. Pastors "worry about the budgets of their congregations and fear that gifts by their members to [other causes] may lead to smaller gifts to the local church" (McCarter, 1994, p. 12). Sociologist Robert Wuthnow writes: "The variation in expectations concerning the role of the local congregation range from those asking that priority be given to the local congregation exclusively for its programs and needs, to those that emphasize local giving as a conduit to a wider array of agencies, to those that openly encourage giving to national and secular charities as well as the local congregation" (1990a, p. 8).

The leaders of exemplary parachurch organizations are aware of the tensions and work hard to establish links among and between the myriad organizations involved in advancing God's will on earth, including efforts to connect with local congregations. For example, Steve Burger, executive director for the International Union of Gospel Missions (UGM), stated, "We are the mission of the church and we must relate to the church. UGM is the vehicle in which the church can fulfill the Biblical charges relating to the poor, the needy and broken" (Pfiffner, 1992, p. 56). A similar view was echoed in August Napoli's comments concerning his work with Catholic Charities of Cleveland. "The church can do more good for the community than any organization I've ever been involved with. It is incredibly exciting to be a part of God's work in Cleveland and to begin to tap the unrealized potential that is here." Finally, Ann McKusick told us, "Fuller Seminary nurtures local congregations in many ways. We look upon our connections with churches as a reciprocal relationship."

If Christian fundraisers are going to be attentive to the spiritual implications and outgrowths of giving, it is vitally important they help make connections between the efforts of parachurch organizations and congregational life. The foundation for the spiritual nurture of most Christians is in the local church. Parachurch organizations wishing to contribute to that nurture are intentional in connecting with the local church. Congregational leaders, for their part, need to recognize and celebrate that God calls people to give to many causes.

As one way of moving beyond competition, Mark Vincent, director of the Mennonite Church's Giving Project, has suggested that congregations encourage members to bring all their gifts, regardless of the purpose toward which the funds are directed, to the church to be consecrated for God's good purposes in the world. In this way, parishioners are reminded that the household of faith is larger and more complex than a single congregation and that all work done in the name of Christ is the work of the church.

Conclusions

This chapter opened with an admonition from Paul's letter to the Philippians reminding all who call themselves followers of God—and that includes God's followers working in fundraising offices—that they are to be "one in spirit and purpose" with other believers. Obviously, budgets must be balanced if Christian organizations are to continue to serve the world and serve God in their various ministries. Fundraising goals must be met for the work to flourish and grow. Still, the good news is that the successes of one truly faithful organization need not—indeed, ultimately does not—come at the expense of another. The ironic outcome of fundraising activities based on a sense of competition among Christian organizations is that they often hurt all causes, even the perceived "winner" in a specific contest for support.

Parker Palmer, writing in *The Active Life,* observed, "If we allow the scarcity assumption to dominate our thinking, we will act in individualistic, competitive ways that destroy community. If we destroy community, where creating and sharing with others generates abundance, the scarcity assumption will become more valid" (1990, p. 127). Whenever a Christian organization places itself in competition with other worthy causes in an either-or paradigm, the whole of God's work on earth is diminished.

There are all kinds of good works to be done and good causes to be supported. The amazing variety of individual human interests we observe surrounding and supporting them can best be understood as God's way of ensuring that resources are available for each and every one. Christian fundraisers can rejoice in the fact that God gives one person an interest in health care issues and another in feeding the hungry; that someone is primarily interested in the plight of children and another in caring for the elderly; that one person has a passion for education and another for evangelism.

As we have suggested, tremendous freedom results when fundraisers take hold of the truth that God has no favorite causes. We have spent much of this chapter looking at four of those freedoms and how they may be experienced and exercised by staff (and volunteers) in ministry-centered development programs. Fundraisers who truly believe that God is enough and that no one ministry is inherently more valuable than another are free to encourage right motives for giving and let donors follow their hearts and feed their souls. Where a holistic vision and a spirit of cooperation have displaced competition, fundraisers are free to share resources and wisdom with their colleagues and free to rejoice in the good gifts that come to other organizations.

Fundraising staff in exemplary programs reflect a holistic perspective on God's work that is based in a deep and productive recognition of the value of a variety of programs and organizations. If the success of a fundraising program is measured solely on the total dollars the staffs bring in the door during the year—and especially where this judgment is made in comparison with other Christian organizations—it is unlikely that the development program will be able to do anything significant that nurtures the spiritual growth of donors. Instead, fundraisers will focus on grabbing as many gifts as possible, by every means possible and without regard to the desires of individual hearts.

Conversely, when Christian fundraisers recognize the need to make room for God to work in donors' hearts, they very soon discover that if there is any encouragement in being united in Christ, it is encouragement to work in harmony with other faithful people. God's generosity is sufficient to enable all God's people to do God's work as it needs to be done now.

6

CLARITY ABOUT
CORE THEOLOGICAL BELIEFS

This I believe: that I shall see the goodness
of the Lord in the land of the living!

—Psalms 27:13

ALTHOUGH WE UNDERSTOOD going into this study that fundraisers from differing Christian traditions are influenced by the theological assumptions they bring to their work, we were not certain that such differences would be immediately noticeable to donors. Furthermore, because our study focused on the fundraising programs of Christian organizations that are unapologetic about their faith-based stance, we anticipated a general over-arching commonality in perspectives on money and its place in the believer's life with God. We were wrong on both counts. What we discovered instead is that theology matters very much in the way organizations approach the work of resource development and that differing theological traditions pursue approaches that do have significant differences.

In ministry-centered fundraising programs, the theological underpinnings of the organization are plainly manifest. Moreover, the distinctive Christian beliefs at the core of the organization are often as important to donors as they are to operation leaders. Indeed, the desire to meet donors on the common ground of a shared faith is a primary characteristic of programs committed to fundraising as a ministry.

However, as the research team behind the book *Money Matters* noted, "The negotiating of beliefs often causes anxiety. An interviewee [or in this case, a potential donor] will feel the need to know: 'Are you one of us or not?' 'Are you committed to our beliefs and way of life or not?' 'Do you believe what I say or not?'" (Hoge and others, 1996, p. 6). It is important, then, that development staff take seriously the subtle yet important theological differences within the Christian church.

In this book, we outline a set of necessary conditions and operating principles for any ministry-centered development program. Still, just how these conditions and principles are implemented depends on the specific theological assumptions the fundraising staff and others in the organization bring to the task of seeking resources. For fundraisers accustomed to formulaic advice and "how to" literature, this conclusion may be disappointing. Yet the development landscape is littered with the sorry remains of well-intentioned programs and derailed careers that were organized around the latest fundraising techniques and trends but ignored the consequences of theological mismatches. "Tensions exist not only in theory but also in the practice of Christian discipleship. What we believe does (and should) affect how we live" (Basinger and Basinger, 1986, p. 8). And, we argue here, theology affects how organizations should think about and go about raising money.

It is from this conclusion that we draw our third operating principle: *an organization and its fundraising program must be clear about the essential theological tenets of its own tradition and how that tradition should shape the work of raising money.* The theological assumptions of the organization will and indeed should influence every aspect of the fundraising program, from the way staff are hired to approaches to donors to how a specific ministry is understood in relationship to the church at large.

Thinking About Theological Differences

James Hudnut-Beumler points to "three alternative theological understandings of giving that emerged out of the Protestant Reformation. First is Martin Luther's conception of giving as an act of thanks for God's unmerited grace. Second is John Calvin's view of the disposition of material resources as stewardship over something that is not ultimately of human ownership. Third is the Arminian/Wesleyan understanding of human acts of giving as volitional responses to divine activity" (1995, p. 81). To this should be added the Catholic concept of the "social mortgage," which suggests that everything we have is publicly engendered—that a whole community has made our wealth possible (Oates, 1995; Tropman, 1995).

As Robert Wuthnow notes, "Some traditions levy standard fees on their members in the form of pew rent or temple memberships. Others enter into moral contracts with their members by asking them for annual pledges, and still others operate entirely from spontaneous donations and specialized solicitations. Expectations vary greatly concerning overall levels of giving and the degree to which giving should be focused on the local congregation or fellowship" (1990, p. 8). These varying expectations reflect, in no small measure, differing theological understandings about the church, membership, wealth, and social responsibility.

No one of these views is more right than the other, and each contributes to a holistic understanding of the intersection of faith and money. However, each view has its own unique and often nonnegotiable aspects. As a result, it is usually not workable to commingle theologies in a single setting if the goal is a coherent faith-centered development program.

An immediate implication of this finding is that it is not possible to suggest a "one program fits all theologies" set of strategies and techniques that will result in a ministry-centered approach to fundraising across the sundry expressions of the Christian faith. We did encounter recurring themes and commitments among the organizations we visited. In each setting, however, the language of solicitation and the approaches to donors were slightly different, as were the staff's attitudes toward the development program.

In every case, it was obvious that some measure of identification with the specific theological tradition of that organization was critical to successful relationships among staff and between staff and supporters of the ministry. David Tiede (1992), president of Luther Seminary in Minnesota, puts it this way: "Our financial strategies must be anchored in the theological moorings of our seminaries. Our schools also have vocations, discerned by our faithfulness to the gospel of Jesus Christ and tested by our commitment to mission in a world of many cultures. Such commitments must be disciplined by intellectual and moral competence."

How Theology Shapes Practice: Some Examples

How fundraisers and others who make decisions about the fundraising program view the relationship between God's sovereignty and human freedom has a tremendous impact on the ways Christian organizations approach the work of resource development. One of the most obvious ways in which differing understandings of God's interaction with humanity show up is in individual and organizational assumptions about prayer and the part it might play in a ministry-centered development program. For some Christian organizations, prayer is almost another facet of the fundraising program, as is illustrated by an example from the Union Gospel Mission of Seattle.

Herb Pfiffner, the executive director, wrote about a time when the mission faced a serious shortfall in funds and yet he refused to turn to a bank for help. "Unpaid bills were stacked on my desk. We prayed fervently. The next morning an envelope containing $100,000 arrived. The donor had never been on our mailing lists. At the end of the same week, a second unsolicited check for just more than $80,000 was received. God not only met our need, He gave us a surplus" (1992, pp. 88–89).

For some ministry-centered development programs, praying with and for donors is an important part of relationships with the organization's most faithful friends. Compassion International, for example, receives between fourteen thousand and fifteen thousand calls a month from child sponsors and other friends of the organization, and many of the calls include prayer requests. Making sure there are prayer partners available to callers accounts for a significant budget item, and the prayer ministry is an important part of what Compassion refers to as "sponsor relations."

Nor is this just an evangelical practice. At Catholic Charities of Cleveland, telephone solicitors are often heard praying with callers. A development director whose office opens on the calling center admitted he occasionally "eavesdrops on the telephone conversations. Some of our callers can really pray up a storm. It brings new energy to my work to listen in for a few minutes," he explained.

Fuller Seminary's Ann McKusick spoke of a personal approach to donors that centers around prayer. Gary Hoag, a member of the Biola University development staff, told us, "We want people to know that their prayers are important, that God's the one who's at work in the lives of students." Wesley Willmer, in *Money for Ministry,* sums up this view as follows: "Recognizing that it is God who works in people's hearts motivating them to give, I believe it is my responsibility to pray for them and ask God to work in their hearts" (1989, p. 24).

Another point of theological importance, and around which there is considerable difference of opinion, is that of the tithe. In our visits, we heard evidence of various understandings of disciplines of giving, although mentions of the tithe dominated. (We have discussed in earlier chapters some of the powerful testimonies we heard from others.)

An alumnus of Biola University remembered being challenged as a student to give "one-tenth of a tenth" to the university and noted that the message had helped make giving a "nonnegotiable priority" for him. Another very generous individual recalled learning about tithing from her grandfather via the "tater" story, the tale of a poor farmer who at the time of harvest counted out his potatoes into two piles: nine for market and one for God, nine for market and one for God. Looking at the meager pile that was God's, the farmer exclaimed, "But how can I do less than give one li'l tater to God?" "I've never forgotten that story," the donor said, "and I've made 'God's taters' a priority in my life."

Other donors were more comfortable describing their giving without the aid of "tithe talk." In these instances, giving was described as "a discipline," "an act of worship," and "an investment in God's work." Several individuals spoke of having been influenced by the example of parents and grandparents who were generous, giving people and of their attempts to challenge their own children to give. A supporter of San Francisco Theological Seminary told us simply, "I've always believed in giving. I was raised that way." We heard similar testimony from members of a family well known for generous philanthropy. As the father, two sons, and a daughter gathered to talk about their giving, they recalled that "Grandma and Grandpa showed us the way, and now we need to show the young ones. What we have is not what we're entitled to keep. What we have is a gift, and we must share it with others."

Most proponents of a literal tithe suggest that the required 10 percent belongs to the local church, with support for other ministries and good causes coming as gifts above the set amount. If an organization's development staff holds to this interpretation or knows that this is the view of the majority of constituent supporters, it has to shape the way it will ask those donors for a gift of significant size. Conversely, if the staff can approach the idea of giving without the guideline offered by this interpretation of the tithe, the parameters within which a gift is sought are far more open. Regardless, if a development person is working with a constituency that has a tradition of tithing (or some other discipline of giving), it will be most helpful for that fundraiser to understand the basic features of practice and the reasons behind them.

Implications of Theology for Hiring

Competition for good development staff causes some chief executives to overlook the importance of matching the personal belief system of a prospective fundraiser with the theological underpinnings of the ministry. As the issues we have just discussed suggest, this may be a grave mistake. For fundraisers to convey, accurately and personally, the uniqueness of the Christian organization to donors, they must thoroughly understand and affirm its theological tradition and, if possible, the tradition of its core of donors. Moreover, if the fundraising staff are successful in securing needed resources, they are likely to become influential participants in organizational decision making.

For these reasons and others, it is crucial that development officers be in sync with the goals and values of the organization. At one point in a discussion of fundraisers from different traditions we sponsored, we heard a fundraiser for an Episcopalian seminary say to her counterpart at a Lutheran school, "I don't think I could speak your language," and so she did not think she could work for his institution. Her point, and ours, is that fundraisers need to have a significant level of comfort with the faith tradition of the organizations they represent. Development staff must understand and be conversant in the particular "God talk" of the Christian organization with which they work. Further, they must be able to integrate the theology of the organization with decisions made in the everyday course of business.

The matter of theological match is significantly different from ideological match and in fact more important. Religious convictions go to the very core of who Christians are as individuals and how they relate to the people around them. It is not enough for a Christian organization merely to seek persons of faith to staff the development office. It is important—indeed, it may be indispensable—that the fundraising staff reflect their particular organization's specific understanding of what it means to be a person of faith. Father Michael Raschko advises, "It would be good if we could first name what we are trying to accomplish overall as pastoral and spiritual leaders and then make our fund raising not only fit that larger project, but also serve it. Fundraising would not then stand out on its own as an isolated task, but it would be integrated into our overall task as spiritual leaders" (1997, p. 54).

Donors are very quick to pick up on inconsistencies between an organization's historic presentation of itself and comments by a development officer whose own theology differs from that tradition, sometimes even slightly. "As development professionals, we must realize that we are much more transparent than we know. . . . We cannot camouflage our agendas. . . . A meaningful step toward effective communication is the ability to present a case with genuine personal conviction" (Sawyer, 1995, p. 49).

For example, it is hard to imagine individuals being able to raise funds effectively for the Mennonite Central Committee if they did not understand or appreciate the Anabaptist commitment to justice and social outreach. Similarly, it would be difficult for a person not sold on the value of denominations within the broader context of the Christian church to understand the unique relationship of denominationally related ministries and a supporting church body. "To truly motivate a gift, we have to learn to speak through the language distinctive to a particular culture of givers. . . . Yet we will only be speaking through these terms to something deeper, something more human, something more spiritual, and something more generically religious. The most basic motivation is this—to place one's heart and treasure in the same place" (Hudnut-Beumler, 1995, pp. 88–89).

Discussions about theological compatibility should begin with the interview process. One of the most effective ways to ensure that a newly hired fundraiser will contribute to fulfilling the mission of the organization is to talk about theology at the earliest opportunity in the hiring process. The person doing the hiring needs to ask the "right" questions. As a longtime development professional put it, "Who the fundraiser is is the important question. This work requires special people, men and women who bring to their tasks the benefit of spiritual insight, perspective, maturity, and an understanding of the big picture from a scriptural basis."

Ministry-centered development programs are staffed by individuals who are professionally competent, spiritually mature, and theologically in tune with the organizations they represent. This is more than attention to codes of ethics and making sure that the fundraising staffs are honest in their interactions with donors. All good development programs, religious or not, adhere to such a standard of operation. What is required is an expanded understanding of what the fundraising program of a faith-based organization can include. Fundraising within the community of faith is not just about money—although dollar goals are important and must be met. "To understand religious giving, we need to penetrate the specifically religious worlds of the donors. This distinguishes the analysis of religious giving from the analysis of secular fundraising" (Hoge and others, 1996, p. 129). Christian fundraising is—or at least should be—about God at work in donors' hearts, and that's an aspect of fundraising that is not learned casually. Prospective Christian fundraisers must bring with them a solid foundation for this understanding.

Along with tips for adjusting to the organization's culture and an introduction to the fundraising priorities of the department, orientation of new staff should include an overview of the theological assumptions within which the ministry operates. Nor should discussions about theology end after the initial period of orientation. As John Frank writes in his helpful book *The Ministry of Development,* "Do not assume that after this initial training . . . development staffs are on board. Continual sharing, training, and encouragement are needed" (1996, p. 78). Even seasoned fundraisers will need time and help in adjusting to a new organization's culture, programs, and vision. Prior experience in fundraising is no substitute for clearly absorbing and appropriating the organizational ethos. In addition, longtime staffers need to be reminded from time to time of the faith assumptions that are basic to the organization. Fuller Seminary faculty member Robert Banks has observed, "To have a theology, you must give some thought to what you believe and develop some coherence in your understanding" (1993, p. 44). This takes time, and it is an ongoing process.

The executive director of a Christian social service agency spoke with pride about the yearlong orientation program provided for new caseworkers. "As we recruit employees, we look for social workers with excellent educational and work backgrounds. We expect professional excellence in everyone we hire, but we also know that's not enough. We are an arm of the church, and our work has to represent what it means to be the church at work in the world. Few new staff bring that understanding with them, so we spend a lot of time helping new employees understand how our theology shapes the way we do things here."

Unfortunately, when this same person was asked if this same sort of help was provided to the development staff, he shrugged off the suggestion. "The training is for the staff involved in direct ministry." His answer helped explain the frequent turnover in the development office.

Being part of a ministry-centered program should strengthen the faith commitments of the staff. At Biola University, staff members spoke of learning from Wesley Willmer, vice president of advancement, what it means to raise money in a way that glorifies and honors God. In the Roman Catholic Diocese of Tucson, newer members of the development team described their work as the place where they've had a chance to grow in their faith. As a result of the encouragement they've received from the director and associate director of development, they feel comfortable in responding when people call the office with problems and prayer concerns.

At Compassion International, weekly chapel services contribute to a staff development program that focuses on nurturing "a servant's heart" in employees, including those who are responsible for raising funds. As a supplement to regular theologically based conversations with the fundraising staff, Ron Lundeen, vice president for development at San Francisco Theological Seminary, has asked the director of the seminary's counseling center to meet with his entire staff twice a year to help the group handle conflict, stress, and planning issues in a spiritually centered fashion. In all these situations, being part of a Christian work environment has contributed to the spiritual nurture of development staff members.

This sort of ongoing attention to the spiritual well-being of the development staff is especially important in light of what fundraisers face in the day-to-day routines of their lives. "Today, fundraisers face difficult questions—relating their energies to their institution's overall priorities, establishing a proper relationship between donors and the institution, determining which information the institution is obliged to share with prospective and actual donors, knowing when a gift should be refused, and determining the obligations of fundraisers to their institutions and the larger community. These issues are made the more difficult because fundraisers . . . are often strongly driven by the bottom line, and have few professional opportunities to consider matters of values or ethics with peers from other institutions" (Brittingham and Pezzullo, 1990, p. v). To this can be added the reality of very limited opportunity for conversations about faith and fundraising.

Theology and Implications for Goal Setting

As was discussed in Chapter Four, ministry-centered development programs operate with the confidence that God will provide whatever resources are required for doing God's work. Assumptions about human responsibility for organizing the work of bringing in those resources, however, differ greatly, depending on the theological grounding of the particular ministry. It is important, therefore, that fundraising staff are comfortable with the logical extensions of the theological assumptions guiding the organization.

To the leadership of some organizations, a carefully crafted plan for reaching the fundraising goals implies lack of faith in God's ability to supply all needs. This is especially true when a theological tradition emphasizes the significance of the "leading of the Holy Spirit." When asked how decisions were made about starting new programs, a board member in such an organization said, "If it's God's will, it's God's bill. We feel it's important to step out in faith with new initiatives. If the dollars don't come in to keep the program afloat, we will shut it down. So far, we haven't had to do that." Fundraisers of a similar temperament and theology are liberated by such a stance and report joy and freedom in their work. In the words of a director of development for one of the Christian organizations, "When we understand the role of the Holy Spirit in the process, we are relieved of some of the stress of being a fundraiser."

Many fundraisers, however, will be uncomfortable with the theological assumptions just cited. Those who value the guidance of clearly stated strategies may be more comfortable with leadership that takes direction from Jesus' story about the foolish virgins who, in their excitement to meet the bridegroom, left home unprepared for the challenges of the night ahead. Despite their good intentions, the virgins' failure to reflect on the situation and state what was needed to meet their goal led to a sad end (Matthew 25:1–13).

A longtime volunteer with Catholic Charities of Cleveland explained that agency's approach to planning for the fundraising program by citing her theological understanding of the role of the individual in the church. "We are an extension of Jesus. When he left, he put us in charge. *We simply can't fail.* The very fact that a soul might be lost because a service wasn't provided is devastating to consider." With consequences of such magnitude hanging in the balance, strategy takes on real urgency for organizations grounded in a theology stressing both free will and human responsibility. Some theologies tell us, in the words of a Russian proverb, that we should "pray to God but continue to row for shore."

Theology and Implications for Shaping Requests for Support

The manner in which Christian organizations go about asking for money provides the greatest opportunity for spiritual connection with a donor but also for abuse. On the one hand, the language of faith can be a powerful manipulative tool that will readily separate some people from their money but may leave them feeling diminished in the process. On the other hand, the language of faith can be used to help believers connect their giving to a deeper relationship with God and thus provide an opportunity for spiritual growth. The author of a book on Christian stewardship asks, "If believers are not taught a Scriptural doctrine of stewardship, can they be expected to give intelligently and can they be expected to realize that giving is indeed as vital a spiritual ministry as witnessing, reading the Bible, and praying?" (Olford, 1972, p. 14).

Theologically reflective development staff consciously and carefully craft appeals that tie faith to giving and that challenge people to think about the act of giving in religious terms. Cautious fundraisers are interested in the question of whether the practice of generous and sacrificial giving can lead people deeper into the life of faith—into a more active spiritual life. But they are also wary of using the language of faith in manipulative ways. They seek to create what Daniel Conway (1989) refers to as a theology of stewardship that recognizes that the "heart and soul of American philanthropy is found in faith and the desire to please God."

Ministry-centered development programs are clear about the core values and ideals of the theological traditions with which the organization is aligned. These values both limit and shape approaches to donors. In faith communities, assumptions about the role and responsibility of the individual are linked to larger theological issues, and these, in turn, can have real consequences for the fundraising program, for better or for worse. As we argued before, our ecclesiology—our understanding of the church—will have a profound impact on our perspective on how this work should be done.

As a parish priest in Tucson told us, "The bottom line is, we're not hitting people up for money. We're bringing the Gospel into their lives, and the Gospel demands a response." Everything done by a fundraising team should be informed by a *shared* sense of who God is, how God is involved with individuals and communities, and how that involvement shapes individual attitudes about giving and receiving.

Methods Matter Too

As we observed in Chapter One, fundraising programs of various ministries are now often the most public face of the church. Individual perceptions of particular Christian organizations—and the church as a whole—are shaped by the way the development staffs go about their work. As one observer puts it, "Our fundraising methods reflect not only the character of our organization, but also its values. They reflect who we are. Whatever methods we use ultimately come from the hearts of the leadership" (White, 1998, p. 134).

The development officers with whom we spoke acknowledged having struggled with whether any and all techniques are acceptable in raising money for Christian causes (for example, premiums, class challenges, giving clubs). Fundraising staff in some Christian organizations have adopted strategies simply because the methods worked in other settings. To do so with seemingly little reflection on what using those strategies might communicate to donors has laid them open to criticism. Other staff and other organizations have adopted some of these strategies while rejecting others, but only after careful reflection on their theological implications. What is essential, as August Napoli, president of Catholic Charities of Cleveland, put it, is for Christian organizations to do more than "wrap church words around fundraising techniques."

It is not easy to agree on implications of techniques in actual practice, as was illustrated when a group of fundraisers came together for a day-long discussion of development as a ministry. One member of the group was passionate in his belief that using secular tools wisely to assist donors to give more easily is simply good development work, despite the appearance in some people's minds of crassness. Others expressed strong reservations. In support of his point, the first person referred to what his local church has done to accommodate the "boomers" in their midst who write checks once a month. The church's stewardship committee sends monthly pledge reminders, carefully timed so that contribution checks can be written while paying other bills. Although he won few converts to his way of thinking, neither was he dissuaded from his advocacy of his church's approach in these matters.

In the end, however, most of the day's participants agreed that if the only intent of a given activity is to raise money, it probably isn't the best choice for a ministry-centered program. The director of development for Compassion International noted that the organization's fundraising staff constantly question the results of the methods they employ in representing the organization to child sponsors and other donors. "It's not enough that something feels good or right to the staff or that it 'works.' We take care to check up on what sponsors hear in what we're doing." Compassion actually runs focus groups to find out what people glean from the material the organization puts out—what message the donors are taking away—not just what is making them give.

Don McClanen, founder of the Ministry of Money, has warned, "You can work the pants off money, but if you're not deeply into Christ and the Spirit, all the talk, theology, biblical study, [and] suffering of the world won't make any difference. It's a spiritual problem. As long as we talk about making stewardship more effective, it won't work. What we're talking about is the transformation of the heart" (Ronsvalle and Ronsvalle, 1996, p. 194). This is echoed by the business officer at an evangelical seminary who remarked that "stewardship and giving are a form of worship." Devlin Donaldson, director of development for Compassion International, told us, "We have two goals in mind—the long-term financial health of the organization and discipling the donors to greater understanding."

The Power of the Carefully Spoken Word

Clarity and consistency in the spiritual facets of the messages presented through fundraising appeals make the organization more appealing to donors to whom the "faith base" of the causes they support is important. As the director of communications for an evangelical seminary told us, "We're determined always to put the mission statement up front." Based on what we heard from many donors, however, too few Christian organizations give sufficient attention to what they are communicating (even if unintentionally) to prospective funders.

A member of the board of trustees observed, "The fact is that we're reluctant to bring our language of faith into the other areas of life; as a result, faith hasn't been brought into fundraising programs." Ministry-centered development programs work hard at choosing words that will connect with donor hearts and elicit right motives for giving. In the words of Father Raschko, these programs work hard "to fit fundraising into the larger scheme of pastoral work" (1997, p. 54) and to do so in ways that are appropriate to the theological tradition within which the organization operates. When this happens, donors do notice and respond accordingly.

When asked what motivated their supporters, a volunteer with Catholic Charities of Cleveland told us, "People don't give to Catholic Charities because *we* are Catholic but because *they* are Catholic." We were also impressed that for some new donors to Catholic Charities of Cleveland, the act of giving was a point of reentry into a faith tradition some had mostly abandoned. Catholic Charities was consciously nurturing that, building a network of active younger donors by offering regular social gatherings and service opportunities for this group. In so doing, it was consciously picking up on the communal element of the Catholic tradition with which people might identify.

A development officer in a very different setting described what he saw happening in donor's lives as "an intimate connection between giving and faith," supported in part by the very way he asks for money. "If possible, during donor visits, I try to encourage the individuals with whom I'm meeting to talk about what God's been doing in their hearts as a result of their giving. I've learned to sit quietly through some long and awkward pauses. But once they start talking, more times than not, the words just pour out." Another fundraiser described her approach to donors as growing out of the theological concept of covenant. "I prefer a relationship built on mutuality that is completely nonhierarchical. I'm especially uncomfortable with approaches to donors that smack of legalism," she explained.

These comments suggest again that people can grow into a deeper faith through the act of giving but that the likelihood of this happening is significantly influenced by how the act of giving is elicited and structured. A director of development for a diocesan fundraising program said, "It doesn't matter how we structure the corporation; the faith base is of critical value—the key piece to most donors." His words were reinforced by the comment of a major donor to his cause: "When a request comes from an organization where people are acting on the basis of faith, it has more credibility."

Donors appreciate when Christian organizations have chosen a different and faithful way for raising money. A contributor to a Christian college told us, "The modeling of the school's philosophy of giving aligns with Scripture, focuses on the right things, and demonstrates competence with fundraising skills." Time and again, donors report that giving does not stand alone as an isolated experience in their lives. It is an integral part of their walk of faith. Giving allows individuals to testify through concrete action to the transforming power of God's grace in their lives. Most are grateful when they encounter a fundraising program that takes seriously the work of God in donors' lives as well as God's work through organizations.

Moreover, "donors also like to communicate on a spiritual or religious level. Donors can sometimes feel profound connections to a fundraiser if they reach an even higher level of exchange about good and evil, morality, ethics, and connections to the most profound questions of life and death. Most fundraisers do not usually think in terms of this level of communication, but these connections can be the most enduring in terms of the relationship between the fundraisers and the donor" (Tobin, 1995, p. 69).

Conclusions

On the surface, it would seem that the chorus line of an old hymn, "I know whom I have believed, and am persuaded, that he is able," is sufficient to bind organizational staff and constituents together in a common purpose. Certainly, a personal faith commitment is a necessary precondition for a successful fit between a fundraiser and a Christian organization. However, as we have suggested, in many instances, it is not enough. Though the faith paths of all Christians may lead back to Jesus, there is great variety in the twists and turns taken by individual believers as they strive to live out their faith.

We have considered what this means for shaping and operating a ministry-centered development program. We noted that it is important that interviews with candidates for fundraising positions include an exploration of theological understanding. We suggested that the theological underpinnings of an organization are often reflected in program planning and goal setting, whether the staff are aware of it or not—and whether the operative theology is aligned with the espoused theology or not. We also argued that the theology of the organization shows itself in the language of solicitations and in the methods and programs employed by the development office.

Several times in this book, we describe the fundraising program as the most public face of most Christian organizations. At this point, we suggest that the fundraising program is also the public voice of an organization, articulating the operative assumptions of its founders and continuing leadership. It is important, therefore, that fundraising staff be clear about, and consistent in, what they say and do. Theology really does matter, and in many more ways than might at first be assumed.

7

GIVING DONORS OPPORTUNITIES
FOR PARTICIPATION

---

*Not that I am looking for a gift, but I am looking
for what may be credited to your account.*

—Philippians 4:17

THESE WORDS FROM PAUL seem a strange admission from a man whose
life in service to God was marked by hardship, deprivation, and repeated
imprisonment. If ever there was a Christian worker who had earned the
right to request gifts from fellow believers, it was the apostle Paul. Yet
even out of his own difficulties, Paul points to motivations other than
practical (or personal) need, deeper motivations, for the work of those
who raise money for Christian organizations.

Christian fundraisers are to look beyond the organization's needs and
goals to the blessings donors will experience from their generosity. They are
to look at the life-enriching relationship with God that can be deepened
through the practice of giving, especially when that giving takes root in and
expresses a person's faith. Paul's example shows us that when Christian
fundraisers can evoke that kind of giving, then donors' hearts grow bigger
and, Philippians 4:18 goes on to explain, the specific need toward which
the gifts are directed will be "amply supplied."

Giving donors real and meaningful ways to participate in the life of the
organizations they support may be crucial to helping them have this kind
of experience of giving. This truth was illustrated in the comment of a

parishioner in Tucson, who at seventy years of age had discovered the joy of giving through his service on the Parish Stewardship Council. "As a young man," he said, "I considered giving to the church a burden and a negative in my life. But now that I've had a chance to see firsthand what can be accomplished when many gifts come together, I can hardly wait to give more. It's a joy."

Despite the scandals of recent years, most people of faith continue to value and support causes that touch their hearts and souls. The majority of Christians firmly believe that the organizations to which they give are doing good work. Conversations with donors illustrate that most take deep satisfaction in being part of something that is larger and greater than themselves.

Unfortunately, in the cases where the rationale for giving is framed only in terms of having an opportunity to change the circumstances of *other* people's lives, donors are rarely encouraged to reflect on how the act of giving might change their own lives. Ministry-centered development programs can encourage that reflection. Sociologist Paul Schervish writes, "Although it does not always occur, the major positive effect of religious consciousness is its potential to affect not just the amount of giving but the quality of the care and involvement of the donor" (1990, p. 65).

Another member of a Catholic parish in Tucson described the character transformation that had taken place in his life as he had grown in his understanding of Christian giving. "At first, my giving was legalistic, but as I continued to give, my attitude changed. Generosity comes from God. I can't wait to be even more generous. I would love to give more." His words are echoed by a longtime supporter of Fuller Theological Seminary: "It makes me happy to be in a position where I'm able to give," she said. "It's extremely satisfying to be able to do something that gets the Gospel out." Another person reported, "I don't look back on giving as a hardship. It has always been a joyful experience."

A strong development program is built on relationships. At the heart of Christian faith is one central, eternal relationship transmitted and sustained by many relationships. It should follow then that donor relations would be a top priority for Christian organizations, and those relations are likely to be strongest where they center around donors' engagement with the ministry being done. Ministry-centered development programs recognize this. For example, during our visit to Compassion International, staff members told us, "We have a passion for caring for children and ministering to the poor. Our job is to find people who share that passion, or in whom we can kindle it, and ask them to share in our ministry."

It is important that fundraisers in faith-centered organizations create opportunities for donors' hearts to follow their gifts and for them to experience the "blessing that issues from generosity" (Peterson, 1995, p. 496). From this observation, we draw the first of three essential operating principles for a ministry-centered approach to fundraising: *the organization and the development program seek to involve donors with the ministry in ways that help their hearts grow bigger.*

Meeting Donors Where Their Hearts Are

Organizational theorists Terrence Deal and Casey Baluss point to the fact that "benefactors give because they believe and have faith in a beloved enterprise." They further note that "nonprofit organizations . . . often fail to recognize the power of who we are, the unique character that induces people to work and give in behalf of a noble cause" (1994, pp. 13–14). There is no denying the fact that fundraisers who seek to nurture donors' hearts, to help donors see and feel the meaning of their generosity, must take time to describe how gifts to the organization are used to meet real needs in the lives of real people. For the purposes of nurturing both their commitment and their spiritual growth, nothing takes the place of meeting donors where their hearts are.

At Compassion International, virtually every person on staff speaks passionately about the organization's commitment to "present the opportunity to sponsor a child in a way that is an extension of the sponsor's faith." When fundraisers are freed to educate donors about these most profound aspects of the development program, about how they become part of the ministry of the organizations, the rewards are significant, both for the donors and for the organization.

Richard Mouw, president of Fuller Theological Seminary, spoke of creating true partnerships with persons who support the organization with their financial gifts. "Donors who feel connected to a work and who are allowed to have a genuine part in the ministry are the best fundraisers. Bonding occurs among donors. This is Christian community at its best— to be involved in reinforcing each other's commitments." Unfortunately, too few donors have found either spiritual encouragement or community through their giving.

Although a fundraiser cannot single-handedly create happy, spiritually alive donors, Christian fundraisers and their organizations and programs can do a great deal to make this possible. Exemplary organizations are intentional about relating to donors and others in ways that allow space and time for God's work in individual hearts. In this way, they help donors find great joy and satisfaction in their giving.

A Christian financial counselor attributed his clients' apparent lack of generosity to the fact that their hearts have not been challenged by a vision. "Most of the folks with whom I work could give at least five times more than they do, but no one's provided them with a good enough reason to do so." To this, Sandra Brown, director of the pastoral counseling center at San Francisco Theological Seminary, added, "Any time we push obligation, we shut the door. Instead, we need to get at what's really important to people, to touch them where they're at. We must genuinely seek to understand how this person puts his or her faith into practice."

A program director at one institution described to us a solicitation call in which the CEO had asked her to participate. When she entered the room where the meeting with the donor already was in progress, she was startled by the obvious agitation and frustration of both men. After a few minutes, the prospective donor asked her to step outside with him. "That man just can't listen," he complained to her. The CEO had asked for a gift in support of a program for which the friend of the organization felt no significant personal connection. As the program director talked with him about his interests, he calmed down. A few weeks later, he returned to the organization with the offer of a substantial gift in support of an aspect of the ministry that fit with where his heart was leading him.

The program director concluded her story with a question: "Did anyone care what was in this man's heart?" Fortunately, the chief executive was wise enough to allow someone more able than himself to work with that particular individual. As a result, a giver's heart grew bigger.

The Gift of Information

A wonderful example of the effort to understand a donor and then to respond in the most affirming way was reported by Richard Mouw, president of Fuller Theological Seminary. He tells of giving a talk about his institution and its needs in which he spoke about how hard it is to raise needed resources for the less glamorous but still critical functions of the seminary, like taking care of its physical plant. A short while later, he received a note and a significant gift from a man whose own work made him aware of and sympathetic to such matters. The donor requested that his gift be used to "fix the plumbing."

Dr. Mouw was of course delighted for Fuller to receive such a gift. He then instructed the maintenance crews to make a photographic record of their work—"before-and-after Polaroids" of the pipes, leaking and fixed. Upon completion of the work, the maintenance staff gave this visual record of the projects made possible by the gift, with their own word of thanks, to Dr. Mouw, who then mailed these items and his personal thank-you to the donor.

This donor was thrilled by the seminary's response. "Nothing could have pleased me more," he told Dr. Mouw. This was a relatively simple and low-cost but very effective way to both thank a donor and affirm his interests and commitments.

This story highlights the good news that donor recognition doesn't have to be expensive, elaborate, or even public. The staffs of ministry-centered development programs have discovered that often the most precious gift they can give a donor is information about a program or project and about how that donor's gift has made a difference. A volunteer with Catholic Charities of Cleveland said, "The more people know, the more they give. It's our job to make the donors feel a part of the work. Giving is a learning process." She described the work of the stewardship committee as "bombarding people with a loving message."

A piece of a person's heart accompanies every contribution. It is essential that organizations honor this gift of self on par with the much needed cash. "It's more than just money that people are giving. It's part of their life. They worked hard to earn what we are asking them to give away," Bishop Manuel Moreno of the Roman Catholic Diocese of Tucson stated. All too often, however, fundraising appeals from churches and parachurch organizations give priority to the needs of the organization over the desires of the giver's heart. They do not recognize the gift of self that might be wrapped up in a gift of money or other resources.

Gifts are the tangible evidence of a donor's belief in the values, goals, purposes, and importance of the ministry. If the organization's goal is to help create channels through which God's love and joy can flow, a personalized, quiet thank-you is usually best. "Information that illustrates a gift at work is one of the most valuable gifts—'premiums'—we can give a donor," observed Joyce Brooks, a member of the Biola University development team. She cited the example of scholarship donors, noting that hearing about how a student is growing as a result of the education a donor's gift made possible is often what touches that donor most deeply. She also described quiet, low-key events where those donors can meet those students and those connections can be made tangible.

The Way to Donors' Hearts: Participation

In contrast, several years ago, a series of interviews with longtime major donors to Christian colleges revealed that a great many of these very generous contributors did not feel valued by the institutions to which they gave. It was not that the schools had been negligent in saying thank you. Indeed, the homes and offices of the donors were littered with objects of appreciation. What these men and women longed for were opportunities for interaction with students and faculty, the chance to feel that they were truly part of the educational mission.

A seasoned fundraiser for Jewish causes puts it this way: "No relationship thrives when one party is always giving and the other party is always taking. The donor can give money, leadership, and also contribute ideas and emotional support to a project. The fundraiser can provide ideas, inspiration, leadership, appreciation, devotion, and a variety of other intellectual, emotional, and spiritual supports to the donor" (Tobin, 1995, p. 76).

Mark Vincent, director of the Mennonite Church's Giving Project, writes (1998), "Our use of wealth is a creative act also, for it gives life to our values. . . . As God's children with a creation identity, we use wealth to give life to other people. We care far more about this than consuming life's blessings or being as frugal as possible." Organizations that place a high priority on nurturing donor faith work hard at providing opportunities, many and varied if possible, for participation. Fred Hofheinz (1991), a program officer in religion at Lilly Endowment, states: "I've observed that, while it's important to have a written case statement which expresses what an organization's mission is and what its plans for the future are, the best case statements are communicated orally—from one person to another—by telling the organization's story in ways that encourage others to become 'partners' in its mission."

Seattle's Union Gospel Mission seeks to involve donors in ways that, according to Executive Director Herb Pfiffner, are faith-centered rather than cause-centered. "We try to keep the focus on what Christ is doing through the mission's programs. Christ is what we are about." To live out the organization's commitment to helping supporters connect their gifts of time and money with their faith, the mission had increased the position of director of volunteers from half-time to full-time. The results have been remarkable. "At first, the program staff was not sure whether the extra work required to find things for volunteers to do was worth the effort. As good comments came back to us about God's work in the lives of the mission's friends, attitudes changed. Making room for volunteers—many of whom are also donors—is now understood as part of our ministry," the volunteer coordinator told us.

Involving donors in the ministry work they support takes effort. It might be fairly easy for Christian organizations with local bases and those whose programs are local in their outreach. It is often more of a challenge for national organizations whose programs are widely dispersed. It may be especially difficult for those whose work is mostly overseas. Nonetheless, geography cannot be used as an excuse for leaving donors out of the work. Christian ministries that are serious about providing donors with opportunities for spiritual growth must be creative in their approaches.

Busy Hands, Connected Hearts

Consider a Christian relief and development agency that provides supplies, most of which are donated, to Christian workers in service all over the world. This organization makes opportunities for volunteers from the area surrounding its U.S. headquarters to come together to sort through donated materials. These volunteers fix some things, throw out what is no good, and repackage things to be sent overseas so that what is needed gets to where it is needed most efficiently. Not only does this give these people—many of whom are donors of money as well as time—a chance to participate in the ministry of that organization, it also ensures that only high-quality materials are shipped.

Another international Christian service organization has a large base of supporters in rural communities. These people are brought together on a regular basis to prepare foodstuffs that can be sent overseas to projects and relief efforts. As a member of the development staff admitted, the organization could probably buy these foodstuffs as cheaply as they get them through this process, "but," she noted, "the work these volunteers do preparing the items is vitally important to their sense of ownership in this organization. It gives all these people a chance to feel part of the work in a way that makes it *their* work, and we would not want to give that up for anything."

Tapping Technology

Even where this kind of participation is simply not possible, organizations with far-flung constituencies can use new technologies in exciting ways to connect the ministry with donors. Web sites provide instant access to information and in some cases allow for immediate feedback about a specific program or gift opportunity. Members of the Golden Mouse Club at Messiah Village, a retirement community sponsored by the Brethren in Christ Church, back up their prayer support for the denomination's missionaries worldwide with on-line words of encouragement through the denomination's Web site. Although many of these high-tech seniors are no longer physically able to travel, e-mail technology allows them to be in frequent contact with mission activities worldwide. It has also provided them with an avenue for a ministry of their own—the ministry of encouragement.

In another case, alumni and friends of a geographically isolated Christian college were able to monitor progress on a long-awaited music building via the Internet. Many had come to believe the project would never happen; instant access to on-line evidence that the building was indeed being built encouraged some of the doubters to make a gift. The Web site also served as a daily thank-you to those who had given early and generously in support of the building. Organizations that depend heavily on direct mail and other less personal forms of fundraising would do well to incorporate the Internet into their donor relations activities. Used well, it can be an inexpensive way of giving a human face to their work.

The Personal Touch

Still, for all the wonders of technology, nothing beats the power of person-to-person communication for building durable and rich relationships. At Compassion International, letters between children and their supporting families breathe life into the child sponsorship program. A staff member told us, "Our president, Wes Stafford, believes in child sponsorship as a change agent in children's lives and the donors' lives. Our goal is that sponsors will see the world through different eyes." We encountered this same sentiment at Biola University, where a longtime supporter told us how he and his wife cried when they opened the letters from "their" scholarship recipients. They spoke of the joy they've found in knowing that their giving "is making a difference in real lives."

Inside Talk

Although we have focused to this point on constituents who are external to the organization, it also behooves the development staff to give attention to others within the organization. Wise fundraisers spend time with program staff, observing first hand what they are doing and listening to them talk about their work. A next step is to involve program staff in telling the stories of their programs to prospective supporters, and eventually, as they come to understand this work better, it may be good to involve these individuals in setting fundraising goals. (As we will discuss in Chapter Eight, some of this involvement is vital.)

We are aware of a Christian college where the development team has worked hard over several years at drawing the rest of the campus community into the fundraising program. Appeal letters are circulated in advance of the mailing date, with a request for prayer on behalf of the outreach to potential supporters. Monthly gift reports are posted outside the development office and on the college's Web site. The entire staff of the college is invited for doughnuts and bagels to celebrate the conclusion of a successful phonathon or the completion of the fiscal year. It's taken time, but development staff report that the question is no longer "How are you doing?" but rather "How are we doing?" Fundraisers are greeted with the assurance, "I'm praying for you." Not so surprisingly, giving from college employees has increased along with their understanding of and excitement about the fundraising program.

In short, whether in person, from a distance, through the aid of technology, or within the organization, the opportunity for participation is key to growing givers' hearts—to providing Christians with their own epiphany that "I am the church." Giving is a learning process, and as Sister Rita Mary, a member of the diocesan staff in Cleveland, explained, "Some act their way into reflection, and others reflect their way into action. So for some, giving may lead them into reflection and transformation." It takes a willingness to employ many approaches to connect with donor hearts.

Overcoming Roadblocks to a Ministry-Centered Fundraising Program

Staff in exemplary programs are aware of possible roadblocks to fundraising as a ministry, and they work to minimize or counteract the obstacles, even when it is not easy. Old behavior patterns are hard to change—for the persons doing the asking and for those who do the responding. If the Christian faith is about anything, however, it's about change. It is this confidence on which fundraisers for religious organizations must begin to act when confronting the following obstacles to a ministry-centered approach to development.

It Takes Time for Hearts to Grow

For most fundraisers, time is in short supply. Theologian Robert Banks has observed, "The fact of the matter is this: our days are overloaded with too many things to do and never enough time to do them all in. We are whisked along through a kaleidoscope of situations, appointments, activities, and responsibilities for most of our waking hours. However much we try to catch up, the watch and the pocket planner regulate our time and help us ration it out" (1993, pp. 72–73). This is especially true for fundraisers. The development team wraps up one fiscal year and is off and running on the next. Fundraisers "win" a campaign, but before they can celebrate, the board has compiled a list of even more ambitious projects to be funded.

Too often, in the rush to keep up with institutional expectations, donors are left in the dust or their interests are ignored. "I still can't believe they asked me for a six-figure gift toward a new music building," an exasperated alumnus of a Christian college exclaimed. "What in the world made them think music is my thing? All my past gifts to the college have been for the athletic program. Someone didn't do the right research." Actually, in this case the development staff were aware of the donor's interests, but under the pressure of deadlines, in their headlong pursuit of an aggressive fundraising goal, they took a chance on changing the man's heart. In the end, they succeeded only in annoying a loyal friend of the college.

Mark Vincent, writing in *Generous Living* (1998), challenges fundraisers to consider "what we're doing that destroys the celebration of giving[.] Why does the invitation to give bring danger to relationships rather than strengthen them? . . . Donors say ministry organizations are insensitive. Many donors experience organizations as bureaucracies that self-serve and are unfeeling toward their constituency." So much for attention to the donor's "spiritual account."

In another illustration, we are reminded of a conversation with a fundraiser for a denominationally sponsored organization. He proudly told us how, as the institution faced a possible deficit at fiscal-year end, he sent a special letter to forty of the most supportive pastors, asking them to mention the giving program from the pulpit. Several congregations responded generously as a result of their pastor's encouragement, and that extra giving helped the organization reach its fundraising goals. When we asked him if he had reported to the pastors on the outcome of the special appeal, he shook his head sadly. In the face of all the busyness of wrapping up the fiscal year and preparing for the next, he had failed to involve the pastors in the celebration of God's goodness. What an opportunity lost.

A ministry-centered development program requires sensitivity to the heart's desire of the other. And it requires acknowledging the validity of where the Spirit might be leading the donor, even if it is not on the same path as the funding appeal of the moment. The surest way to build relationships is to relate to donors as individuals. We were taken by the words of a donor to Fuller Theological Seminary who said of the president, "He always knows your name."

A one-size-fits-all approach to donor relations is not likely to minister to individual hearts. A volunteer with Catholic Charities of Cleveland explained, "The Holy Spirit puts people where they should be. You don't give because of what someone else is. You give because of what you are." Wesley Willmer states that "a godly perspective suggests people should give for reasons of love, vision, compassion, and stewardship. Organizations seeking a godly perspective have a special obligation to encourage this higher, spiritual motivation in donors" (1989, p. 17).

In addition to paying attention to the desires of donor hearts, fundraisers who wish to encourage the hearts of donors must take time to match the request for funds to what the donor is able to provide. A longtime supporter of an outreach program for children told us about an appeal she had received asking for support for a several-million-dollar renovation of the organization's national headquarters. "I guess my $20 a month doesn't count for much," she said sadly. By failing to take time to sort out donors for whom this particular appeal was most appropriate, well-meaning fundraising staff communicated to a faithful friend that her gifts were of limited consequence. In so doing, the development staff robbed her of the joy she usually experienced when giving.

Unfortunately, a lot of what occurs in the name of resource development for ministry in Christian organizations resembles the children's game of tag. Fundraisers, pressured to meet this year's too-high goals, race after donors, pausing just long enough to hit them with a request for support and shout, "You're it! You're the donor today." It's not surprising that more and more persons of wealth are choosing to play another game: hide and seek.

A generous woman in California described her experience with fundraisers in the violent terms of the street, referring to the uncaring approach of some organizations as "drive-by shootings." "In one day," she said, "fundraisers from three ministries stopped by for a visit. Not one of them took time to ask about my life or what my goals were for my giving. They didn't even pretend like they wanted to know me. I feel like I've been ambushed." It is unlikely the board members or chief staff officers of any Christian organization would feel good knowing a donor felt this way about how she was asked for support.

A seminary president described his ambivalence about the donor-fundraiser relationship as follows. "The spiritual weariness of the job has sometimes overcome me on just this point: How with integrity, can one become the friend and even the pastor to folk with lots of money to give away? How might one become that friend and pastor to someone in their very resistance to giving money to you? It is a hard question. I empathize with wealthy folk who are constantly suspecting that the interest of other folk in them relates mostly to money" (Shriver, 1992, p. 20).

Donors are rarely encouraged to provide feedback on how giving has changed their hearts, and so most fundraisers do not know how donors perceive their work, at least not in this regard. Along with the happy stories of God's blessing in individual lives, organizational leaders who seek to hear what donors have to say about the messages and methods used by the organization should be prepared for stories that are not so joyous. The fact is that both types of tales are helpful in assessing how the organization is doing with donor relations. In short, it's not enough simply to state that donor relations should be a high priority. Fundraisers, CEOs, and board members need to back up their words with action. An annual review of the fundraising program that includes soliciting candid feedback from donors and other important constituents is a good first step.

If the organization's aim is to help create channels through which God's love and joy can flow, it must pay attention to what is happening in donors' hearts as a result of the way in which the organization goes about raising money. Robert Wuthnow writes, "Research has focused more on the mechanics of giving and on the motivations leading people to respond to appeals for money than on the place these experiences may have in individuals' spiritual journeys. We need to pay more attention to these accounts. . . . We need to understand better how they nurture the spark of faith and hope on which the spirit of charity thrives" (1990b, p. 283).

Although very much committed to meeting the fundraising challenges given to them, the ministry-focused fundraisers we met are able to balance the drive to reach their goals with a sincere desire to do what is best for the donor. They see themselves as facilitators, offering the individuals with whom they work opportunities to pursue their dreams and to participate in the work of faith in the world. This is no less so when their efforts result in a gift going to another ministry.

They have the freedom to take the time necessary to build relationships with potential donors and to link donor interests in real and genuine ways with the ministries they represent. They are free to devote time to helping donors discover the intimate connection between giving and faith. Bob Heslinga, director of development for the Roman Catholic Diocese of Tucson, explained, "Stewardship is the process of building up the household of the Lord. How do we do this corporately? It must be reflected in our priorities."

Fundraising as a Ministry Also Takes Money

If time is in short supply for Christian ministries, financial resources are usually even more limited. The simple truth of the matter is, however, unless money is allocated in a Christian organization's budget to support activities that truly nurture donors in their spiritual growth (not merely fertilizes them for monetary harvest), those activities will generally not happen. Apathy and ignorance of what it takes to succeed in fundraising are barriers. Even worse are situations where the chief development officer actually has to fight to maintain travel budgets, hold on to staff positions, or integrate up-to-date technology into the fundraising program.

No amount of hard work, past experience, or charisma can compensate for a lack of internal support. Fundraising must be understood as a shared responsibility, and it is up to the chief executive to lead the way by accepting his or her share of the load. Unfortunately, most organizations do not focus much on reinvesting into constituency, and those that do reinvest often find resistance and accusations of waste. However, when we questioned staff at the exemplary organizations about the "value" of investing in donor relations, these ministry-oriented fundraisers told us that it can be no other way.

Ed Anderson, the chief financial officer at Compassion International, explained that the president and the board place a high priority on maintaining close contact with the child sponsors, and they have put the organization's money into this commitment. "To eliminate the budget line for 'sponsor relations' would hurt Compassion in two areas—both 'customer service' and ministry to donors would suffer. An organization's budget must match its ministry goals. Here at Compassion, we work hard to make sure everyone understands what we're trying to do and where the organization is headed in the long term."

The good news, as has already been suggested, is that the most appreciated donor recognition "gift" may be relatively easy and inexpensive to provide. It is information, and providing information to donors often costs very little. It certainly is less expensive than premiums and plaques and is generally far more meaningful to a donor. As Christian organizations focus on communicating about the real benefits that donors' gifts create—the impact of an individual gift on the fulfillment of an important mission, the change that these gifts make possible in the lives of others—donors' hearts grow bigger.

Finally, fundraisers must also have the freedom to continue a relationship even when the effort will no longer "pay off" in fundraising terms. An example of this principle is found at Biola University, where a member of the planned giving staff devotes a majority of his time to assisting elderly annuitants and other donors with health care, housing, and financial planning concerns. In most cases, these individuals have already given all they have to give. Nonetheless, the university continues in its relationship with these longtime friends, keeping trust with brothers and sisters in Christ. The staff described the time allocated to this work not as an expense for the department but as "a ministry of care and friendship." It is no surprise that a donor to Biola would tell us, "I feel safe in my giving. There's no sense that it's just my checkbook they want. As a result, they've got my heart and my gifts."

A Friend in Need: The Challenge of the Hurting Donor

A number of fundraisers talked about the challenge of working with individuals who give to the organization out of personal pain. While acknowledging that this is probably not a new phenomenon, the number of hurting donors seems to be on the increase. Christian organizations are struggling to find ways to respond appropriately to the emotional and spiritual needs of some donors. It may be true that "a friend in need is a friend indeed," but for a fundraising staff already working at full tilt, it can be tough to figure out the best way of responding to donor needs.

As noted in Chapter Six, many Christian organizations seek to respond to the emotional and spiritual needs of their friends through a ministry of prayer. It is common for gift response cards to include a space where donors can forward a prayer request along with their gift. Many other Christian organizations receive prayer requests by telephone, and a number have people on staff whose job it is to pray with callers. At Compassion International, the "phone crew are among the highest-grade and highest-paid nonexempt employees," a member of the development staff explained. Compassion is so clear about its desire to attend to the spiritual welfare of donors that it has added a chaplain whose time is devoted to organizing the prayer ministry and to following up with donors who request prayer support. David Dahlin, assistant to Compassion's president, stated, "Donors have been faithful in their commitments to Compassion. In turn, we will stand with donors in their time of need with prayer and a telephone call."

For organizations in closer proximity to their donors, as is the case for the Union Gospel Mission of Seattle, donors sometimes expect more than the promise of a prayer or a note of encouragement. The mission's development staff spoke with concern about donors who expect the organization to provide a level of pastoral care that they are not equipped to provide. "Ours is a ministry to the poor and the homeless. To be asked to minister to the difficult family situation of a wealthy donor takes us into new territory." Though finding the appropriate response may not be easy, UGMS staff are determined not to abandon donors in need. They lend a listening ear when they can, offer simple advice where appropriate, and try to refer individuals with more serious emotional or spiritual needs to others who can be of greater assistance.

This is a point at which partnerships with local congregations can be especially helpful. It may be that the most loving thing a fundraiser can do is to encourage the individual to become involved with a church community. The staff at the Roman Catholic Diocese of Tucson told us, "People do let the office know of their problems and prayer concerns. The bishop takes this very seriously. He always responds with a note, and he may ask a pastor to call on the person."

It is not a bad thing if fundraisers admit that it is not their place or role to pastor donors. Development officers have to face up to their own limitations of time, training, or temperament for intensive counseling situations. Nor should it be interpreted as abandonment to refer a hurting supporter to the care of a local congregation; done with true care and compassion (and appropriate follow-up), it is unlikely to be seen that way by the donor. A referral can be the best way to help a donor. It can also serve as a model of the kind of cooperation between parachurch organizations and congregations that should characterize the life of the church.

Conclusions

We have focused in this chapter on the need to give donors the greatest possible opportunities to experience themselves as true participants in the work they support. Development consultant John Frank has described Christian development work as "creating opportunities to involve God's people in God's work." We absolutely agree that, in the ideal, it should be that. However, we think that all of us involved in such efforts need to recognize that just writing a check often does not feel like "involvement." That is why we have stressed the need to do the things that help donors become involved in other ways too.

The ways we ask people in the first place, trying to recognize the passions they might have and to offer them real opportunities to express those passions in a gift, are crucial. So too are the ways we thank them and show them that their gift has made a difference by providing illuminating and timely information. Finally, trying to find a variety of ways supporters can actually give of their time and energy (if they desire), as well as their money, is an excellent thing for every Christian organization to do. We recognize there are obstacles that may arise to creating this sense of involvement and participation for donors, and we have seen examples of how some organizations overcome or circumvent these.

The words from Saint Paul with which we began this chapter are a beautiful reminder of what should matter most to Christian fundraisers. The goal of development work in Christian organizations should be twofold: to raise the dollars necessary to advance the work at hand and also to give attention to "what may be credited to [the individual's] account." In sum, our goal should be for donors to grow in faith and joy through the opportunities for sharing and belonging we make available to them.

In the work of Christian fundraising, donors should be offered opportunities to experience themselves as part of the family of God's children, wherein the work of caring for one another is known as a blessing as well as a duty. Robert Wuthnow describes this dynamic when he observes, "I suspect that many people have felt deeply blessed by the outpourings of kindness and generosity they have seen in their churches, among their friends, and in their neighborhoods. Religious literature, sermons, and testimonials are filled with accounts of such experiences. Often the logic involved is easy for the skeptic to pick apart. But for the faithful, these accounts demonstrate the possibility of God working in human hearts, the value of someone praying earnestly in faith, and the reality of caring and helping within the human community" (1990b, pp. 282–283).

On the surface, the principle highlighted in this chapter seems so obvious that we should not have to mention it. Yet what we discovered in our research is that fundraisers too often forget or fail to make time for the individuals whose gifts they seek. As a result, donors report feelings of abuse, disappointment, and cynicism—hardly emotions that encourage givers' hearts to grow bigger (or more fond of the ministry in question). By contrast, exemplary programs seek to make room for donors and to honor the fact that when they give, they give—and want to give—of themselves as well as their resources. In this they point the way for all Christian organizations in the work of fundraising.

8

INTEGRATED ORGANIZATIONAL PLANNING

God of Guidance,
Give us direction so we may know
which way to choose and which to refuse;
which course to claim and which to reject;
which action to take and which to avoid.

—Responsive reading from *The Hymnal: A Worship Book*

MOST ADULT AMERICANS remember the Lone Ranger, a mythic hero whose Wild West adventures were played out to the strains of the *William Tell Overture*. He was assisted in his good works by his faithful companion, Tonto, but there was no doubting the hero of the series. Like many of today's "best" fundraisers, everywhere the Lone Ranger went, people marveled at his ability to set things right. And when the job was done—again reminiscent of the trend in modern-day fundraising shops—he set out for the next troubled situation with little more than a wave of his hat and a "Hi, ho, Silver, away!" He had no need for a long-range plan. His goal was simple: get the job done and move on. No roots. No accountability. No volunteers. It was his show.

This approach worked as a premise in the movies and on TV, and it may have even worked for a few fundraising operations in years past. But for today's development programs, especially those dedicated to the spiritual nurture of donors, there's no place for Lone Rangers. Strong fundraising programs are grounded in and supported by an organizationwide understanding of fund development that is both strategic and holistic. Fundraising, to be truly successful, cannot be seen as something separate from the rest of the organization. It must be understood as everyone's responsibility, even if the day-to-day aspects of the development program are entrusted to a few specialists. This is what we saw in the exemplary programs we were privileged to visit, and this is the point we make in this chapter.

Careful and prayerful planning encourages what Friedrich Nietzsche referred to as "a long obedience in the same direction" (1907, p. 106). Planning opens the way for God to "enlighten our minds, purify our hearts, strengthen our wills, and lead us to live as faithful followers of Jesus"—to finish the prayer that began this chapter. Integrated planning that involves the development staff along with personnel from across the organization creates the safe environment within which a ministry-centered fundraising program can operate. In short, a carefully shaped plan can answer the question that less informed members of the program staff are prone to ask: "What does fundraising have to do with it—or at least with my work?"

Before leadership and staff ever put pens to paper (or fingers to computer keyboards), it is also important to ask whose goals will determine the course and character of a fundraising program. Planning consultant Janet Boguch writes, "Successful fund development does not happen as the result of an enthusiastic and educated person's energetically and doggedly leading the way and doing most of the planning and executing of the activities" (1994, pp. 73–74). The strongest development efforts are those that flow from a comprehensive institutional plan and reflect the best thinking of a cross section of an organization's stakeholders—including development, program, and administrative staff. It is important that leaders set out clearly and publicly what an organization is intended to accomplish over a specific period of time. This is just as true for Christian organizations as any others.

A good comprehensive plan, then, includes establishing fundraising goals within the framework of a larger agenda and articulation of and commitment to the organization's basic values. The larger institutional plan sets the course for the development program by identifying and pricing out priorities and options for the current year (or longer). A full development plan can and should elaborate on those priorities and options and specify how they can be met.

While development staff must understand and appreciate larger institutional goals, strengths, and limits, others in the organization must be willing to listen to and respect the advice of development staff on the question of how much money can be raised within the available period of time. Fundraising doesn't just happen, and a good organizational plan is more than a wish list. If the development staff are able to show why a funding goal is out of line, their concerns should be taken seriously. A spirit of mutual accountability and appreciation for each other's work is indispensable.

Once goals have been established, it is up to the development staff to interpret the agreed-on plans to the "right" donors, matching organizational priorities with individual passions. When this happens, donors' hearts can grow bigger at the same time an organization's agenda is being advanced. From this observation, we draw the second of three essential operating principles for a ministry-centered approach to fundraising: *organizational leaders recognize the importance of integrated planning and include the development staff in the process of shaping larger goals.*

This chapter focuses on how integrated planning contributes to the goal of growing donors' hearts. Our intention here isn't to provide a step-by-step guide on preparing a plan. Rather, we seek to build a case for why leaders of Christian organizations should make planning a high priority and for whose benefit the planning is done. Specifically, we spell out four advantages that flow from an organizationwide, integrated approach to planning. We also suggest how each of the four helps focus development staff and others in the organization on the central issue of God's work in donor hearts. The advantages are as follows:

- Good planning provides consistency.
- Good planning establishes limits.
- Good planning encourages accountability.
- Good planning enables evaluation.

An organization that has charted a course for its future is far more likely to move ahead with courage and effectiveness than one in which the leadership eschews planning. Good planning enables boards and staff to take stock of where the organization stands in the present, decide where they want it to be in the long and short term, chart a course to get there, and monitor progress along the way. When a change in the plan is required, it can be made with a clear understanding of why the change is needed and the advantages of the proposed new direction.

Consistency

Organizational consistency is vitally important to successful fundraising. Few things are as unappealing to donors as "wishy-washiness" in an organization's talk about its future. Nothing is more likely to turn away thoughtful donors than a sense that an organization's goals are unclear or constantly changing or if there is the same sense about its plans for reaching its goals. There is a high price to be paid in lost donor loyalty from "letting an organization swerve from its traditional roots, disconnect from its cherished values and rites" (Deal and Baluss, 1994, pp. 7–8). Supporters are right to be leery if, just when an organization seems poised to move in one direction, a new course of action is announced.

An intelligently crafted long-range plan suggests to potential donors that an organization is serious about its future effectiveness, that careful thought has been given to how the proposed future can be secured, and that the organization is competent to carry out its stated mission. To be presented with concrete evidence that an organization is committed to following through on its plan—that it is not just a piece of paper, "for show"—is reassuring to donors and others involved with the organization. When an organization is consistent in its program or service focus and its fundraising efforts, it creates a context in which donors can be consistent in their giving.

Conversely, fundraising staff are crippled in their efforts if the organizational ground is constantly shifting under their feet. Several fundraisers we interviewed described their frustration at starting out the year with one set of fundraising goals in mind, only to be asked to raise additional funds "on the side" for projects that had not been included in the organization's plan or the budget for the year. One story we heard captured the elements of many others.

"Just when it seems we've gotten a handle on what we're supposed to be doing this year, the executive director walks in the door with another funding need," a director of development for a community-based social service agency reported. "It's really tough to plan in our situation. It would be so much better if we could lay everything out at the beginning of the year and take the time to match donor interests to various priorities. Instead, we're always scrambling to fit a new priority into ongoing conversations with donors." A good plan provides the basis from which development staff can move ahead with confidence, safe in the knowledge that the rug will not be pulled out from under their fundraising efforts just as they are beginning to experience success.

Limits

In any vibrant, outward-looking organization, there are certain to be more good ideas than there are funds to support them. An organizational ability to say no to some good opportunities is crucial to setting realistic fundraising goals. Just because a need presents itself or the ministry is asked to take on a new challenge doesn't mean it's the right thing to do. As the president of a small, denominational seminary stated, "The range of programs and special projects we could pursue are almost without limit, but there's only so much one seminary can do. We keep a close eye on our constituency, and we try not to run too far ahead of what we believe the church and individual donors are able to handle."

Potential new programs should be tested against the organization's long-range plan and its collective sense of vocation. All new initiatives must support carefully and prayerfully considered priorities of the organization. Herb Pfiffner, executive director of Seattle's Union Gospel Mission, observed: "The problems of this city are immense, and we got over a long time ago the notion that it's up to us to solve them all single-handedly. God has called this organization to a particular work, and while we may add to the program from time to time, we don't stray very far from our original purpose." The work of preparing a plan forces an organization to assess its current position and determine with renewed purposefulness where it is headed.

Two organizations told us of goal setting and planning for the development program that was influenced by past experience—one negative and the other positive. As a result of previous lessons learned, board members and others in these organization were not about to send the development staff out alone to set a goal and to try to raise the money. In one case, the organization was feeling its way back cautiously from a fundraising calamity. In the other case, the organization was continuing on a long-traveled path of strategic planning and careful financial accounting. The lessons derived from both situations are worth telling.

At the time of our visit, the Roman Catholic Diocese of Tucson was in the midst of an ongoing effort to pay off a substantial operating deficit caused by a failed foray into broadcasting a number of years earlier. We mentioned in Chapter One that a planning team composed of parish priests and laypeople met to talk about what they wanted the diocese to do. From their brainstorming about what might be possible if there were no debt, they discovered that much of what they listed as "high-priority" items could actually be accomplished without great expenditures and despite the debt.

As a result of working through the debt, Catholics in Tucson learned to work together in new and innovative ways to stretch resources. This has led to an interesting discussion of how much money the diocese should seek to raise. Diocesan leaders have discovered that it is possible to do more with less and without weakening core programs. Whatever the direction and results of future fundraising efforts, this is surely a good thing in terms of helping the members and staff of this diocese be better stewards of God's resources.

In a different kind of example, we point once more to something Compassion International has done. Several years ago, the leadership team at Compassion put in place a plan that limits growth of the organization to no more than 10 percent a year. In explaining the decision, David Dahlin, assistant to the president, stated, "Compassion has purposefully limited its growth because we don't want to go beyond our means. Corporate planning determines how we will spend and raise money." Each department in the organization is asked to prepare an annual report that includes both an overview of the previous year's activities and plans and objectives for the coming year. From these various departmental plans, an organizationwide planning team establishes program priorities that are in turn used to guide budget decisions. "We know we can't afford all the good things we would like to do," Chief Financial Officer Ed Anderson explained. "Careful planning shows us where to say no." In earlier discussion with other staff there, we were also told that the "controlled growth" plan was important to ensure quality in expanding programs. That kind of attention to quality in programs makes it easier to raise money and helps donors feel a greater joy in their giving as they are assured their gifts are really making a difference.

A particularly insidious form of inconsistency that can be warded off by good planning is the temptation to "chase the money." A humorous example of this is shown in a cartoon where a fundraiser from "ABC Ministries" sits across the table from a panel of funder representatives saying, "You say you want evangelism? We can give you evangelism."

When development staff lack the guidance of an institutional plan, there can be a tendency to make up programs to fit a funder's priorities in lieu of institutional priorities, to position the organization to get what appears to be easy (or at least plentiful) money. Going after money and then creating a program if and when the funds are received can be a legitimate course to take, but only if the new program fits with the organizational mission—and only if a thoughtful decision to launch out in a new direction is informed by a thorough understanding of the risks and start-up costs involved.

The fact that a funding opportunity has materialized does not necessarily mean that the organization is ready, able, or wise to take the next step. The decision to go after new money must be carefully examined in terms of the intended direction of the organization over the long haul. Sometimes there are very good reasons for preserving the status quo, even if it means forgoing possible funding.

We saw this at an organization where the leadership team turned down the opportunity for a substantial grant to start a youth project after determining there wasn't sufficient interest among the program staff to sustain the initiative for the longer term. This was not an easy decision, and the executive director continues to think about what ideally might have been, but he knows it was the right thing to do. "It hurts to turn aside a potential grant, but it would have hurt us more to launch a major project without the wholehearted support of key individuals," he said. Deliberate and informed discussion of how a new initiative fits with existing programs can safeguard against venturing into territory where the organization does not have, and probably cannot generate, the resources to go.

Accountability

There's nothing like putting plans in writing to hold an organization's "feet" to the fires of accountability. In his book *Money for Ministry* (1989), Wesley Willmer of Biola University wrote, "Donors have a right to know how their gifts relate to the goals for which the money was raised. Full disclosure is essential to honest communication and long-term relations" (p. 23). If an organization has declared itself to be heading in a certain direction, donors and development staff alike are justified in questioning an unexpected expenditure or the introduction of a new program that seems to come out of nowhere. When an organization routinely comes to donors seeking gifts in support of items that are outside the budget, the practice will undermine donor confidence and run the development staff ragged.

A good example of this could be seen in one Christian social service agency where additional unbudgeted capital expenditures amounting to as much as 15 percent of operating budget occur annually and where raising these additional funds as "special requests" was putting considerable strain on the development staff. Although this was, for the most part, a well-run organization, the special expenses were generally for unanticipated repairs or replacement of things like roofs and vehicles.

When we asked why the organization did not budget for these expenditures and plan for the fundraising, we were told it was because the specifics of those expenditures—exactly what the money would be needed for—were so hard to predict. They also said the organization did not want to be asking its supporters for money they were not sure was needed. The unfortunate result of this good intention not to bother donors with requests for funds that might not be needed in the end was an appearance of poor management and possibly poorer stewardship. We had to wonder what some of the organization's donors would think if they saw financial statements showing the organization typically spending 10 to 15 percent more than was budgeted.

Good financial and strategic planning, however, could resolve both these issues. This organization could regularly budget money for depreciation of major assets and could predict those costs fairly reasonably on a historical basis. This would allow fundraising staff to plan on seeking those funds every year as part of the budget and be able to ask donors for just what is needed. Such planning could only improve both the fundraising program and the overall effectiveness of the organization and so would almost assuredly build donor confidence.

Talking about the importance of accountability to donors, Henry Rosso, founding director of the Fund Raising School, observed: "The organization is strongest when the prospective donor can accept the validity of the income and expense projections relative to past accomplishments and future program delivery. If financial accountability through the planning process can demonstrate efficient use of resources for effective programs, then good stewardship has begun" (1991, p. 23). Good planning and stronger accountability go hand in hand.

The staff of almost all development offices have the expertise to provide an accounting to donors of how gifts for current or special projects have been used, and for the most part, donors are satisfied with what they hear from the causes they support. However, when an organization ventures into the area of planned giving, donor expectations of the organization regarding stewardship of gift funds and timely reporting are, quite naturally, a great deal higher. Here organizational leaders must take great care to establish clear and strong lines of accountability and do so before the first gift is ever received.

We observed one organization where board members had encouraged the development staff to take advantage of the growing interest in planned giving in the constituency. This seemed a good idea for an organization looking to build an endowment, especially in light of the greater emphasis being placed on planned giving in the fundraising world generally. After reading a few brochures on the subject, the CEO gave his OK to the venture.

So the organization began issuing gift annuities. But it did so without first educating itself about the investment responsibilities involved in managing annuities and without developing investment policies for the new program. What's more, it did so without asking the finance department staff whether they had the capacities to handle the project. As a result of having leapt into a fairly sophisticated form of planned giving before thoroughly exploring what it entailed and before preparing other departments to handle their responsibilities, the organization may now end up having to make payments to some annuitants out of its operating funds. This mess could have been avoided by integrated planning efforts.

Evaluation

For the most part, planning is a forward-looking process. However, the best plans are built on hard-nosed evaluations of previous years' activities and achievements and then lay the groundwork—set out a plan—for evaluating the effectiveness of what is to be done in coming years. Good planning begins with asking probing questions: Which programs worked especially well, and why? Which failed, and why? What activities resulted in a pleasant surprise for the service constituencies or staff? What outcomes would the staff rather not see or repeat in coming years?

In the words of planning experts John Redding and Ralph Catalanello, "Planning is a continuous evolving process, with plans being questioned, refined, and modified based upon the most current information about environments as well as through insights gained from implementation efforts" (1994, p. 24). The purpose of a plan is to guide the organization in its forward movement. However, as the old adage suggests, unless we understand our history, we are apt to repeat it. And while some things bear repeating, other things are better left behind.

Moreover, what is true for the whole organization (and its programs) is true for the development office too. It is important that development staff take time out occasionally to check what has been accomplished to date in the programs and also what is happening with fundraising goals and efforts. In the case of fundraisers working in Christian organizations, evaluation should include checking their own efforts both in terms of dollars garnered for the organization and in efforts to shape the program to facilitate God's work in donor hearts.

Ongoing—or at the least annual—evaluation makes for smarter planning for the year ahead and helps staff identify areas for possible improvements or change. Wesley Lindahl, a longtime member of the Northwestern University development staff, suggests that evaluation should occur at three levels: actual dollars raised versus dollar goals; actual staff activity versus goals for number of visits, telephone calls, letters, and so on; and development's contribution to the organization's overall goals. He writes, "The cash and activity numbers are usually easier to gather, especially in a large nonprofit organization, but monitoring of the final organizational goals is what really matters" (1994, p. 87). Evaluation of this sort requires that fundraisers check in with donors, find out how the development team is doing in representing organizational priorities, and convey the essence of it programs, as well as funding challenges.

We are arguing that for Christian organizations, a primary goal should be that donors will grow in their faith through their giving. Specific activities carried out by staff can contribute to meeting this goal, and it is possible to keep track of how well fundraisers have done in following through with those activities. But certainly an evaluation of God's work in donors' hearts is qualitative in the extreme. It requires that development staff venture into territory where it is not usual for them to go with donors. However, we are not alone in observing that "most individuals do not have many interesting opportunities to talk about their personal feelings about giving. . . . Most individuals welcome the opportunity to discuss what they think and feel about an issue" (Tobin, 1995, p. 67). And out of our interviews we have seen that when development staff initiate these types of conversations, the results are usually gratifying and always informative.

The resource development team at Compassion International, for example, reports that talking with donors about how they're feeling about the organization's fundraising efforts has been a wonderful learning experience, for staff and donors alike. "Occasionally we hear things that are hard for us to accept. When that happens, we remind ourselves that's why we're out there talking to child sponsors and other donors. For the most part, however, we've been affirmed in what we're doing, and that affirmation feeds our future work," a member of the staff said.

The pace of fundraisers' schedules, especially funders who work for smaller Christian organizations, is such that finding time for thoughtful evaluation of past performance can be tough. Nonetheless, looking back is crucial to moving forward with confidence and enhanced effectiveness. In addition, evaluation that includes listening to donor stories can be a crucial element of a fundraising program that helps grow donors' hearts.

Planning: Good for Donors Too

Few Christians would recommend impulse buying as wise stewardship of one's resources. So it is most strange that Christian organizations are notorious for encouraging donors to engage in impulse giving. Ironically, pushing supporters to make quick and unexpected giving decisions usually results in smaller gifts than what might have been received had the persons who support the organization been allowed to plan their giving. Christian financial planner and author Ron Blue notes, "It has been my experience that when a family plans to give, whether a tithe or a greater amount, and follows that plan, they will tend to give substantially more than the family that gives out of the excess, for there is rarely any excess" (1989, p. 80).

If financial planning is good for an organization, then surely planning is also a good practice for individuals. Indeed, it is unfair and unwise for fundraisers to assume that donors do not have plans for how they wish to give their money. Development staff who care about God's work in individual lives will encourage donors to prepare a plan for their giving and will commit themselves to refrain from encouraging donors to deviate from what they believe God has called them to do with their money.

As a case in point, we recall an unexpected conversation during a weekly Rotary Club meeting. Upon learning about our research project, a man who introduced himself as a "major donor to a number of well-known Christian organizations" asked if we wanted to know what he thought of the fundraisers he had met. We said we would, and this is what he told us: "They act as though I'm their personal automated teller machine. Every time the organizations I support get in a financial pinch, they drive up, hit me with a request, and wait for me to spit out the money." Apparently, none of the several organizations this man supports had made the effort to truly connect with him, and as a result his heart is growing weary, not bigger. It is important that Christian organizations remember that money is not the ultimate point of this effort; it is the work that fundraising makes possible—and, indeed, the growth of the kingdom of God.

Staff in three exemplary programs offered remarkably similar comments. At Compassion International, virtually every person stressed the organization's commitment to "present the opportunity to sponsor a child in a way that is an extension of the sponsor's faith." Chi-Chung Keung, a development officer at Biola University, said, "I care more about where the individual is at spiritually than what he can do financially." In Cleveland, Sister Mary Rita spoke of stewardship as "central to parish life and to our lives as people of faith. The end result of the dollars contributed is much more than the stated goal—there is a greater goal. We are the church. We are called to live the reality. We long for integration." When organizations make it a priority to think carefully of what the development program is really about, the rewards are significant, both for the individual and for the organization.

"I get it," said a volunteer who had just been through a fundraising workshop. "We don't ask someone to give to build a new library. We ask them to give because of what that library means for the preparation of pastors." This volunteer indeed "got it," but his moment of epiphany didn't just happen. His "getting it" was the result of careful and consistent communication about the bigger goals of the fundraising program. Planning helps organizations keep the bigger goals visible to all and can help key participants see how to communicate them more effectively.

The Question of Power

Another issue that has to be faced squarely and can be addressed by thoughtful, integrated planning has to do with where power comes from in an organization. While fundraisers who define their work as an integral part of the organization's ministry long for a good plan to guide their work, there are other fundraisers—too many, we believe—who much prefer operating on their own. The "lone ranger" approach described at the beginning of this chapter has been adopted by some development staff members to safeguard their positions and to give themselves an advantage in the organization. They know well the other "golden rule," the one that states, "He (or she) who controls the gold rules."

There is nothing inherently wrong with fundraisers wanting to have a hand in suggesting possible new programs or directions for their organization. Often the development staff include people who have very appropriate and valuable experience for that purpose, and they may have good ideas for improving or augmenting programs. But they should be listened to because of the experience or creativity or wisdom they have to offer—not because they might control some purse strings.

As fundraising consultant Joseph Mixer notes, "The more dependent the agency is on private funding, the more opportunity and power the chief development officer has to implement change" (1993, p. 149). To this we add a word of caution: the more dependent the agency is on private funding, the more opportunity and power the chief development officer has to push a personal agenda or build up a personal "kingdom" because he or she controls access to that funding. This can create very significant problems for any organization. In truth, the dynamic we are describing could happen with any Christian fundraiser in relation to any organization he or she serves. However, we want especially to point out a particular set of circumstances where this phenomenon can become most troublesome.

We have seen this problem emerge with the most difficulty where separate foundations have been created for the purpose of making it easier for an organization to attract and manage planned gifts or certain kinds of foundation or government funding. Although a foundation may be a useful vehicle, several factors can converge to create major problems. If the foundation director is aggressive and driven by personal ambition, if the foundation is successful in attracting significant gifts, and if lines of accountability between the organization and the foundation have not been clearly defined at the outset, the relationship with the foundation can quickly become convoluted and even dangerous. The foundation that was created to serve the parent organization may come to act in ways that are in conflict with the goals and priorities of the parent organization or attempt to manipulate them. That is the opposite of what is intended; it is placing God's tools into the service of mammon.

Some of the most common examples of this appear in the world of public library fundraising, where boards of successful library foundations allocate funds to projects that they may deem important but library boards or staff would not support (Jeavons, 1994a). Clearly, this kind of situation would be inappropriate, and potentially damaging, for Christian organizations that wish to operate with complete integrity and to have a part in growing donors' hearts. Though we have seen little of this in the universe of Christian organizations, it is dangerous and must be addressed before it becomes a problem.

Conclusions

Careful, integrated planning brings great advantages. In its absence, difficulties tremendous and costly (in financial and spiritual terms) are likely to arise. Obviously, given the focus of this book, we have been talking mostly about the advantages and difficulties for fundraising and development work. It has become clear to us that the planning needed to create a safe and productive environment for fundraising, an environment where it can be done as a ministry, must involve more than the development staff. It must involve stakeholders from every corner of the organization.

We have looked at how such planning—when done thoughtfully and carried out skillfully—can provide consistency to the whole organization's efforts, including those of the development program. Planning can provide useful limits and helpful accountability. We examined how it can help ward off crises and saw illustrations of some of the kinds of crises that can arise in the absence of such planning. We suggested that a similar kind of planning is good for donors' efforts to be good stewards and consistent givers and should be respected.

As suggested in earlier chapters, fundraising can be lonely work if it is carried out in isolation from the rest of the organizational activity. Nowhere is this more true than with regard to the issue of planning. It is difficult for fundraisers to know what direction to take, what to choose and what to refuse, what course to claim and which to reject, what action to take and which to avoid in the absence of a clearly stated organizational plan.

The danger in such a situation is one of two possibilities. On the one hand, development staff can be paralyzed into inactivity, not knowing what to do in the face of a directionless agenda. On the other hand, development staff might wander off in their own direction, pursuing goals that are not in the best interest of the organization as a whole. In either instance, donors are left to figure out for themselves what the organization is about and in that context are likely to become less generous or even quit giving to the organization altogether.

Exemplary programs, however, recognize the importance of integrated planning and include the development staff in the process of shaping larger goals. Development programs that are rooted in an organization that does effective long-range and strategic planning are far more likely to project consistency to donors, to provide limits within which the staff and donors function, to engage in honest evaluation, and to encourage accountability. That is finally a benefit to all involved and creates a context in which both fundraising and giving are more likely to be personally and spiritually satisfying experiences.

9

SPIRITUALLY
MATURE LEADERSHIP

*The spiritual leader influences others not by the power of his
own personality alone but by the personality irradiated and
interpenetrated and empowered by the Holy Spirit.*

—J. Oswald Sanders

WHEN FLANNERY O'CONNOR wrote "A Good Man Is Hard to Find," she
could have been talking about what many Christian organizations experience when looking for development staff. Fortunately, the majority of
Christian organizations now include women on their fundraising teams.
Still, O'Connor's observation, broadened to be gender-inclusive, applies
to the struggles most confront. More and more Christian organizations
(and their development programs), facing growing needs, are adopting
challenging goals for the future, which are in turn leading them to seek
new and specialized staffing and the highest-quality leadership.

These organizations usually assume that success in one fundraising setting will ensure success in another. As a result, development officers are
sought out more often on the basis of their previous accomplishments
than for their fit with the mission of the organization now recruiting them.
The discussion of the importance of theological compatibility in Chapter
Six highlighted some of the potential problems with this approach, and
our studies of Christian organizations tell us that the assumption that success in one setting will ensure success in another is not valid.

If an organization is looking for a "messiah" who can save the program with spectacular fundraising skills, it will surely be disappointed. Even when expectations are less grandiose, skills alone, though crucial, will never be enough. Success in fundraising goes far beyond skills.

Real and lasting success requires a good fit between an organization's values and culture and the values and style of the fundraiser representing it. Even more important, it requires an ability on the part of the fundraiser to embrace the cause or organization wholeheartedly, along with the spiritual vision that shapes it. When we asked about staffing patterns, one longtime Christian fundraiser observed, "There are too many people in the business who don't understand the cause they represent. There needs to be a measure of intimacy." The most effective development officers are interested in advancing a cause rather than just advancing their careers.

We have observed that when ministry-centered organizations search for new development officers, they look for persons who understand and embrace their mission and make a commitment to achieve it. Yet this is a surprisingly uncommon practice more generally. Few organizations even state their mission, vision, or institutional values when advertising a development position. Evidence of this can be clearly seen in the "job openings" section of any issue of the *Chronicle of Philanthropy*. Most organizations—including those that are faith-based—seem to be looking only for "a proven record of success," specific expertise or geographical affinity, rather than for a person who will fit well with and make a commitment to the specific purposes and values of the organization.

The vice president of a management search company has observed, "In real life, because management does not focus, or does not know what it wants or is confused about what it wants, a whole slew of bad candidates (from the point of view of filling the job) are passed through a series of lugubrious interviews, with no one precisely sure (least of all the candidate) as to what is wanted. . . . The result is a failure of imagination and the continued stagnation, bankruptcy, and regression of the organization" (Irish, 1975, pp. 71–72).

Lack of attention to these matters certainly hurts the fundraising programs of many organizations. In the case of Christian organizations, attention to spiritual qualities of the candidate must rank as one of the most important factors to be considered. From this observation, we draw our third and final essential operating principle for a ministry-centered approach to fundraising: *the development program seeks out, supports, and is guided by spiritually mature and reflective leadership.*

Exemplary organizations are fortunate to have a chief development officer who is able to think theologically about fundraising. Furthermore, the staffs we interviewed were encouraged, and their skills were being enhanced, by a chief executive who has come along beside them as a co-learner in what it means to approach development as a ministry. We believe this is the key component in the ability of these exemplary programs to help donors' hearts grow bigger.

Characteristics of Spiritually Mature Leaders

When we have talked with others about this particular principle, the first question asked is almost inevitably, "Does this mean that every chief development officer must have had seminary training?" To this we answer no; that would be an unnecessary and unrealistic expectation. Indeed, there are countless development people in religious organizations who have a theological education but do not integrate that training with the way they raise money. Nor does a seminary degree ensure a thoughtful, spiritually reflective approach to development. There are many more development officers with theological backgrounds than there are Christian organizations that approach development with the spiritual well-being of the donor in mind.

Though many of the fundraising leaders we have met over the past few years in exemplary organizations have some theological education, we saw in them more than just formal training in theology. Three characteristics in particular stand out.

First, spiritually mature individuals have a clear sense of calling and personal purpose. In his book *Leading with a Follower's Heart* (1990), Eugene Habecker, president of the American Bible Society, writes, "If 'being' precedes 'doing,' and I am convinced that is the case, then wherever God calls me to serve, I need to display in both my personal and my organizational actions what He calls me to be as a Christian" (p. 192).

Second, spiritual maturity is reflected in an ability and willingness to ask critical questions about the conventional wisdom of the fundraising profession. These individuals are quick to draw good ideas from wherever they may be found, but they are just as quick to test those ideas against the standard of what they believe God desires for this particular work. In Henri Nouwen's words, "Every word spoken, every advice given, and every strategy developed" is tested by a "heart that knows God intimately" (1989, p. 30).

Third, spiritually mature development staff have an interest in bringing together the principles of their faith with the principles of fundraising in novel and creative ways. Spiritual maturity shows itself in those moments when the rhetoric about wishing to do development in a different way is backed up through creative thought, words, and actions.

A Different Kind of Search

A newsletter from a fundraising consulting firm offered the following wise, if seemingly obvious, advice for seeking development staff: "To search means, first, to know for what you are searching" (Gonser Gerber Tinker Stuhr, 1998). Before a position description is drafted or an advertisement is placed, chief executives and boards of Christian organizations should spend time discussing the personal qualities and values they feel are necessary to judge adequately whether a potential candidate fits with their organization. The persons who will conduct the search need to consider *all* the attributes—spiritual gifts, skills, experience, and knowledge—necessary to ensure good performance in the context of their particular organization.

It is important that chief executives and boards seek development staff who are living out their commitment to Christian service through the work of fundraising. This includes discussing with prospective staff how they view the ideal relationship between donors and the organization. It is essential that potential staff are able—and are asked—to testify to what the experience of giving means to their own relationship with God. We think here of the faculty member at Biola University who told us, "Nothing in my Christian life works if I'm not giving."

Above all, Christian organizations must seek individuals who can speak freely about their own faith commitment. In the words of Henri Nouwen, "The question is not: how many people take you seriously? How much are you going to accomplish? Can you show some results? But: are you in love with Jesus?" (1989, p. 24). If this is what Christian organizations want, then they need to recognize that finding a different kind of development officer requires a different kind of search and a different set of questions.

Ironically, the questions usually asked in interview sessions with prospective development staff are probably the wrong questions. At least that is the case if what is sought is a fundraiser who is spiritually reflective about his or her work. The truth is, the questions most often described as "wrong" or off-limits in today's litigious environment are actually the right ones, if what is being sought is a person who can be an effective part of a team focused on doing fundraising as ministry. Two stories illustrate this point.

The first involves a luncheon conversation we held with a group of development officers from the seminaries that make up the Graduate Theological Union at Berkeley. In discussing how they were selected for their jobs, they all agreed that it is necessary for the chief executive to have some understanding of how fundraising "works" in order to choose a chief development officer. At the same time, they were quick to add that this is not sufficient to recruit the right kind of person for seminary development work. "Presidents should focus more on the candidate's philosophy of fundraising and whether this matches what the president and the institution wish to accomplish through the development program," we were told.

"There needs to be a value check," another person responded. "The president should ask questions like, 'What's most important to you as a development professional?' and 'Why do you want to be at this place and at this time?'" The fundraisers gathered around that table were adamant that "you have to have a commitment to the specific mission of the organization. The connectedness with place and purpose is all-important."

The other illustration comes from Ron Lundeen, vice president for advancement at San Francisco Theological Seminary. He recalled that his decision to accept the position at SFTS came only after the president began to ask him the "wrong" questions—questions about what was most important in him, about his commitments to family, church, and friends, and about his understanding of divine call and God's will for his life. "The president had confidence in my fundraising skills. That's why he approached me in the first place. He was checking out my theological fit with the seminary and with his own view of development."

Lundeen is a man with a strong sense of vocation. He did not want to work at a place where these were not important questions. From what we observed in our visit to SFTS, asking the wrong questions clearly uncovered the right person for the job. That president should be applauded for having the courage and wisdom to ask them.

Tender Loving Care

Once spiritually mature leaders have been found for the development programs of Christian organizations, it is crucial that chief executives support these people in many ways. Certainly they must offer practical and institutional support. In addition, though, the chief executives must encourage these individuals to continue to grow in their theological understanding of the work to which God has called them. These fundraising leaders must also be encouraged to pass this understanding along to the persons with whom they work and to involve donors, whenever and wherever possible, in a conversation about what it means to give money in ways that express and deepen their faith. In this way the chief executive, by lending public support to these activities, plays a crucial role in creating an environment in which a ministry-centered development program can flourish.

To paraphrase Harry Truman, when we are speaking about fundraising, "The bucks start here," with the chief executive. The president or executive director needs to spend time with the fundraisers, educating them to the purposes and mission of the organization and discussing with them how donors can support and be part of that mission in ways that contribute to the donors' spiritual development. The CEO should lead or at least encourage discussions of what it means to raise funds in a way that helps givers' hearts grow bigger. In addition, chief executives should model for the development staff (and all staff) the importance of giving attention to one's own spiritual condition when one is serving in a Christian organization. In the words of a respected authority in the development world, "The chief executive must serve as the principal advocate for the mission, the primary architect of the vision, and the inspirational force for the continuing advancement of the organization into the future" (Rosso, 1991, p. 289). In the ideal setting, the chief executive in a Christian organization also leads the way toward a thoughtful, theologically rich understanding of what the organization seeks to accomplish through the ministry of fundraising.

A few years ago, Clyde Cook, president of Biola University, was praised for attending a fundraising workshop for presidents of Christian colleges for his third consecutive year. "Even Mickey Mantle had to report for spring training," he said with a shrug and a smile. Embedded in this one comment is a secret of the university's exemplary development program. Cook's response spoke volumes about his understanding of the importance of his role as the institution's chief fundraiser and the need to continuously improve his performance and his ability to integrate his faith with this role. The development staff at Biola University are fortunate to have a leader who has equipped himself to be of greatest assistance to the program.

Asking the Right Questions

If every inquiry from the chief executive to the development staff has to do with gift totals and reports on dollar goals, it is not likely that the staff will feel free to take time to think spiritually about their work. A sadly illustrative story along these lines came from a woman who has since left fundraising. She spoke of returning to the office with the good news that a donor who had been asked to give $25,000 in support of a special project had responded with a gift of $50,000, an increase that the donor attributed to God's working in his heart. "That's nice," the executive director said. "Now all you need to do is find twenty more gifts just like that one." The joy the fundraiser had carried back in her heart was wiped away with a single, careless comment.

It is not surprising that staff in situations such as the one just described will seek their fundraising advice and counsel from wherever it may be found, without thinking about the assumptions that undergird the advice. That is an unfortunate but all too common occurrence with potentially troubling consequences, for both the particular Christian organization and the larger church. Bishop William McManus, commenting on the decline in giving among Catholics, points to the fact that two decades ago, church agencies that were facing enormous financial pressures sought a quick fix to their problem. So they turned to professional fundraising counsel whose primary goal was the bottom line and not the spiritual reasons for giving. "Consequently," he observes, "the church's fund raising techniques became almost entirely secularized, being not much different from those used by a myriad of good-cause organizations and agencies in need of quick money for their activities" (1990, p. 119). In his view, this marked the beginning of a low period in the understanding of the average Catholic for what giving means for one's faith. The same can surely be said for almost the whole of the Christian church.

Equipping the Board for Spiritual Leadership

Boards have leadership responsibilities in these matters too. The board should stand with a chief executive in helping others appreciate the importance of development activities that build up donors' hearts. This makes it crucial that board members understand the principles of a ministry-centered fundraising program and be able to talk knowledgeably about the organization's development efforts. Working together, the president and the board chair (and others, if helpful) should design a study plan for the board that includes both a review of biblical and theological teachings about money and faith and opportunities for board members to share personal stories of what giving has meant in their faith journey.

It is likely that some trustees will be uncomfortable with the discussion in the beginning, but the rewards of such conversations can be tremendous, as a trustee from San Francisco Theological Seminary reported. "A fundraising effort that is spiritually based, that has specific goals for ministry, and that is carefully managed and realistic is empowering to trustees. We feel like we know how to help, and it's a very positive experience," he said.

A study plan is especially helpful for boards and chief executives of organizations that are considering adding a development program or enlarging what may now be a minimal effort. However, this exercise can be just as useful for boards where the fundraising program is well developed and has enjoyed a history of success. This was evident at Biola University, where a trustee told us, "The philosophy of the department is well circulated. The board is involved—'a stand-with approach'—as an encouragement to the staff. There's a good system of checks and balances. All this contributes to organizational openness to the work of the development office."

In addition to specific times set aside for reflection, it is helpful for boards to keep track of comments and questions about the fundraising program that come up during the natural course of general board sessions. This is an excellent way to assess the impact of board education on board practice. After all, reflection should lead to change. It should be expected that the kinds of questions board members ask will be different as trustees explore the idea of fundraising as an extension of the organization's stated ministry. In time, board queries should come to include attention to God's good work in donor hearts as well as God's good work on behalf of the organization's bottom line. When that happens, directors can know that their commitment to board education has been worth the effort, both personally and for the organization they serve.

Importance of a Spiritual Fitness Program

Advice abounds on the importance of keeping physically fit when one is employed in a stressful occupation such as fundraising. In fact, it is the trendy thing these days (for those who can afford it) to retain the services of a personal trainer for help in designing and carrying out a plan of action for physical fitness. Furthermore, persons who are serious about succeeding in their careers, especially those new to a position, are encouraged to seek out a professional adviser or counselor who can provide an outside, neutral evaluation of how one is doing on the job. The professional adviser helps put criticism and setbacks in focus and serves as a sounding board for frustrations as well as new ideas.

Far less often, however, are people encouraged to seek out a spiritual adviser or spiritual director. Yet for those who view the work of fundraising as a ministry, it is just as important to give attention to spiritual fitness as to one's physical or professional condition. It is crucial, both for the future health of the Christian organizations they serve and for their own personal well-being, that development staff in religious organizations work at keeping themselves spiritually fit and right with God. David Hubbard, former president of Fuller Theological Seminary, offered the following advice to Christian fundraisers: "As a group, we have a drive to achieve. And, I am afraid, most of us have a desire to be liked. This makes it hard for us to say no when we should. However, the central tasks of loving God, caring for family, and carrying out the mission of the institution call us to say no, to build a rhythm into our lives that won't be there unless we build it" (1993, comm. 4).

At a minimum, a spiritual fitness program includes personal devotions or meditation, regular attendance at worship, and some sort of active service in the context of the local congregation. For the Christian fundraiser, it should include more. The pressures of raising funds in high-stress environments can sap spiritual reserves. This in turn opens the door to actions that run counter to Christlike behavior. The differences between right activities and approaches to the work and questionable ones are dangerously subtle. Gray areas abound in fundraising. It takes the clear light of God's leading to see our way in the shadows. Robert Banks, a member of the Fuller Theological Seminary faculty, has written: "If character plays a vital part in our ability to act Christianly in everyday situations, we cannot overlook the importance of those contexts which most helpfully shape it. . . . Unless I am clearing time for God to show Himself to me and love me, to reveal His dreams for me and deepen my affection for Him, to talk to and with me, and to empower me through the wide range of ways He makes His Spirit available to me, I will never get very far in developing an integrated Christian life" (1993, p. 137).

In addition to the activities of individuals on their own, most of us can also benefit from the added insight of a caring spiritual adviser or spiritual friend. We were impressed by the wisdom of a vice president for advancement at a California seminary in recognizing and acting on this truth. Almost immediately upon arriving on the campus, he sought out a faculty member with a reputation for wisdom to be a spiritual partner and counselor to him in his work. This seasoned development professional recognizes all too well the pressures and temptations confronting fundraisers, even, or perhaps especially, in the context of Christian organizations. Determined not to veer from his commitment to a ministry-centered approach to fundraising, he recognized his need for help in discerning and holding to the course.

Interestingly, he told us that he and his spiritual confidant do not talk a lot specifically about the seminary's development program, although that is an open topic for discussion. Rather, their time together is spent reading Scripture, praying, and speaking about God's work in both their lives. These times with his spiritual adviser give him perspective on his work and help remind him of his reasons for working at the seminary.

It may be that this development officer's experience is somewhat unique in that he is surrounded by a whole faculty of possible spiritual counselors, but we don't think so. All persons of faith have within their sphere of friends and acquaintances persons to whom they could turn for spiritual help and guidance. If they do not, they should make it a priority to seek out such persons and get to know them.

Integrating Faith and Practice

Over the past fifty years or so in this country, a chasm has developed between faith and secular society. This is nowhere more evident than in the separation that exists between the life of work and the faith of people in the workplace, a phenomenon on which a number of scholars have commented (see, for example, Neill and Weber, 1963; Marty, 1969; and Wuthnow, 1994a, 1997). Only rarely are men and women of faith, including those employed by Christian organizations, encouraged to think about their work in a Christian way, in the context of faith.

Robert Webber, author of *The Secular Saint* (1979), writes: "The average Christian does not realize the complexity of the problem of the Christian in culture. For this reason the typical responses to the problem appear superficial and without substance. In general these responses fall into three types: indifferent, reactionary, and pious" (p. 26). Webber's observation applies to the fundraising staffs of Christian organizations as surely as to Christians involved in any other field of work. The three responses are outlined here and shown in Figure 9.1.

Indifferent Response

We have met Christian fundraisers who feel no need to seek connections between their private faith and their public work of resource development. These individuals move from seminar to seminar and book to book, gathering up the latest tips for fundraising success but never stopping to consider the assumptions behind the suggestions or the nature of the organization from which they came. Theirs is a pragmatic approach to learning, based on the premise that if it works in the short term, it must be good. For them, talk about the integration of faith and fundraising

Figure 9.1. Integrating Faith and Fundraising: Flawed Responses.

Indifferent

(Separate spheres of life:
simply unconnected)

CHRISTIAN
FAITH

PROFESSIONAL
LIFE

Reactionary

(Somewhat similar activities but guided by different principles:
Christian fundraisers can learn only from other Christians)

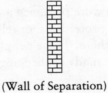

CHRISTIAN
FUNDRAISING

(Wall of Separation)

SECULAR
FUNDRAISING

Pious

(Secular fundraising practices are borrowed and made acceptable by
overlaying them with quotes from scripture and other
Christian language and images)

CHRISTIAN
LANGUAGE
AND IMAGES

SECULAR
FUNDRAISING
PRACTICE

seems like much ado about very little. They are unaware of or, even worse, indifferent to the possibility of fundraising as ministry.

Reactionary Response

At the opposite end of the continuum are Christian fundraisers—"reactionaries," in Webber's view—who refuse to learn from anyone or any source except those that carry a Christian "seal of approval." They will attend only workshops and seminars sponsored by Christian organizations, and they limit their reading to books by Christian authors (for some, this means only writers of their own denominational or sectarian stripe). They depend on a handful of experts identified as theologically "safe" to interpret the conventional wisdom of fundraising for them. Unfortunately, because they have not educated themselves in the basic assumptions of their chosen work or gained a wider perspective on it, they have no way of judging the professional or religious validity or soundness of the advice provided to them. These people are not equipped for the intellectually as well as spiritually challenging work of shaping fundraising as a ministry.

Pious Response

The middle ground between these two extremes belongs to what Webber calls the "pious" response to integration of faith and work. This approach is characterized by attempts to sanctify or "Christianize" conventional fundraising wisdom by applying scriptural texts and other spiritual words and images to secular practice—that is, to "wrap fundraising technique in 'God talk.'" In this approach, it is all too common for the context of the scriptural text to be ignored or distorted as fundraisers attempt to apply timeless principles to a specific twenty-first-century practice. This is a shallow approach to integration of faith and fundraising and does little to advance conversation and more fruitful practice among Christian fundraisers of varying theological traditions or between persons of faith and others involved in fundraising.

Preferred Response

In contrast to these three flawed understandings of the possible or appropriate interplay between faith and work, the chief development officers of the exemplary programs we examined have been thinking about the integration of faith and fundraising for many years. These spiritually mature development professionals appreciate the complexities of the work to which God has called them, as well as the variety of ways in which God works in the world, and they seek to avoid the sort of superficial responses that Webber outlines. Their faith is at the very core of their professional identities, illuminating and guiding every program choice and every interaction with donors.

They are eager learners and are not afraid to draw new ideas from many sources. At the same time, they are intentional in testing principles and advice with what they know of God's ways and God's will. Their faith serves as a sort of permeable barrier, letting in what is good and sorting out whatever does not meet the test of Gospel values (see Figure 9.2).

It is encouraging to us that faith-informed wisdom about fundraising is beginning to have an impact on the wider profession as a number of spiritually mature fundraisers have become known across the whole of the development world for their competence and their contributions to the profession. (Several of the people leading the exemplary programs we studied are such individuals.)

As was previously stated, the requirements for a first-rate Christian fundraiser include all the skills and attributes of any other top-quality development person and more. In the paradigm of fundraising as a ministry, what is called for are new ways—and specifically theological ways—of looking at, assessing, and possibly improving old ways of doing the work of raising money (look back at Table 1.1 in Chapter One). It must be acknowledged that there is much common ground between secular and faith-based approaches to fundraising; their domains of possibility overlap. Still, the possibilities presented in the ministry paradigm go well beyond what is hoped for or sought through a traditional program.

Figure 9.2. Integrating Faith and Fundraising: Preferred Response.

Integration

(Christian faith and spiritual perspectives permeate
and shape personal and professional practice)

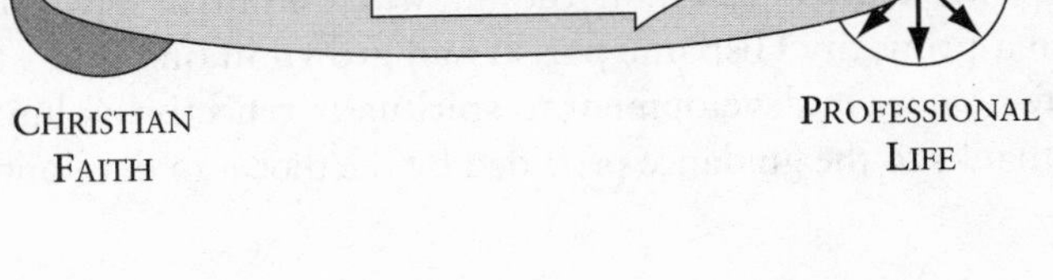

INFUSION

CHRISTIAN
FAITH

PROFESSIONAL
LIFE

The Path to Integration

All this means that the acquisition of knowledge about "professional fundraising" is the foundation on which any solid career as a development professional is built. Yet the Christian fundraiser is called to a larger realm of possibility and ministry. We believe that individuals who are new to the work of fundraising in the context of a faith-based organization should be encouraged to think about what they do in terms of their faith, in addition to building their professional skills and knowledge, from the very beginning. Even then, it is likely that most novices will be so busy with and worried about "learning their job" that they will have little time or energy for deeper reflection. That is to be expected and probably all right. Spiritual and professional maturity, like all other kinds, takes time and experience. The process cannot and probably should not be rushed.

It is sad, however, when Christians who make a career of fundraising never grasp what it means to integrate faith and work, never see what is possible if they were to put faith at the very center of how they conceive of themselves and their chosen career. They may be content with the "success" that comes from professional expertise and doing things "by the book," but they will have missed many wonderfully satisfying and joyous possibilities for experiencing God at work in the world through and in their own lives and work.

Importance of a Guide

Interviews with Christian fundraisers at various stages in their careers point to the importance of mentor relationships and of a supportive work environment in helping fundraisers move toward spiritual maturity. The structure of the organization must at least allow for, and ideally should encourage, individual change and growth. Great, then, is the good fortune of a newcomer to fundraising who also has the privilege and advantage of working with and learning from a spiritually mature development officer. As the staffs of the exemplary organizations we visited can attest, the possibilities for integrating faith and work are far more quickly understood, and the maturation curve is considerably shortened, in the presence of a good teacher.

We saw this truth in action in Tucson, where a parish stewardship committee in a primarily Hispanic parish had grown in one year's time from complete novices in development to spiritually reflective volunteer fundraisers, thanks to the guidance provided by the diocesan development staff.

Determined to introduce Christian stewardship as a next step to the parish's evangelization program, the congregation sent one its own members to a fundraising workshop where she learned how to apply fundraising principles in a Hispanic cultural context. Upon her return, the stewardship committee, working with her and Bob Heslinga, director of development for the diocese, took the information she had received and adapted it to their own setting. This included preparation of vision and mission statements that outlined where the group believed God was directing the parish community and a list of stewardship goals.

At this point, the stewardship committee was ready to test its newfound vision, expertise, and enthusiasm on a small fundraising project, and not surprisingly, a need presented itself. Within three months, they had succeeded in raising $32,000 for repairs to the church roof. This first foray into asking parishioners directly for money (outside the usual Sunday offertory) achieved far more than providing for some much needed repairs, however. It demonstrated to the stewardship committee the direct link between giving (and the readiness to ask others to give) and evangelization.

It is important to observe that the leaders of this small campaign had all been through the parish's evangelization program, as had many who gave. Father Raul Treviso, pastor of Saint John the Evangelist Catholic Community, told us, "We discovered that people who have been evangelized understand the importance of giving. They're ready. We see other people who are very committed to the parish with their time, and in some cases their money, but they haven't had a conversion. They haven't changed, and they aren't ready for stewardship education."

When we asked Father Raul about what the year's experience had meant to him personally, his face lit up with joy. "I went into this very uncomfortable with the idea of asking people for money, but along the way, I've discovered a new side to myself," he said. "It's still not easy for me to ask for money in one-to-one situations. However, when I see what giving means for the people, I'm excited. This is good for us." Father Raul and the rest of the stewardship committee had moved from feelings of uneasiness about their own powerlessness to "get" people to give more to the ease found in recognition of the true source of power—the Holy Spirit at work in people's lives.

Development Work as a Ministry of Stewardship Education

There is an additional and perhaps most important reason for Christian organizations to seek and encourage development staff who are spiritually mature. Recent research warns that a not-so-funny thing has happened on the way to America's churches. The majority of pastors, we are being told, have decided they'd rather talk about God without mentioning mammon, ignoring the subject of Christians and money except for the once-a-year obligatory stewardship sermon (see, for example, Ronsvalle and Ronsvalle, 1996; Wuthnow, 1994a, 1997; Hoge and others, 1996).

Theologian and churchman Loren Mead warns, "It is as if church leaders, particularly clergy, assume that money itself is evil—a strange theological position for those whose scriptures include the story Jesus told about the talents" (1995, p. 14). Similarly, researcher Neely Dixon McCarter writes, "Pastors do not like to allude to use of money in sermons; they prefer that lay people manage the annual solicitation of pledges. . . . Deeply buried in their consciousness seems to be the notion that money—not the love of money, as the Scriptures suggest—is the root of all evil" (1994, pp. 11–12). The leader of one of the exemplary programs we studied, who had been a pastor himself, commented on this problem too. He said that in his experience, "Most clergy are really dualists, who see money as the chief symbol of the material world, which they see as inherently evil. They only want to focus on spiritual things and see money and fundraising as, at best, a distraction."

One consequence of these attitudes is that stewardship education is virtually nonexistent in many churches. Many persons of faith have been left to learn about giving where they may. By default, the majority of churchgoers today are being introduced to the whys and hows of giving not by their pastors but via fundraising appeals from the myriad religious organizations that dot the North American charitable landscape. This situation presents both a challenge and an opportunity for the leaders of Christian organizations, and it suggests that a development program should be understood as something more than just a source of funds.

This is an awesome additional responsibility to assign to persons who already feel overburdened with aggressive fundraising goals and the challenges of ever-increasing organizational needs. Indeed, it is too great a responsibility to be handled by the development staff alone. So everyone in a Christian organization, and most especially the persons who make decisions about how gift dollars are used, should join in making sure the fundraising program is structured in ways that provide opportunities for the stewardship education and ongoing spiritual development of donors.

The plain truth is, the way in which Christian organizations go about raising money is a very powerful form of stewardship education, and the fundraising staff are stewardship educators (often the only ones encountered), whether the work is thought of as such or not. When development officers show as much concern for the faith and "giving IQs" of donors as for the financial health of the organization, fundraising can be a powerful and motivating sermon. "Right" stewardship education doesn't just happen. It requires intentionality, institutionwide reeducation, and above all the full commitment of the president and the board to reenvisioning the development program as a ministry.

Conclusions

Although the subtitle of this chapter, "A Pearl of Great Price," may seem to overstate the importance of spiritually mature leadership, we simply cannot emphasize too strongly how important such leadership is. Only theologically reflective and spiritually mature leadership can move a development program toward the place where a concern about the spiritual condition of donors is held in creative (and productive) tension with concern about the financial condition of the organization. Of all our findings in this study, perhaps the most clear and consistent is the recognition that spiritually mature leadership is indispensable in creating any ministry-centered development program.

We have written in this chapter about the characteristics of such leaders in and around development programs, including chief executives as well as chief development officers. We have also discussed how those involved in the highest levels of organizational leadership, the boards and CEOs, have to be willing to conduct a different kind of search if they hope to find and recruit such leaders for their development programs. Finally, we have talked about the things that must be done to nurture and sustain such leadership over the long haul—things that must be done by both the leaders themselves and the people around them. We concluded our discussion with an effort to map out the path of spiritual maturation and integration for both leaders of development programs and the programs themselves.

To find and sustain this kind of leadership for their development programs requires that Christian organizations seek out men and women whose personalities, in the words of J. Oswald Sanders, have been "irradiated and interpenetrated and empowered by the Holy Spirit." The steps to spiritual maturity are several and will be varied for different people. The process of maturation will likely be—with encouragement and support—slow and steady, but it is well worth the wait and the work. In our view, spiritual maturity is an essential feature of the leadership of a fundraising program that encourages donors' hearts to grow bigger.

PART THREE

THE FUNDRAISER'S MINISTRY

10

FUNDRAISING AS A CALLING

[From] Paul, a servant of Jesus Christ, called to be an apostle
and set apart for the gospel of God . . . to all in Rome
who are loved by God and called to be saints.

—Romans 1:1, 7

THUS DID THE APOSTLE Paul address his epistle to the church in Rome. The notion of "calling" or "vocation" has a central place in the Christian tradition and its vision of the life of faith. This has been true since the origins of this tradition. Calling has often been closely associated with a deeper commitment to live one's faith more fully and especially with a commitment to ministry.

It is surely not insignificant that the last of the key characteristics that we found is necessary for a Christian organization to have success in making fundraising a ministry is a commitment to finding and supporting spiritually mature, theologically reflective leadership. What we observed in each exemplary organization we studied is that the leaders of such development programs saw their own work as a ministry. They each spoke of having a sense of calling to the particular position they were filling.

By the end of our studies, we saw clearly that to have a fundraising program that works as a ministry is probably not possible unless the people who do this work see it is a personal ministry for themselves. We also saw that this work seems to be more fulfilling to those who enter into it this way or come to experience it this way. It is more fulfilling to, and done better by, those who experience themselves as answering a call from God and carrying on a ministry for God and the faith community they serve.

165

In light of those observations, we devote this chapter to reflecting on some different aspects of conceiving and entering into the personal work of fundraising as a ministry. Here we invite Christian fundraisers to reflect on the possibilities for making their work more personally and spiritually satisfying and enriching. This enrichment comes from understanding this work as a calling. To this end, we want to do several things here.

We begin by examining the whole notion of calling or vocation, looking at its roots in the biblical and Christian traditions. Then we consider how vocation sometimes enters into, but sometimes is at odds with, contemporary ideas about what it means to be a "professional." We want to look at three specific issues:

- How an experience of calling or vocation may be particularly important to people of faith within the Judeo-Christian tradition

- How a sense of vocation may relate to a personal inclination toward and commitment to a particular type of work or specific position (apart from any faith commitment)

- How one's spiritual sense of vocation interacts with conventional, secular, professional expectations about what is appropriate behavior in doing one's work

A Sense of Vocation

The notion of calling or vocation appears in many forms in the Bible. How has it been understood in the Judeo-Christian tradition? What does it mean to have a calling? What is the role of vocation or calling in shaping one's life as a person of faith?

First, in the biblical and Christian traditions, calling has often been understood as the basic source of one's personal identity. In the Old Testament, many of the persons who played key leadership roles in the Israelite community came into their identity as they answered a calling from God. This pattern begins with Abraham and Isaac, continues with Moses and the Judges, and is central to the stories of many of the Prophets. The power of the experience of "being called" in forming one's identity is very clear in these early stories. Indeed, it is such a powerful experience that we see people's names change—as they did for Abraham (Genesis 17:5) and Jacob (Genesis 32:8)—when they receive their calling.

For many Christians, the most familiar and prominent example of this connection between calling and identity is found in Paul's biography. Few figures in the early church have a story of conversion and service as dramatic as Paul's. It is instructive to see how Paul describes himself in light of his experience of God's directing the course of his life.

At the beginning of the Epistle to the Romans, Paul identifies himself as "Paul, a servant of Jesus Christ, called to be an apostle." Then again, at the beginning of the First Epistle to the Corinthians, he describes himself as "Paul, called to be an apostle of Christ Jesus by the will of God." It is important to see that in introducing himself in this way, Paul no longer identifies himself as one would expect for a man of the ancient Roman or Hebraic culture. He does not tell his readers whose son he is or what town he hails from or his occupation or station in life—all the things one would anticipate hearing from a highly educated Jew who was also a Roman citizen. These were all far more common and appropriate ways for people to explain who they were in those times and cultures. Instead, his readers are to know who Paul is, because Paul knows himself this way, by what he is called to be, "an apostle of Christ Jesus." Beginning his letters as he does, Paul highlights his spiritual calling as the source of his worldly identity.

Second, this calling is also the source of his spiritual identity. Paul no longer describes himself as a Jew, no longer as a Pharisee, no longer as an expert in the law, but rather as one who is a servant of Jesus Christ. Paul is now a follower of Christ, and that is the defining fact of his existence, because that is what he is *called* to be.

Moreover, for someone like Paul, it is because his calling is the source of his spiritual identity that it shapes his worldly identity. The two are inexorably linked. His calling becomes that aspect of his life through which all other aspects are integrated.

Paul's example, and that of others, highlights how a spiritual sense of calling can be the nexus through which spiritual people knit together all the aspects of their lives into a unified whole. Despite the countervailing norms of modern Western society, this can imply a union of the personal and the professional. That kind of integration is surely one function of calling Paul envisions when he exhorts the Ephesians to "live a life worthy of the calling you have received; being humble and gentle; being patient, bearing with one another in love" (Ephesians 4:1–2). He is saying that for Christians, the calling to be a follower of Christ should be the defining factor in both our identity and our actions.

In that context, we need to see a third crucial understanding about callings in the biblical tradition, which is also manifest in Paul's story: that a calling is "to be" as much as it is a calling "to do." Put another way, one's calling to be a Christian is as much about what one is like and one's relationships with others in daily life as it is about performing specific kinds of service. (It may be that too, though, and we will discuss that aspect of vocation momentarily.)

Let us not forget that the primary calling of all Christians is to be like Christ. In this broadest sense, a calling tells us, above all else, whom we serve—the same One whom Christ served. The question of to whom we give our ultimate loyalty in all the decisions we make and all the things we do is a critical question in all aspects of our lives. It is certainly critical to the effort to live a life of faithfulness, whatever one's worldly profession or station.

A Calling to Specific Work

The wonderful Christian writer Frederick Buechner talks about calling in different terms. Musing on the meaning of vocation, he says, "It comes from the Latin, *vocare,* to call, and means the work [one] is called to by God. . . . The kind of work God calls you to is usually the kind of work that (a) you most need to do, and (b) the world most needs to have done. The place God calls you to is the place where your deep gladness and the world's deep hunger meet" (1992, pp. 185–186).

Focusing more on calling as a question of the kind of work one does, Buechner says that this too is a matter to consider in the light of faith. Beyond the broader question of discipleship—"Whom do we serve or follow?"—he points to narrower questions about how a person finds or selects the kind of work in the world that allows the living out of one's faith most fully in the occupational sphere of life. Buechner suggests that these narrower questions should involve consideration of one's gifts, talents, and interests, as well as the needs of the world as one understands them. The work we feel the greatest passion for and perhaps feel best equipped to do, if it is also work we can see that the world really needs done, may be our calling.

One of the problems we may first encounter in thinking about our own vocation in these terms—thinking about it as a framework within which one can integrate the values of faith and one's gifts and skills with the requirements and opportunities of worldly work—is that society's traditional views of what kind of work should be described as a calling have been too narrow. A couple of hundred years ago, only a few positions or types of work were viewed by most people as things one might be "called to." Essentially, these were the same positions that were first identified as "professions."

In the early 1800s, at least in the Anglo-American world, the work of ministers, doctors, lawyers, and perhaps teachers constituted pretty much the only "professions." A decision to enter into one of these fields was the only decision about a choice of work one would have typically described as a calling. As industrialization set in and our society grew more complex organizationally, a whole host of other lines of work came to be identified as professions. Today engineers, scientists, and technology experts and researchers of many sorts, people involved in a wide range of service careers, and managers of various types are all described as professionals.

Even so, the range of work that most people would now consider a calling is still rather limited. For many people, the question of whether fundraising is that kind of work—whether it is a profession in either the technical or the moral sense—remains unanswered.

"Professional" status is sought after in our culture. It is desired because that status generally brings with it prestige, better pay, and certain kinds of power. To sociologists, the defining characteristics of a profession are that the work involves specialized knowledge, generally requiring a lengthy education and intensive training; commitment to public service; and the power to make autonomous decisions on matters of significance to society (Flores, 1988). Traditionally, the professions were also defined by their capacity to restrict entrance to their ranks as well. For example, only doctors got to say who else could be a doctor.

Only one of the characteristics just cited necessarily overlaps with the qualities that should mark work that fulfills a Christian sense of vocation: commitment to service. But then maybe our society's usual identification of profession with calling may be too strong. As Christians, we should recognize that people may feel called, in the sense of divinely led, to any kind of work, paid or not, where they might use their spiritual gifts and practical skills to serve others in a way that allows them to live out and give witness to their faith.

Christians from traditions where vocation was traditionally identified with ordination or serving in a formal ministerial role may have a hard time accepting a broader view. Among the various Christian fundraisers we interviewed, the ones who had the most trouble thinking of their job as a ministry usually came from one of two backgrounds. Either they came from a traditional Catholic background, where they thought of people with a vocation as the religious; or they were from evangelical upbringings, where normally a calling had to take one to a mission field or a pastorate. Yet upon reflection, most of them—like most people we know—could look at their own life experience and recognize numbers of people who seemed clearly to be living out a calling to Christian service and witness as merchants or barbers or cooks or plumbers or receptionists.

So why should it not be possible, or even likely, that someone could experience a calling to fundraising? Is there any reason this should not be experienced as a kind of work in which one can integrate one's faith commitments, one's spiritual gifts, and one's practical talents with the need to make a living and the desire to be of service to the world and the church? Given that fundraising is increasingly acknowledged as a profession, this possibility might make sense even in terms defined by our secular culture. The truth is that many people who do the work of Christian fundraising do experience their role and what they do as a ministry and a calling. Further, they do it better because they embrace that experience.

Conflicts Between Calling and Profession

That said, we must also recognize the potential problems in the connection between professional work, as the larger society around us now understands that, and living out one's vocation, as we are talking about it here, in a professional role. Potential sources of conflict range from commonplace social assumptions about what it means to be a professional, which may be at odds with what is required to do ministry, to some specific facets of the work to be done, which may be incongruent with our personal and spiritual values. There are in fact aspects of the conventional, professional approach to fundraising that can interfere or conflict with the ability to experience this work as a calling.

The first conflict in approaching fundraising as a calling arises in relation to the secular culture's definition of what it means to be a professional. For example, certain widely accepted attitudes regarding professional decorum and professional relationships would seem to require keeping one's personal feelings and biases out of one's work. These attitudes are communicated in the training of most professionals.

Case in point: doctors and lawyers have long been taught that they are not supposed to let their feelings about the personal characteristics of their patients or clients affect how they treat them or defend them. In fact, when people say they have a "strictly professional relationship" with someone, they mean that personal feelings and revelations are excluded from the relationship. To ensure this requisite objectivity or detachment means (in the conventional view) that professionals must guard against emotional involvement in their work.

Yet one of the joys of working for the church is that it usually provides a context in which it is acceptable and even desirable for personal and spiritual values to be united with professional commitments. If ministry is about being an instrument through whom God can work—and God is the creator and source of all our gifts, our talents, our noblest passions, our best attributes, and even our foibles—we have to put all of ourselves at God's disposal and bring all of ourselves to the work we do. Openness and a certain degree of personal vulnerability are required of those who would minister to others.

If ministry is about making God's presence visible and meaningful to others, then those involved in this have to bring their own experience of God's grace and love into the work for this to happen. Ministry is often entirely about being personally involved with the people one serves. So the larger cultural bias toward separating personal feelings, interests, and faith commitments from professional service cannot stand here, at least not if this work is to be a calling and a ministry.

This is not to say that the workplace in a Christian organization should be like a congregation where pastoral care, mutual support, and spiritual nurture of the staff can take unlimited amounts of time and energy, as some might wish. Nor is it to say that for individuals working in these surroundings, professional relationships with colleagues, clients, or donors should center entirely on their shared faith. All of them need to be mindful of the work they are there to do, the goals they are working toward, and how to get there in keeping with the value structure they share because of their faith. Ministry also requires competence and focus.

We must not lose sight of the fact that if we are called to the work of fundraising (or any other kind of work) with a Christian organization, we are called to *work*. We do nothing that reflects favorably on our faith community, our God, or our cause if we do not do that work as well as it can be done. For a true integration of faith and work, the work must be as solid and honorable as the faith. And if one is called to this work as a ministry, it is the complete integration of the spiritual and professional toward which one must strive.

There are also potential conflicts between the typical practices or strictures of certain professions and the ways one would choose to do some kinds of work as a ministry. We know that some of the conventional assumptions and tactics of secular fundraising are not fully compatible with Christian values. These assumptions and tactics raise questions that we must resolve before we can adopt them in Christian organizations.

We have noted that perhaps the most important function of the basic calling Christians experience, the calling to discipleship, is to help people be clear about whom they are to serve in both their personal and their professional lives. In every profession, many things can come to dominate one's behavior, and every profession holds up standards of conduct, goals, and ideals for effective performance and high achievement, as well as implicit and explicit understandings about what constitutes success. Everyone feels some pressure to meet those expectations. In fundraising, some of these are readily reconciled with Christian values and a calling to serve God. Others are harder to reconcile, but it may be important to do so. Still others are irreconcilable with a calling to serve Christ and so should be rejected. These are personal choices and judgment calls every Christian fundraiser has to make.

Questions for Reflection

To this point, the discussion has been largely theoretical. To make it more concrete and personal, let us focus on some specific questions that are likely to arise for anyone who approaches work in Christian fundraising as a calling and a ministry. Three questions are basic, deriving from the foregoing discussion:

- Whom do you serve in this calling?
- In what ways do you (or should you) approach your work as a fundraiser differently as a Christian, especially if you are working for a Christian organization? (This question could be reframed to apply to any person of faith working for any kind of religious organization.)
- What are the potential conflicts between the fundraising profession's values and your values as a Christian?

Here we want only to suggest a direction for reflection, very briefly, in response to each of these questions, in the hope that these questions might foster continuing reflection at other times and perhaps in other directions.

Whom You Serve

Whom do you serve? Among the possible answers to this question are your institution or organization, your boss, or yourself. One more possible answer, of course, is "God, first and last." To give this last answer and mean it does not mean you cannot serve the others mentioned as well. Ideally, there should be no conflict, at least not between serving God and serving a religious organization and its leadership, if that organization and its leaders are also faithfully serving God.

We know, however, that sometimes organizations or their leaders lose their way. Sometimes they make choices that are not about fulfilling their stated mission or serving whom they say they exist to serve. Sometimes there are conflicts. Often these are about priorities; sometimes they are about integrity.

What if your Christian organization asks you as a Christian fundraiser to push a donor into making a gift she is not ready to make? Suppose that you recognize that the gift will meet an important need and you are fairly confident you can elicit it, even though it may cause some problem for the donor and may undermine her experience of giving as a celebration of grace. Do you go after the gift?

Or perhaps your organization is providing donors with information that seems intended to manipulate them or that paints an incomplete or biased picture of the situation. Yet it has proved effective in the past at raising money for truly wonderful work. What do you do?

If you serve the organization, because it's your job, or yourself, because it's your career, the answers to these questions will probably go in one direction. Whereas if you serve God, because this work is a calling, the answers will probably go in a different direction. This is one way in which understanding your work as a call to ministry may make a difference.

Fundraising as a Christian

How might fundraising be different, as the personal work of an individual, because one is a Christian, especially if one is working for a Christian organization? We have explored many aspects of this theme in this book. There are two fairly concrete questions to wrestle with at this point.

One is to ask, "How are my relationships with donors (and others) shaped by my faith commitments, perhaps by their faith commitments too, and by the desire for these relationships to reflect the values of faith?" A second is to ask, "What specific social, moral, and spiritual attitudes and values are affirmed or promoted by the ways I encourage people to give, and how do those correspond to the ideals of my faith?"

If all Christian fundraisers examined their conduct around these two questions, they might be surprised—perhaps encouraged, perhaps troubled—by what they found. Undoubtedly, for most of us, our faith does shape the way we relate to others, including donors and colleagues, in very positive ways. Still, we might also find areas where we would like to do better and hope that our personal and professional behavior would give a clearer witness to our faith.

Professional Versus Christian Ideals

We have alluded before to potential conflicts between Christian values or ideals and the value or ideals of the fundraising profession. These issues are often subtle and complex, and we do not want to give the impression here that we see Christian and professional ideals as always being in conflict. In fact, our sense is that many Christian fundraising programs need more, not less, of a commitment to "professionalism"—in the sense of trying to do things as well as they can be done.

Still, we also see places in the practice of fundraising where Christian and professional values or assumptions will be in tension. The question, we think, should then be, "How can we make these tensions constructive rather than destructive?" Let us look at just a few cases.

One example would be the "bigger is better" assumption. This is a pervasive prejudice in the culture in which we exist that has permeated the fundraising world. There is a pronounced tendency to go for bigger campaigns, bigger lists, and bigger gifts. But let us not forget that the Bible affirms the value of smallness, too. The description of the church at its best in the Book of Acts is not the description of a "megachurch" but rather of a network of small house churches. The Bible is full of verses and stories that affirm the importance of small steps in faith (see Luke 16:10 or the wonderful story of the healing of Namaan in 2 Kings 5). Jesus reminds us in the story of the widow's mite—a story of special relevance for fundraisers—that God does not necessarily attach the same values to large and small that the secular world does. As Christians, neither should we.

The point is that despite the biases of our profession, what we see as only a small gesture might be, in God's eyes, the act that is most important. It might be the first step in a lifetime of giving that may be significant for the future of the church. There might even be a time when a small campaign is better than a large one. If we are committed to doing this work as a ministry, we should be attentive and open to these possibilities.

A second example might be the preference in our culture for the permanent over the transitory. This is an especially obvious bias in the world of nonprofit organizations, many of which were set up to solve specific problems or fulfill a narrowly defined mission but none of which ever seem to be planning on finishing their work and going out of business. Rather they all seem to be planning to go on forever, regardless of whether they outlive their mission or their inspiration.

This translates as an overarching bias in the profession of fundraising toward pursuing endowment funds. But there are downsides to endowment, especially for organizations that should be drawing their strength from the inspiration and commitment of the individuals who first shaped them or those to whom they should be accountable now. Although building a large endowment may allow an institution to direct more resources to programs and services in the future, it may also have the effect of insulating that organization's leadership from the people they serve.

In contrast to the rage for endowment, one exemplary Christian service organization, the Mennonite Central Committee, maintained a practice of refusing endowment gifts for 75 years. Any gift, large or small, had to be used up in five years, a period long enough to plan the wise use of even a very large gift. It has recently begun to accept endowment gifts, because it wants to be able to respond to the dreams of those who wish to leave a lasting legacy to support the organization. However, MCC still does not solicit such gifts, and (we were told) has no plans to do so. Furthermore, it requires that such gifts must be undesignated; they cannot be specified for particular purposes, but must be available to support the ongoing Christian relief and service work for which MCC is so well known.

Has this organization lost some gifts from people who only want to create an endowment? Quite possibly. But it has certainly kept something just as important, something an endowment fund cannot buy. That is MCC's continuing focus on sustaining a solid, living relationship with their supporting constituency, the denomination whose name they bear.

The Mennonite Central Committee is widely recognized as one of the best Christian international development agencies, both in terms of the work it does and in terms of the witness it makes and the opportunities it creates for Christians to grow through service. (A study of such groups a few years ago showed this to be true; see Jeavons, 1994b.) It has maintained its remarkable focus, quality of service, and spiritual vitality, at least in part because it has maintained such strong, intimate relationship with the denomination it represents. Moreover, the members of that denomination (and others) have remained steadfast and eager in their support of it because of its quality and focus.

This organization knows it has to pay attention to the spiritual and practical guidance of the "living church" because it does not have the option of living off the "dead hand of the past." The members of the living church know they have to support it—and do so generously—because it serves and represents them well.

There are, sadly, many examples of organizations that have drifted off their missions or intentionally changed course—often in troubling ways—because their resources became so plentiful that they ceased being responsive and accountable to the people who set them up or depend on their programs. Many Christian organizations have drifted into work that no longer reflects the concerns of a people of faith, perhaps a community or tradition whose name the organization bears, in part because they could live off of an endowment and not worry about the wishes and vision of founders and subsequent generations. There are positive aspects to being dependent on the widow's mite, especially if an organization wants to serve and stay close to the church.

Moreover, the Bible does not tell us that institutions should be eternal. Only God's love and God's reign are described as enduring from generation to generation. The Scriptures do tell us that we should "not be anxious about tomorrow"; but not because we have acquired a healthy endowment. Rather they tell us that we should feel that way because if we are doing what God asks of us, we can count on God's abundance to provide whatever we need.

This is not to say that endowments are evil or have no legitimate purpose. It is just to lift up one more example of how some of the most basic conventional assumptions about and goals for fundraising often need deeper and more careful scrutiny in a Christian context. If a Christian fundraiser's work is finally about helping to build the kingdom of God, we would do well to remember that this will be a kingdom where "the first shall be last and the last shall be first" (Matthew 19:30). In that context, all conventional assumptions, including the most tried and true professional assumptions, may need to be stood on their heads, at least occasionally.

Conclusions

Our studies have convinced us that conventional assumptions are most likely to be turned upside down to serve and honor God when the individuals engaged in the work of Christian fundraising come to that work, or come to experience it, as a calling. Such people, we believe, are more likely to question conventional wisdom in fundraising, applying it where appropriate but rejecting it where it is not, in order to be sure the needs for funds do not undermine the commitments of faith.

Such people are more likely to be appreciative of the smallest gifts as well as the largest. Such people are more likely to be attentive to the messages they convey in the ways they ask and more likely to be concerned about the human and spiritual qualities of their relationships with donors (and others) because they see those relationships as commitments and expressions of faith. Such people are more likely to see the attention and care they give to these matters as being about serving and honoring God, rather than just doing their jobs or advancing their careers, and so, ironically, probably do their jobs better.

We want especially to emphasize here that there is also much to be gained and to celebrate from the fundraiser's point of view in approaching this work in this way. Why? Because those who approach and experience their work in this way are connecting with a source of deep satisfaction. They are bringing their professional lives into a space where the profoundly fulfilling integration of faith and work is possible. They are thus much more likely to occupy that space as professionals where, as Frederick Buechner put it, "their deep gladness and the world's deep hunger meet." By divine design, that is always a place of extraordinary blessing.

We hope that all Christian fundraisers will listen for their callings, if they have not already, and consider how they might try to root themselves in that space of potential blessing in this work every day, day in and day out.

II

FUNDRAISING AS
AN INVITATION TO COOPERATE
WITH GOD'S GRACE

*God has shown us, people, what is good. And what
does the Lord require of us? To act justly, and to love mercy,
and to walk humbly with our God.*

—Micah 6:6–8

IN CHAPTER TEN, we looked at the meaning of vocation to reflect on how fundraising might be seen and experienced as a calling by individual Christians engaged in this work. Examining biblical and spiritual concepts of vocation while thinking about our larger culture's view of the professions and professional conduct suggested how undertaking the work of fundraising as a personal ministry might greatly enrich our experience as well as improve the quality of this work. It also suggested some ways in which doing this work as a ministry might lead us into conflict with more conventional, secular expectations about how we should think and act as professionals.

Before we bring this volume to a close, we want to offer a meditation on this work of fundraising for Christians and Christian organizations. We want to reflect on the potential for fundraising, undertaken as a personal ministry by Christians for Christian organizations, to have a prophetic function, as that term is best understood. In our view, Christian fundraising can have a prophetic function when it points all those involved—organizations, fundraisers, donors, and potential donors—to the deepest aspirations God holds for us all, to God's vision of what is good, as that vision has been proclaimed by Micah and the other Prophets.

After that, we will briefly review the conclusions we have drawn from our research in light of this most challenging vision of what a true ministry of fundraising could be. We will revisit a few key points to suggest how they might become a focus of ongoing reflection and discussion for Christian fundraisers. Finally, we will articulate what we see as the most important challenge Christian organizations and Christian fundraisers face as we all move into the third millennium. But let us begin with one more story and meditation. The story is from Scripture.

A Prophetic Vision of Fundraising

Our starting point for this meditation is the story of Elisha's encounter with a woman in financial distress. This is not a text to which we have seen fundraisers make reference very often. Yet it is, we believe, one that offers another perspective on the work of Christian fundraising that might be both challenging and important. This story highlights the ways in which there can be a prophetic aspect to the endeavor of raising resources for the work of the community of believers. However, before delving into the story, it is important to say a few words about the meaning of prophecy and prophetic ministry.

Prophetic Ministry

According to the *Oxford English Dictionary,* the word *prophet* means "one who speaks for God, or a deity, as an inspired revealer or interpreter of God's will." This is generally not the first or most common understanding held today, even by Christian people, of what it means to be a prophet. Too often even Christians' first understanding of prophecy reflects a narrow and superficial view of a prophet as "one who can predict the future."

However, that has never been the essence of prophecy in the biblical tradition. This common misunderstanding of what it means to be prophetic often leads to a problematic reading of important texts by Christians and others. Starting with this misunderstanding, those texts—the Book of Revelation is a good example—are often misappropriated as tools to speculate about specific occurrences in the future or about the meaning of contemporary events rather than approached as avenues for study and meditation that can lead toward a deeper understanding of God's will. (For a helpful discussion of this tradition and these texts, see Eller, 1974.)

The true biblical vision is much better represented in the *Oxford English Dictionary*'s definition.

The essence of prophecy in the biblical tradition is the act of pointing to the truth God has revealed about how the world should be, the direction in which creation should be moving, and the role we human beings should play in all that. The essence of prophecy is the ability to see and articulate how the will of God should be visible—or made manifest—in any situation and then perhaps to point to the potential consequences if we human beings do not do what the will of God requires. (That is why the biblical prophets speak so often about issues of justice and mercy and hypocrisy, and it explains why speaking about what the future may hold can sometimes be the secondary characteristic of a prophet's ministry but is not the most important purpose of his or her words.) Prophetic ministry is marked by the ability to examine any situation with an understanding of what God would hope for in that context.

Example of a Prophetic Ministry

With that understanding, let us a consider a story about identifying and meeting a need for resources in this context.

> The wife of a man from the company of prophets cried out to Elisha, "Your servant my husband is dead, and you know that he revered the Lord. But now his creditor is coming to take my two boys as his slaves."
>
> Elisha replied to her, "How can I help you? Tell me, what do you have in your house?"
>
> "Your servant has nothing there at all," she said, "except a little oil."
>
> Elisha said, "Go around and ask all your neighbors for empty jars. Don't ask for just a few. Then go inside and shut the door behind you and your sons. Pour the oil into all the jars, and as each is filled, put it to one side."
>
> She left him and afterward shut the door behind her and her sons. They brought the jars to her, and she kept pouring. When all the jars were full, she said to her son, "Bring me another one."
>
> But he replied, "There is not a jar left." Then the oil stopped flowing.
>
> She went and told the man of God, and he said, "Go, sell the oil and pay your debts. You and your sons can live on what is left" [2 Kings 4:1–7].

This story holds powerful lessons, both for our lives in faith more generally and for our work as Christian fundraisers specifically. To understand these lessons, to begin to grasp their implications, we should, first, look at the context and details of this situation as presented; second, consider carefully what the key actors here did; and third, examine the outcomes closely.

SITUATION. There are two key actors here. First we have "a widow of a man from the company of prophets," which means a man who committed his life to serving and following God, probably in a kind of supportive role to Elisha. Then we have Elisha, a prophet himself—or "the Prophet, with a capital 'P' "—who is widely recognized as the key spiritual leader and divinely inspired teacher of his time in Israel.

The widow is in dire straits because her husband's death has left her with no income and no assets. (Then as now, being a true "man of God" apparently was not the path to financial security.) Indeed, she is worried now that her family's creditors will take away her sons if she cannot pay the family's debts, but she has no idea how she can do that.

The financial need here is real and pressing. It is not the result of anyone's miscalculation or folly or greed. It must be met for a good and moral purpose, to avoid the breakup of this family and indentured servitude for the sons. But this widow has no assets at all, nor skills or services she can offer others to get the money she needs.

ACTIONS. So the widow goes to the "man of God," the prophet Elisha, seeking his advice, and he does several things. First, he ascertains what resources she has to work with—in this case, "nothing . . . except a little oil." Second, apparently seeing how the will of God can be fulfilled in this situation, he tells her to seek help from her neighbors. Yet the way he tells her to seek that help does not make much sense to us and must not have made sense to her either, because he tells her to go and ask them for any empty jars they have.

Nevertheless, he tells her to be bold in seeking this odd form of charity and "not to ask for just a few." Then, he tells her, she should take these (presumably many) empty jars and pour her little bit of oil into them. Finally, in one last instruction that seems to make the least sense of all, he tells her "to set each one aside when it is filled." (How one, much less many, could be filled with only "a little oil" we do not know.)

Given these strange directions, what does the widow do? She enlists the aid of her sons and does exactly what Elisha told her to do, even though this seemingly makes no sense at all as a way to solve her problem.

OUTCOMES. The immediate and visible outcomes that result from the widow following this odd plan are that her neighbors provide help by offering her their empty jars, and she ends up with an abundance of oil. In fact, she ends up with so much oil that when she sells it she has enough money to pay the debt and keep her family together and then have enough left over so that "she and her sons can live on what is left." This last point is no small consideration for a widow in that culture, for she would have no other available means of support.

We can infer additional important results from these events. The widow, we can assume, learns a remarkable lesson about trusting in God's providence. In the words of a familiar hymn, "all that she needed, God's hand has provided," and very likely her faith and trust in God grew deeper. She also probably grew closer to her community, having been willing to ask for help and then having received it.

In addition, the members of the community may have grown in faith and generosity. They, too, must have marveled at the strange course and yet wonderful results of these events. They were presented with a legitimate need to give, and though the request made to them may have seemed odd, they responded nonetheless. They then had the satisfaction of seeing how their generosity—and their cooperation with God's plans—made a difference for this woman and her sons.

Reflecting on These Lessons

So, what might we learn from this story? First it tells us about the value and rightness of trusting in God's providence, in God's abundance and active care for us. It teaches the importance of being willing to act in faith when we have to do so to meet real needs for good and moral purposes. This woman faced a critical need for resources for a moral purpose. She sought divine guidance about how to meet that need, seeking the prophet Elisha's advice. Then, trusting that God was speaking through the prophet, she followed his directions, even though they may have seemed strange. She acted in faith, and the need was met.

Second, the story tells us something about the potential for good that can be realized when we are willing to ask others for help in achieving good purposes or in doing God's work. The widow asked her neighbors, the members of her community, for assistance. She was bold in asking, because the need was critical and the purpose right and because she was clear she was acting with divine guidance. What is more, even though what she was asking for must have puzzled many she asked, they responded generously—probably because the need was obvious and legitimate but perhaps also because they could see she was acting and asking "in faith."

In the end, the community probably grew closer and stronger and more generous for being involved in a good work like this together. In addition, those who gave probably felt their faith grow deeper. For when they responded in a way that promoted justice and served mercy, they saw how it did make a difference and it was good.

Third, the story tells us something about the importance of following divine guidance, when we have worked and prayed hard to discern and understand that guidance, even if what we are being directed to do is counterintuitive or perhaps even makes no sense. We need to remember that the God we wish to serve and follow is the God who "chose the foolish things of the world to shame the wise" (1 Corinthians 1:27). Indeed, we need to remember that things sometimes have to work this way so that other people's faith can be encouraged and nurtured.

Why would that be? Because sometimes it is only when things work in this way that others can see that it is the grace and power of God—and not human striving or cleverness—that is fixing what needs to be fixed, that is bringing something good to pass. As Christians, we proclaim our belief that this is the gracious and creative God whose work we are doing. Scripture tells us that the better world we are trying to build is one where "many who are first will be last, and many who are last will be first" (Matthew 19:30). If we are willing to live our whole lives—especially our professional lives—with this truth in mind, then appearing wise in conventional terms should never be our first concern.

Indeed, the course Elisha told the widow to follow must have looked to her and others like shear folly. (No doubt a good fundraising consultant could have given her more sensible and more sophisticated advice about how to solicit the resources she needed.) Yet the apparently odd course to which Elisha directed her clearly allowed her legitimate needs to be met. Moreover, it did so in a way that should have made it clear to anyone watching that it was the power and grace of God at work here—in the generosity of the neighbors responding to the strange request as well as the miraculous sufficiency of resources that were available when all was said and done.

Some Key Questions

So finally, we contend, this story holds up for all of us the most challenging but most important standards to aim for in shaping and doing the work of Christian fundraising as a ministry. Perhaps, to focus more sharply on those standards and move our programs and our work in that direction, all of us involved in Christian fundraising might regularly and candidly reflect on three key questions, which might go as follows:

- Does the work we are doing as Christian fundraisers testify to a deep and certain trust in God's grace and abundance?

- Does it invite all those who are able in our various communities to participate in God's work by appealing to their best qualities and their highest ideals and by asking them in appropriate ways to give generously and faithfully for a good and moral purpose?

- Does it demonstrate our commitment to seek, discern, and follow divine guidance, even when the course of action into which it is leading us seems curious or even foolish?

If we, as Christian fundraisers, regularly ask ourselves these questions about our work and can honestly answer yes, we can be confident we are doing ministry. Our work will then have the potential to be prophetic in the best sense, helping the people we encounter in this work see the reality of God's infinite generosity and God's unfailing love for all creation. Moreover, it will have that potential because it would also lift up the capacity for profound generosity that exists in all of us—a potential that God wants us to realize in every aspect of all our lives.

A Brief Summary

This rhetoric may sound enthralling to everyone who identifies as a Christian and who cares about building up the household of God. No self-respecting Christian fundraiser would say, "Of course I don't care about the spiritual nurture of my donors; I just want their money"—at least not in public!

Yet we also know that sometimes Christian fundraisers act in ways that make donors feel just that—as if the people asking them for money have no interest in their faith or in their welfare, spiritual or otherwise. A number of donors actually told us quite bluntly that they felt they were being treated "like automated teller machines" or, worse yet, that they "had been mugged by a fundraiser." Christian fundraisers themselves expressed uneasiness about the ways some Christian organizations raise money and treat donors. So we know that translating our idyllic-seeming rhetoric into action is not easy.

That is why we have spent most of this volume identifying and exploring resources all of us can draw on to shape and guide the work of Christian fundraising so that it can become a ministry. We began with a careful critical analysis of current fundraising practices among Christian organizations and a hard look at the conventional (secular) assumptions that shape many of those practices. This was followed by a look at the Scriptures and at the history of the church. We explored spiritual and practical ways to do fundraising more effectively as people of faith, in ways truly in keeping to the vision of the Gospel.

We examined six key characteristics of Christian fundraising that give it the character of a ministry. We had set out in our research to find and understand the various resources, principles, approaches, and practices available to Christian fundraisers who want to make their work the kind of ministry that strengthens the whole church and all its members. Based on the characteristics we found in exemplary organizations we studied, we articulated six essential conditions and operating principles we believe are required to create and sustain fundraising programs that nurture donors and potential donors spiritually, that grow givers' hearts and nourish their souls.

Let us review briefly the six key characteristics of fundraising as a ministry in a final invitation for readers to reflect, challenge, debate, and discuss.

1. Nothing is more important for any Christian fundraising program than trusting in God's abundance and grace and endeavoring to communicate that to others in all the ways giving is discussed and people are asked for support. One must begin with this conviction and then strive to make sure it is made manifest in all one's approaches to and interactions with donors. We noted that to do fundraising in this way requires the basic commitments of setting goals appropriately, avoiding inappropriate or self-inflicted crisis appeals, and trying to accentuate the positive elements of the work the money supports and of the lives of the people who are served.

2. The second essential is to do away with the unhealthy spirit of financial competition among Christian ministries, recognizing that God has no favorite causes. We have noted, based on what we have seen in organizations that are doing fundraising as a ministry, that new and wonderful creative freedoms come to Christian fundraisers who can operate outside the narrow competitive focus on financial success. These include the freedoms to let donors follow their hearts, confront problematic motives for and conditions on a gift, take the time needed to cultivate relationships, share resources and wisdom with other organizations and fundraisers, and rejoice in the triumphs of other ministries.

3. In matters of combining faith and practice, we cannot talk always in generalities. Theology matters, down to its very particulars. It is important for organizations that want their fundraising programs to be extensions of their ministry to be clear about their own core theological beliefs and assumptions so that those can guide their choices about fundraising practices. We pointed out the implications of this in matters of hiring and program planning as well as strategic choices about language, methods, and techniques for fundraising solicitations.

4. One of the most important outcomes of operating on a strong theological foundation, with a clear commitment to express that in ministry, is an eagerness to give donors the greatest opportunities for participation in the ministries they support. Most of us know how profoundly we can be ministered to in the process of doing something for another person. We are often changed by our efforts to serve others. Actually seeing—and better yet, getting a feeling for—the ways in which the work we support financially makes a difference in someone else's life is sometimes the most wonderful gift we can receive as donors and is often the greatest stimulus for even greater generosity. So giving donors an opportunity to participate in some way in ministries they support may be uniquely valuable in growing givers' hearts. Though we recognized a number of the factors that may make this difficult, we also offered a range of realistic suggestions and examples of how this can be done well nevertheless.

5. Doing fundraising in this way is a complex effort, even more so for large or multifaceted Christian organizations, and the context makes it very easy for core principles and commitments to get compromised or even lost altogether. That is why we make a strong appeal for careful, integrated planning as an element of governance and management of the organization as a whole and for the development program in particular. Without such planning, it is almost impossible to do fundraising as a ministry. Planning can provide both consistency and needed limits to programmatic and fundraising efforts, encourage organizationwide accountability, and ward off crises. The cautionary tales of Chapter Eight should remind us all of the importance of planning for the health of a whole organization.

6. Spiritually mature, theologically reflective leadership is of the utmost importance. Our examination of Christian organizations has left us absolutely convinced that the conditions and operating principles we have just revisited cannot possibly be achieved and implemented, much less sus-

tained, without effective leadership—in this context meaning leaders who have a thorough understanding of both fundraising and matters of faith. The ability to function in a leadership role as a "reflective practitioner" (Schön, 1974), integrating the insights of faith with the competencies of professional practice, was a striking and distinctive feature of all the key leaders of fundraising programs that had the quality of ministry about them. Equally striking was the sense of calling each had in this work. We noted the characteristics of such leaders, what is needed to find and support such leadership, and the pattern of evolution of spiritually mature leaders and programs in fundraising.

Operating Within a Larger Culture of Ministry

Finally, we need to observe here that working in this way—being mindful of core beliefs and values and truly attentive to the spiritual welfare of current and potential donors—may not be possible unless the development program is nested in and contributes to a larger organizational "culture of ministry." The exemplary fundraising programs we saw were extensions of organizations that wanted every aspect of their work to embody their spiritual values. These organizations were willing to do the hard work required to create an atmosphere where this could happen. Only when the whole organization is truly committed to ministering to all persons with whom it interacts and appreciates the possibilities for this that fundraising presents will there be the necessary commitment of time and resources for fundraising to be a ministry. It is clear to us that the CEO must play a critical role, in addition to that of the chief development officer, in creating such a culture.

The Challenge Before Us

We offer these insights in gratitude to those who helped us see them. We hope this examination will promote a deep, vital, and extended conversation among Christian fundraisers. We believe that the work of Christian fundraising can and should be conducted in a way that provides spiritual nurture to all the people involved. To match this vision with practice, there is a profound need for a broad, sustained dialogue about how to carry out fundraising as a ministry.

All of us involved in Christian fundraising feel challenged to raise the money we think is required to support the good work God has called us and others to do in the world. Surely that is true. But just as surely we should feel the equally important challenge to grow givers' hearts and feed their souls—and our own! For all future efforts to make a good and true faith visible in the world depend on the growth of all those hearts in love, in generosity, in compassion, and in faithfulness. For people of faith, the act of giving—elicited and received in the right way, as an act of grace and faith—can be a powerful occasion for such spiritual growth.

On the other side of the coin, if we raise the money we need now at the cost of undermining or misdirecting people's faith, we do no favor to our cause or our God. If we raise money by giving people a vision of a God who cannot provide all we really need, a God who is never enough, a God who does not really offer us a life more abundant, then our work is an affront to the Gospel, a denial of everything Jesus taught.

Deeply caring, very competent, and wonderfully faithful Christian fundraisers have shown us some of the ways needed money can be raised for God's work now. They have modeled processes of fundraising that contribute to the creation of all the resources—most important among them, faith-filled people—needed for God's work in the future. They have given us examples of how we can grow givers' hearts in this work. There are surely more ways all of us can find to do fundraising like this, if only we will all make this a focus and a commitment in our work and explore these possibilities together.

We envision a time when all of us who are involved in the business of asking for money for Christian organizations can do this in a way that offers people a clear view of God's grace at work in the world. We envision a time when we collectively learn to use the mammon of the world to point to God's love and grace as the single most important force at work in the world and in all our lives. When we come to that time, Christian fundraising will be a true ministry, a pastoral and prophetic activity, of the church.

Indeed, if we keep these ideals and goals in mind and do the hard work needed to embody them in Christian fundraising programs, this work can be a ministry with profound significance. It can be a ministry that is prophetic in the biblical sense of the word. When Christian fundraisers can ask people for support in ways that are clearly invitations to cooperate with God's grace as those people experience it and feel that grace at work in their hearts, they will be helping to grow those givers' hearts.

We hope this volume begins a dialogue that will enrich and ground the Christian fundraising practice of all who share this vision.

REFERENCES

Alcorn, R. *Money, Possessions, and Eternity.* Wheaton, Ill.: Tyndale House, 1989.

Banks, R. *Redeeming the Routine: Bringing Theology to Life.* Wheaton, Ill.: BridgePoint/Victor Books, 1993.

Barrett, D. "Annual Statistical Table on Global Mission." *International Bulletin of Missionary Research,* Jan. 1996, p. 24.

Basinger, D. W., and Basinger, R. G. "Introduction." In D. W. Basinger and R. G. Basinger, *Predestination and Free Will: Four Views of Divine Sovereignty and Human Freedom.* (11th ed.) Downers Grove, Ill.: InterVarsity Press, 1986.

Bassler, J. *God and Mammon: Asking for Money in the New Testament.* Nashville, Tenn.: Abington Press, 1991.

Blue, R. W. "How to Have More Money to Give." In W. Willmer (ed.), *Money for Ministries.* Wheaton, Ill.: Victor Books, 1989.

Boguch, J. "Organizational Readiness for Successful Fund Development: A Systematic and Holistic Approach." In R. C. Hedgepeth (ed.), *Nonprofit Organizational Culture: What Fundraisers Need to Know.* New Directions for Philanthropic Fundraising, no. 5. San Francisco: Jossey-Bass, 1994.

Brittingham, B. E., and Pezzullo, T. R. *The Campus Green: Fund Raising in Higher Education.* ASHE-ERIC Higher Education Reports, no. 1, 1990.

Buechner, F. *Listening to Your Life.* San Francisco: HarperSanFrancisco, 1992.

Clary, E. G., and Snyder, M. "A Functional Analysis of Volunteerism." In *Working Papers from the Independent Sector Spring Research Forum, 1990.* Washington, D.C.: Independent Sector, 1990.

Clary, E. G., and Snyder, M. "A Functional Analysis of Volunteerism." In M. S. Clark (ed.), *Review of Personality and Social Psychology: Prosocial Behavior.* Thousand Oaks, Calif.: Sage, 1991.

Conway, D. "A Theology of Stewardship." *In Trust,* 1989, *1*(2), 4.

Curtis, S. *A Consuming Faith: The Social Gospel and Modern American Culture.* Baltimore: Johns Hopkins University Press, 1991.

Deal, T. E., and Baluss, C. S. "The Power of Who We Are: Organizational Culture in a Nonprofit Setting." In R. C. Hedgepeth (ed.), *Nonprofit*

Organizational Culture: What Fundraisers Need to Know. New Directions for Philanthropic Fundraising, no. 5. San Francisco: Jossey-Bass, 1994.

Drucker, P. *The Effective Executive.* New York: HarperCollins, 1966.

Eller, V. *The Most Revealing Book of the Bible: Making Sense out of Revelation.* Grand Rapids, Mich.: Eerdmans, 1974.

Flores, A. (ed.). *Professional Ideals.* Belmont, Calif.: Wadsworth, 1988.

Foster, R. J. *Money, Sex, and Power.* San Francisco: Harper and Row, 1985.

Frank, J. *The Ministry of Development: An Introduction to the Strategies for Success in Christian Ministries.* Dallas: EDM Press, 1996.

Gardner, N. "Seeking Smaller Donors Is Now a 'Capital' Idea." [http://www.nptimes.com/april1.html]. Apr. 1, 1999.

Gonser Gerber Tinker Stuhr, *Bulletin,* March 1998.

Habecker, E. B. *Leading with a Follower's Heart.* Wheaton, Ill.: Victor Books, 1990.

Hodgkinson, V. A., Weitzman, M. S., Noga, S., Gorski, H., and Kirsch, A. *Giving and Volunteering in the United States, 1994.* Washington, D.C.: Independent Sector, 1994.

Hofheinz, F. "For Money, Look to the Future." *In Trust,* 1991, 2(1), 7.

Hoge, D. R., and others. *Money Matters: Personal Giving in American Churches.* Louisville, Ky.: Westminster/John Knox, 1996.

Hubbard, D. A. *Ten Commandments for Development Officers.* Washington, D.C.: Christian College Coalition Publications, 1993.

Hudnut-Beumler, J. "Protestants and Giving: The Tithes That Bind?" In W. Ilchman and C. Hamilton (eds.), *Cultures of Giving: How Regions and Religions Influence Philanthropy.* New Directions for Philanthropic Fundraising, no. 7. San Francisco: Jossey-Bass, 1995.

Irish, R. K. *If Things Don't Improve Soon I May Ask You to Fire Me.* New York: Doubleday, 1975.

Jeavons, T. H. *Public Libraries and Private Fund Raising: Opportunities and Issues.* Evanston, Ill.: Urban Libraries Council, 1994a.

Jeavons, T. H. *When the Bottom Line Is Faithfulness: The Management of Christian Service Organizations.* Bloomington: Indiana University Press, 1994b.

Lindahl, W. E. "Multiyear Evaluation of Fundraising Performance." In J. M. Greenfield (ed.), *Financial Practices for Effective Fundraising.* New Directions for Philanthropic Fundraising, no. 3. San Francisco: Jossey-Bass, 1994.

Lynn, R. W. *Why Give? Stewardship: A Documentary History of One Strand in American Protestant Teachings About Giving.* Based on comments presented at a gathering of Lilly Endowment grantees engaged in research on the topic of the funding of American religion, Indianapolis, Oct. 1998. Diskette available from the author.

Marty, M. *The Modern Schism: Three Paths to the Secular.* New York: Harper-Collins, 1969.

McCarter, N. D. "Why the Job Is So Tough: Contrary Currents, Finances Haunt Most Chiefs." *In Trust,* 1994, 5(4), 11–14.

McManus, W. E. "Stewardship and Almsgiving in the Roman Catholic Tradition." In R. Wuthnow, V. A. Hodgkinson, and Associates, *Faith and Philanthropy in America: Exploring the Role of Religion in America's Voluntary Sector.* San Francisco: Jossey-Bass, 1990.

Mead, L. "O Sacred Immovables: Confronting the Barriers to Change and Growth." *In Trust,* 1995, 6(4), 13–15.

Miller, L. "Religious Institutions Are Invoking Premiums to Inspire the Wealthy." *Wall Street Journal,* Mar. 10, 1999.

Mixer, J. R. *Principles of Professional Fundraising: Useful Foundations for Successful Practice.* San Francisco: Jossey-Bass, 1993.

Moore, R. L. *Selling God: American Religion in the Marketplace of Culture.* New York: Oxford University Press, 1994.

National Conference of Catholic Bishops. *Stewardship: A Disciple's Response.* Washington, D.C.: United States Catholic Conference, 1993.

National Society of Fund Raising Executives. *Donor's Bill of Rights.* Alexandria, Va.: National Society of Fund Raising Executives, 1994.

Neill, S. C., and Weber, H.-R. *The Layman in Christian History.* Louisville, Ky.: Westminster/John Knox, 1963.

Newtithing Group. "Fact Sheet: Newtithing Group's 'Affordable Donations 1999.'" [http://www.newtithing.org/content/fact.sheet]. Apr. 1999.

Nietzsche, R. *Beyond Good and Evil.* (H. Zinmern, trans.). London: Oxford Press, 1907.

Nouwen, H. *In the Name of Jesus.* New York: Crossroads, 1989.

Oates, M. J. *The Catholic Philanthropic Tradition in America.* Bloomington: Indiana University Press, 1995.

Olford, S. *The Grace of Giving: Thoughts on Financial Stewardship.* Grand Rapids, Mich.: Zondervan, 1972.

Palmer, P. J. *The Active Life: A Spirituality of Work, Creativity, and Caring.* San Francisco: HarperSanFrancisco, 1990.

Payton, R. W. *Philanthropy: Voluntary Action for the Public Good.* New York: American Council on Education/Macmillan, 1988.

Peterson, E. H. *The Message: New Testament with Psalms and Proverbs.* Colorado Springs: Nav Press Publishing Group, 1995.

Pfiffner, H. A. *More Than a Thousand Points of Light.* Seattle: Union Gospel Mission, 1992.

Raschko, M. B. "Theology of Stewardship." In *Stewardship: Disciples Respond.* Washington, D.C: National Catholic Stewardship Council, 1997.

Redding, J. C., and Catalanello, R. F. *Strategic Readiness: The Making of the Learning Organization.* San Francisco: Jossey-Bass, 1994.

Ronsvalle, J., and Ronsvalle, S. *Behind the Stained Glass Windows: Money Dynamics in the Church.* Grand Rapids, Mich.: Baker Books, 1996.

Rosso, H. A. "The Trustee's Role in Fund Raising." In H. Rosso and Associates, *Achieving Excellence in Fund Raising: A Comprehensive Guide to Principles, Strategies, and Methods.* San Francisco: Jossey-Bass, 1991.

Sawyer, J. C. "Listening in Fundraising." In D. A. Brehmer (ed.), *Communication Management in Fundraising.* New Directions for Philanthropic Fundraising, no. 10. San Francisco: Jossey-Bass, 1995.

Schervish, P. G. "Wealth and the Spiritual Secret of Money." In R. Wuthnow, V. A. Hodgkinson, and Associates, *Faith and Philanthropy in America: Exploring the Role of Religion in America's Voluntary Sector.* San Francisco: Jossey-Bass, 1990.

Schmidt, J. D. "Developing Lifelong Relationships with Donors." In W. Willmer (ed.), *Money for Ministry.* Wheaton, Ill.: Victor Books, 1989.

Schmidt, J. D., and Willmer, W. *The Prospering Parachurch.* San Francisco: Jossey-Bass, 1998.

Schön, D. A. *The Reflective Practitioner.* New York: Basic Books, 1974.

Shriver, D. W., Jr. "Visions and Nightmares: The Leader's Call to See Reality— and Change It." *In Trust,* 1992, 3(3), 16–21.

Thomas Aquinas. *Summa theologiae.* (O. P. Batten, trans.). New York: Blackfriars/McGraw-Hill, 1964. (Originally published 1273.)

Tiede, D. L. "Finance and Faith." *In Trust,* 1992, 4(1), 2.

Tobin, G. A. "Between the Lines: Intricacies of Major Donor Communication." In D. A. Brehmer (ed.), *Communication Management in Fundraising.* New Directions for Philanthropic Fundraising, no. 10. San Francisco: Jossey-Bass, 1995.

Tropman, J. E. *The Catholic Ethic in American Society: An Exploration of Values.* San Francisco: Jossey-Bass, 1995.

Vincent, M. Untitled. *Generous Living,* June, 1998, p. 1.

Webber, R. E. *The Secular Saint: The Role of the Christian in the Secular World.* Grand Rapids, Mich.: Zondervan, 1979.

White, J. E. "Integrating Faith into an Organization's Fund-Raising Practices." *Generous Living,* May 1998.

Willmer, W. K. "Considering a Godly Perspective in Providing Money for Ministries." In W. K. Willmer (ed.), *Money for Ministries.* Wheaton, Ill.: Victor Books, 1989.

Wuthnow, R. *The Restructuring of American Religion.* Princeton, N.J.: Princeton University Press, 1988.

Wuthnow, R. "Religion and the Voluntary Spirit in the United States: Mapping the Terrain." In R. Wuthnow, V. A. Hodgkinson, and Associates, *Faith and Philanthropy in America: Exploring the Role of Religion in America's Voluntary Sector.* San Francisco: Jossey-Bass, 1990a.

Wuthnow, R. "Improving Our Understanding of Religion and Giving: Key Issues for Research." In R. Wuthnow, V. A. Hodgkinson, and Associates, *Faith and Philanthropy in America: Exploring the Role of Religion in America's Voluntary Sector.* San Francisco: Jossey-Bass, 1990b.

Wuthnow, R. *God and Mammon in America.* New York: Free Press, 1994a.

Wuthnow, R. *Sharing the Journey.* New York: Free Press, 1994b.

Wuthnow, R. *Crisis in the Churches: Spiritual Malaise, Fiscal Woe.* New York: Oxford University Press, 1997.

THE AUTHORS

THOMAS H. JEAVONS is currently the general secretary of Philadelphia Yearly Meeting of the Religious Society of Friends, the largest Quaker judicatory in the United States. He is also a visiting fellow at the Yale University Program on Nonprofit Organizations. He earned a B.A. degree in philosophy from the University of Colorado (1975), an M.A. in theology from the Earlham School of Religion (1978), and a Ph.D. in management and cultural studies from the Union Institute (1992). He also holds a graduate certificate in business administration from Georgetown University.

Before coming to Philadelphia Yearly Meeting, Jeavons was the founding director (from 1992 to 1996) of the Center on Philanthropy and Nonprofit Leadership, as well as a professor of public administration and philanthropic studies, at Grand Valley State University. He has also been a director of programs for the Association of American Colleges, the executive secretary of Baltimore Yearly Meeting, and a program coordinator for the American Friends Service Committee.

His previous publications include *When the Bottom Line Is Faithfulness: The Management of Christian Service Organizations* (1994), *Public Libraries and Private Fund Raising: Opportunities and Issues* (1994), and *Learning for the Common Good: Liberal Education, Civic Education, and Teaching About Philanthropy* (1991), as well as numerous chapters and articles. His continuing scholarly interests include the history and practice of philanthropy, the roles of religious traditions and organizations in American culture, and the governance and management of all kinds of nonprofit organizations.

REBEKAH BURCH BASINGER is an independent fundraising consultant and researcher, working primarily with Christian colleges and seminaries. She earned her B.A. in English at Trinity College (1975), her M.A. in English at Wichita State University (1981), and her Ed.D. in educational leadership and policy studies at Temple University (1991). Before starting her own business, she was a college administrator and fundraiser for twenty years, including three years as the director of the Foundation for Independent Colleges of Pennsylvania.

Basinger's main research focus has been on fundraising in the college and seminary setting, with a special interest in the role of trustees in the development function. She has presented and published on a range of fundraising topics, including annual fund programs, foundation and corporate relations, and working with women donors. Most recently, her research has focused almost exclusively on the fundraising programs of religious organizations and the implications of that work for the spiritual lives of donors.

Basinger serves on the boards of several Christian organizations, including *In Trust: The Magazine for Leaders in Theological Education* and MAP International. She is the past publisher of *Christian Scholars Review* and is currently editor of *YES!*, a magazine of the Brethren in Christ Church.

INDEX

A

Abraham and Isaac, 166
Abundance: accentuating the positive and, 83–86; attitude of scarcity versus, 73–74, 83–84; communication of, 74–75; confidence in God's, 71–86, 182, 184, 185; crisis appeals and, 81–84; realistic goals and, 75–81, 135–137; turning toward, 73–74
Account, personal, 114, 129
Accountability, 137–139, 175–176
Active Life, The, 97–98
Acts, Book of, 45, 174; 6:1-6, 39
Affiliation, as motivation, 39, 40; in Old Testament, 43, 44
Alcorn, R., 89
Altruism, 40
Amos 4:4-5, 41
Anabaptists, 61, 104
Anderson, E., 126, 136
Annual fundraising cycles, 81–82
Appeals: crisis, 73–74, 81–84; emotionally manipulative, 7, 65; instrumental, 65; positive, 84–86
Aquinas, T., 60, 64, 66
Aristotle, 47
Arminian/Wesleyan perspective, 100
Arrogance in fundraising, 24
Asking: contemporary approaches to, in United States, 65–66; Gospel mission instructions and, 48–49; Greek and Roman attitudes toward, 47–48; historical approaches to, in United States, 63–65; language of, 110–112;

methods and techniques of, 109–110; New Testament perspective on, 47–53; theological differences and, 101–103, 108–112. *See also* Christian fundraising; Fundraising; Fundraising as ministry
Atonement money, 41
Authority, appeal to, 62–63, 66–67

B

Baby boomers, 110
Baluss, C. S., 80, 116, 134
Banks, R., 106, 123, 153
Barrett, D., 35
Basinger, D. W., 100
Basinger, R. G., 100
Bassler, J., 47, 50, 51, 52–53
Bee, R., 91
Begging, 47–48
Beliefs, theological. *See* Theological assumptions and differences; Theological fit
Better Business Bureau, 25
Bible: importance of guidance of, 56; prophecy and prophets in, 179–184; sibling rivalry in, 87; teachings of, on calling or vocation, 166–168; teachings of, on giving and asking, 11, 36, 37–54. *See also* New Testament; Old Testament; *specific book headings*
"Bigger is better" assumption, 174–176

Biola University, 9, 102, 137, 148; board development at, 152; donor participation in, 118, 121; donor relationships of, 91, 102, 127, 141; staff development at, 106

Blessings: from generosity, 116; to givers, in Old Testament, 43

Blue, R. W., 141

Board members: fundraising/giving capacity of, 80–81; fundraising guidelines for, 81; spiritual leadership of, 151–152; theological fit of, 80; wealthy versus nonwealthy, 80–81

Boguch, J., 132

Brethren in Christ Church, 121

Brittingham, B. E., 107

Brooks, J., 118

Brown, S., 117

Buechner, F., 168, 177

Burger, S., 96

C

Cain and Abel, 87

Calling or vocation: Biblical resources on, 166–168; Christian fundraisers' perspectives on, 169–170; concept of, 6; conflicts between, and profession, 170–176; of fundraisers, 12, 165–177; identity and, 166–168; questions for reflection on, 172–176; to specific professional work, 168–170

Calvin, J., 100

Caritas, 60

Catalanello, R. F., 139

Catholic Charities of Cleveland, 9; confidence of, in God's abundance, 74; donor participation in, 118; donor relationships of, 124, 141; fundraising method of, 109; holistic/ noncompetitive approach of, 92, 96–97; planning approach of, 108,

141; prayer approach of, 102; spiritual communication of, 111

Catholic Philanthropic Tradition in America (Oates), 61–62

Charity, in middle ages, 58–60, 66

Chief development officer. See Development officers; Development staff; Leadership

Chief executive officers: study plan for, 152; support of, for development staff, 149–150; support of, for spiritual fundraising, 150–151, 187. See also Leadership

Christian colleges: donor conditions in, 93; donor satisfaction in, 119, 123; staff involvement in, 122

Christian fundraising: assertions about, 18; assumptions that have shaped, 30–32; Biblical resources on, 37–54; contemporary approaches to, 7, 65–66; defined, 5; ethical framework of, 22; focus and goals of, 22; history of, 12, 36, 54, 55–67; ideal outcomes of, 22; ongoing dialogue about, 12–13; versus other fundraising, 17–18, 173; overview of, 11–12, 100–101, 184–187; as pastoral activity, 29–30; philosophical and cultural underpinning of, 22; problems with, 23–27, 30–32, 66–67; prophetic function of, 178–184; as public face of Christianity, 8, 35–36, 112–113; theological assumptions in, 100–101; traditional paradigm of exchange in, 30–32, 63, 66–67; traditional versus fundraising-as-ministry paradigm of, 21, 22–23; ultimate objective of, 23; view of the church and, 32–34. See also Asking; Fundraising as ministry

Christian fundraising research study: background on, 6–13; findings of, precis of, 19–21; methodology of, 8–9

Christian organizations: competition versus cooperation with, 87–98; defined, 2–3; giving patterns and, 34; integrated planning in, 131–144. *See also* Congregations; Parachurch organizations

Chronicle of Philanthropy, 83, 146

Church: early, fundraising practices of, 57–58, 59; history of fundraising in, 55–67; history of, in United States, 61–65; importance of fundraising practices to, 66; importance of view of, 32–34; in middle ages, 58–60, 66; post-Reformation, 61

Clary, E. G., 40

Classical philosophy, philanthropy in, 47–48, 58–59

Cleveland, Catholic Charities of. *See* Catholic Charities of Cleveland

Codes of ethics, minimalistic, 4, 22

Commercialism, 30–32

Communication, internal, 121–122

Communication with donors: about fundraising practices, 110, 125, 140; about results of gifts, 25–26, 117–118, 120–121, 126–127, 137–138; deceptive versus truthful, 24, 25–26; of God's abundance, 74–75; language of faith in, 110–112; person-to-person, 121; technology for, 120–121; theological differences and, 108–109, 110–112. *See also* Donor relationships; Information sharing with donors

Community improvement, classical tradition of philanthropy for, 58–59

Community obligation, as motivation, 39, 40; authority in, 62–63; in New Testament, 45, 51–52, 54; in Old Testament, 40–42, 43, 44; tithing and, 43; in U.S. mainline churches, 62–64

Compassion International, 9; donor participation in, 74, 115, 116, 121; donor relationships of, 102, 126, 140, 141; fundraising methods of, 110, 140; holistic/noncompetitive approach of, 88, 90, 95; long-term goals of, 110; paradigmatic story from, 10; planning approach of, 136; positive approach of, 83, 84; prayer ministry of, 102, 127–128; staff development at, 106

Competitiveness: Biblical examples of, 87; eliminating the spirit of, 89–90, 185; freedoms of holistic approach versus, 90–96, 98; fundraising without, 87–98; between parachurch and denominational congregations, 96–97; scarcity and, 87, 97–98

Comprehensive planning. *See* Integrated organizational planning

Congregations: authority of, 62–63; competition between parachurch organizations and, 96–97; decline in, versus growth in parachurch organizations, 35–36; fundraising in, 3; history of fundraising in, 62–65; referring donors to, 128; weekly collections of, 3, 5

Connections, 2, 112; between calling and profession, 168–177; between faith and practice, 154–159

Consistency, organizational, 134

Constantine, Emperor, 58

Consumer culture, 30–32

Conversion, 55, 67

Conway, D., 108

Cook, C., 150

Cooperation and collaboration: among fundraisers of different ministries, 87–98, 185; of development with other organizational functions, 131–144

Corban, 45

1 Corinthians, 167; 1:27, 183; 9, 50; 9:11, 52; 13:3, 49–50

2 Corinthians: 4, 72; 8–9, 50–52; 8:10, 50; 9:12, 54; 11:7-11, 51

Counsel: fundraising, 65; of God, 183; referring donors for, 127–128; spiritual, for development leaders, 151–154, 158–159

Covenant, 111

Crisis appeals, 73–74, 81–84; abundance-minded, 83–84; breaking the cycle of, 81–84

Cultural and political context: of church in United States, 62; of early church, 57–58, 59; of medieval church, 58–59; of New Testament perspective, 47–48; of Old Testament perspective, 41; of professional vocation, 168–170, 178

Curtis, S., 30

Cynics, the, 48

D

Dahlin, D., 127–128, 136

de Tocqueville, A., 27

Deal, T. E., 80, 116, 134

Deception in fundraising, 23, 24–25

Definitions, 4–6

Denominational congregations. *See* Congregations

Denominational differences. *See* Theological assumptions and differences

Deuteronomy: 14:28-30, 42; 15:10, 45; 26:10-11, 42; 26:12-15, 43

Development education: for board members, 151–152; interorganization cooperation on, 94–95; theological discussion and, 105–107; theological/spiritual, 147, 152–154, 158–159

Development function: broad view of, 32–34; goals of, 129; integrated organizational planning and, 131–144; stewardship education by, 159–161

Development officers: advisors and mentors for, 151–154, 158–159; characteristics of spiritually mature, 147–148; evaluating theological fit of, 148–149; importance of theological fit versus fundraising expertise of, 145–147; integration of faith and practice for, 154–158, 187; interviewing prospective, 148–149; search for and hiring of, 145–147, 148–149, 161; spiritual maturity in, 145–161. *See also* Leadership

Development staff: chief executive officer support for, 149–150; competition versus cooperation among, of different ministries, 89–90; hiring of, implications of theology for, 103–107, 112, 148–149; involvement of, in organizational planning, 131–144; ongoing theological discussion with, 105–107; orientation for, 105–106; power issues of, 142–143; size of, 78–80; spiritually mature leadership of, 145–161. *See also* Fundraisers

Didache, 57

Discipleship: calling to, 165, 166–168, 171–172; stewardship and, 6

Divine guidance, importance of following, 56, 183, 184

Donaldson, D., 110

Donor fatigue, 85

Donor motivation. *See* Motivation, donor

Donor participation, 114–130, 186; information gifts for, 117–118, 120–121, 126–127; information technology for, 120–121; joy of giving and, 115–117; obstacles to, overcoming, 122–127; Paul's view on, 114; taking time for, 123–126, 129–130

Donor relationships: in fundraising as ministry, 18–19, 116–118, 187–188; goal setting and, 76–77; holistic perspective in, 90–92; spiritual communication and, 110–112; taking time for, 123–126, 129–130; in traditional versus fundraising-as-ministry approach, 4, 7–8, 23–27; without possibility of payoff, 127. *See also* Communication with donors

Donors: benefits of integrated organizational planning to, 140–142; giving patterns of faithful versus nonfaithful, 34; ministering to hurting, 127–128; planning of, 140–142; realistic assessment of giving potential of, 76–77, 124; respect for, 24, 90–92; sensitivity of, to organizational consistency, 134; sensitivity of, to theological fit, 104, 111–112; treating, as means to an end, 24, 25–26; treating, equally versus unequally, 24, 26

Donor's Bill of Rights (NSFRE), 4

Drucker, P., 78

E

Early church, fundraising practices of, 57–58, 59

Ecclesiology, 32–33

Ego-defensive function, 40

E-mail, 26, 120–121

Elisha, 180–184

Eller, V., 179

Endowments, 26, 174–176

Entrepreneurial evangelism, 66

Ephesians 4:1-2, 167

Epistles, 45. *See also specific headings*

Ethics: conflicts between profession and calling and, 170–176; in conventional versus fundraising-as-ministry paradigm, 22; minimalistic codes of, 4, 22

Evaluation: planning and, 139–140; for spiritually mature leaders, 152

Evangelical Christianity: concept of calling in, 169–170; concept of stewardship in, 6; entrepreneurial, 66; parachurch organizations and, 3

Exchange paradigm, 30–32, 43, 63, 66–67

Exemplary organizations: listed, 9; summary of practices of, 19–21, 184–187. *See also* Biola University; Catholic Charities of Cleveland; Compassion International; Fuller Theological Seminary; Roman Catholic Diocese of Tucson; San Francisco Theological Seminary; Union Gospel Mission of Seattle

Exodus: 23:10-11, 42; 30:11-16, 39, 41

Expectations, reasonable, 76–77

F

Faith: degree of, as predictor of giving, 34; fundraising and expression of, 1–13; giving in, 28–30; integrating fundraising practice and, 154–159; workplace and, 154, 171

Fear, as motivation, 39, 40; Jesus' teachings on, 46; in middle ages, 59, 60, 66

Federal Accounting Standards Board, 25

Feedback, asking for donor, 110, 125, 140

Financial planning, 137–139. *See also* Integrated organizational planning

Flores, A., 169

Focus groups, 110

Foster, R. J., 28

Foundations, power issues in, 143

Francis of Assisi, Saint, 17

Frank, J., 105, 128

Freedoms of holistic perspective, 90–96, 98

Fuller Theological Seminary, 9, 77, 153; donor relationships in, 116, 117–118, 124; donors' joy in giving to, 28, 115; holistic/noncompetitive approach of, 95, 97; prayer approach of, 102

Fund Raising School, 138

Fundraisers: board members as, 80–81, 82; calling of, 165–177; cooperation among, of different ministries, 89–98; cooperation of, with other organizational staff, 131–144; function of, 32–34; integration of faith and practice for, 154–158; interviewing prospective, 105, 112, 148–149; motives of, 11, 38–39; number of, 78–80; ongoing theological discussion with, 105–107; orientation for, 105–106; power issues of, 142–143; spiritual growth of, 11, 106–107, 151–159; spiritually mature leadership of, 145–161; theological fit of, 103–107. See also Development officers; Development staff; Leadership

Fundraising: as a calling, 165–177; Christian fundraising versus, 17–18, 173; connections in, 1–2; and expression of faith, 1–13; problems in, 11; utilitarian focus of, 4, 11. See also Asking; Christian fundraising; Fundraising as ministry

Fundraising as ministry: Biblical resources for, 11, 36, 37–54; as a calling, 165–177; challenges of, 187–188; conditions necessary in, 20, 74, 88, 99, 185–186; confidence in God's abundance and, 71–86, 185; defined, 5; donor par-ticipation and, 114–130, 186; elements of, summarized, 12, 19–21, 185–187; ethical framework of, 22; exemplars of, 9, 67; focus and goals of, 22; goal setting for, 75–81; as growing hearts, 10–11, 74, 123–126; historical resources for, 12, 36, 54, 55–67; holistic perspective in, 87–98, 185; ideal outcomes of, 22; integrated organizational planning in, 131–144, 186; integration of faith and practice in, 154–159; as invitation to cooperate with God's grace, 178–188; obstacles to, overcoming, 122–127; operating principles for, 20–21, 116, 133, 146, 186–187; paradigmatic story of, 10–11; philosophical and cultural underpinning of, 22; prophetic function of, 178–184; reasons for, 18–19, 32–36; spiritually mature leadership of, 145–161, 186–187; summary overview of, 184–187; theological differences in, 99–113, 185–186; traditional fundraising versus, 4, 7–8, 17–18, 22–23; ultimate objective of, 23; vision of, 21, 22–23. See also Asking; Christian fundraising; Exemplary organizations

Fundraising counsel, 65

Fundraising language, in traditional Christian fundraising, 24

Fundraising methods, theological differences and, 108–109. See also Asking

G

Gardner, N., 77

Generosity: classical view of, 47–48, 58–59; spiritual growth in, 10–11, 27–30, 34–35, 182–183

Generous Living (Vincent), 123

Genesis: 4:1-14, 87; 17:5, 166; 32:8, 166

Geographical obstacles, donor communication and, 120–121

Gift annuities, 138–139

Gifts: big versus small, 174–176; goal setting for, 75–81; matching requests for, to donor's ability to provide, 124

Giving: assessing donors' potential for, 76–77; Biblical resources on, 37–54; decline in, among Catholics, 151; decline in, in United States, 74; in faith, 28–30; impulse, 140–141; as occasion for grace, 27–28; to parachurch ministries versus congregations, 96; planning for, 140–142; spiritual growth in, 27–30, 34–35. *See also* Joy in giving; Motivation, donor

Giving and Volunteering in the United States (Hodgkinson et al.), 34

Goals: board member capabilities and, 80–81, 82; fundraising staff needs and, 78–80; setting, implications of theology for, 107–108, 112; setting, integrated organizational planning for, 131–133; setting, permanent versus transitory, 174–176; setting realistic, 75–81, 135–137. *See also* Integrated organizational planning; Planning

God: calling to service of, 172–173; confidence in abundance of, 71–86, 182, 184; importance of following guidance of, 183, 184. *See also* Grace

God and Mammon: Asking for Money in the New Testament (Bassler), 47

"God talk," 156

Golden Mouse Club, 121

Gonser Gerber Tinker Stuhr, 148

"Good Man Is Hard to Find, A" (O'Connor), 145

Gospel mission instructions, 48–49

Grace: fundraising as invitation to cooperate with, 178–188; giving and, 27–28, 29; giving as act of thanks for, 100; Paul's view on giving and, 52

Graduate Theological Union, Berkeley, 148–149

Gratitude or love, as motivation, 39, 40; in New Testament, 46; in Old Testament, 43; theological perspective of, 100; in U.S. church, 63, 64

Great Collection, 50–51

Greed, Paul's concern with creating an impression of, 50

Greek tradition, 47–48, 58–59

Guilt, as motivation, 39, 40

H

Habecker, E. B., 147

Hearts, allowing donors to follow their own, 90–92

Hearts, growing, 10–11, 74; evaluation of, 140; integrated organizational planning and, 133; taking time for, 123–126, 129–130; through donor participation, 116–117. *See also* Spiritual growth

Hebrew culture, 41

Hell, threat of, 46, 60

Heslinga, B., 126, 159

High-pressure tactics, 91

Hiring: of development officers, 145–146, 148–149; implications of theology for, 103–107, 112, 145–147

Hoag, G., 102

Hodgkinson, V. A., 34

Hofheinz, F., 119

Hoge, D. R., 99–100, 105, 160

Holistic perspective, 87–98, 185; eliminating the spirit of competition for, 89–90, 185; implications of, 90–96

Holistic planning, 131–144. *See also*
  Integrated organizational planning
Holy Spirit, calling of, 6
Honesty in fundraising, 24–25;
  accountability and, 137; positivity
  and, 84–85. *See also* Deception in
  fundraising
House churches, 174
Hubbard, D. A., 153
Hudnut-Beumler, J., 100, 104–105
Huguenots, 61
Hymnal, The: A Worship Book, 131

I

Idealism, 40
Identity, calling and, 166–167. *See
  also* Calling or vocation
Ideological fit, 104. *See also* Theologi-
  cal fit
Imitation of Christ, The (Kempis), 28
Impersonal fundraising, 24
Impulse giving, 140–141
In Trust, 89
Independent Sector, 74
Indiana University, Fund Raising
  School, 1
Indifferent response to integrating
  faith and practice, 154–156
Individual, New Testament focus on,
  47, 58
Indulgences, sale of, 55–56, 59, 60, 65
Information sharing with donors,
  25–26; for accountability, 137; to
  encourage sense of participation,
  117–118, 120–121, 126–127. *See
  also* Communication with donors
Information technology, 120–121
Instrumental function, 40, 65, 184
Integrated organizational planning,
  131–144, 186; for accountability,
  137–139, 175–176; advantages of,
  to donors, 140–142, 144; advantages of, to fundraising and organi-

zation, 133–140, 143–144; for
  consistency, 134; evaluation and,
  139–140; for limit setting,
  135–137; Lone Ranger approach
  versus, 131, 142; power issues and,
  142–143. *See also* Goals; Planning
Integration of faith and practice,
  154–158, 187; indifferent response
  to, 154–156; path to, 158; pious
  response to, 155, 156; preferred
  response to, 156–158; reactionary
  response to, 155, 156
Integrity, New Testament perspective
  and, 52
International organizations, donor
  involvement in, 120–121
International Union of Gospel Missions (UGM), 96
Interviewing: of prospective development officers, 148–149; of prospective development staff, 105, 112
Irish, R. K., 146
Isaiah: 1:17, 42; 29:13, 44–45
Israelites, 41, 42, 43

J

James 2:1-4, 25
Jeavons, T. H., 143, 175
Jeremiah 22:3, 42
Jesus: on abundance, 74; on asking,
  48–49; calling of all Christians to
  be like, 168; on connections, 2; on
  giving, 28, 30, 32, 45–46; giving as
  imitation of, 28; on love, 25; on
  planning, 107–108; on socio-
  economic status, 26. *See also* New
  Testament
John: 4:16, 25; 8:32, 25; 10:10, 74;
  15:9-13, 25
1 John: 3:17, 46; 4:18, 46
Joy in giving, 28; attitude of abundance and, 74; fundraising that
  fails to provide, 24, 124–125;

holistic perspective and, 91; Paul's view on, 52, 53, 54; providing opportunities for, 115–117; taking time for, 123–126, 129–130

Justice and fairness, as motivation, 39, 40; in New Testament, 45–46, 54; in Old Testament, 42, 44

K

Kempis, T. à, 28
Keung, C.-C., 141
Key terms and concepts, 4–6
Kingdom niche, 88
Kingdom without walls, 96–97
"Kingdom work," holistic perspective on, 87–98
2 Kings: 4:1-7, 180–184; 5, 174
Knowledge function, 40
Koinonia, 50–51

L

Leadership, spiritually mature, 145–161, 165, 186–187; board members and, 151–152; characteristics of, 147–148, 161; chief executive officers and, 149–151; development officers and, 145–149, 150–151; integration of faith and practice for, 154–158; spiritual fitness program for, 152–154. *See also* Development officers
Leading with a Follower's Heart (Habecker), 147
Letters to donors, 121
Leviticus: 19:9-10, 42; 19:33-34, 44; 27:30-32, 42
Lilly Endowment, 6, 119
Limit setting: for fundraising goals, 75–81; for organizational goals, 135–137
Lindahl, W. E., 139–140
Lone Ranger approach, 131, 142

Long-range planning. *See* Goals; Integrated organizational planning; Planning
Love or gratitude. *See* Gratitude or love
Luke: 7:32-36, 45; 9:3-5, 48; 10:1-12, 48; 16:10, 174
Lundeen, R., 76, 106, 149
Luther, M., 28, 55–56, 59, 67, 100
Luther Theological Seminary, 89, 101
Lynn, R. W., 6, 61–62, 63, 64, 74, 89

M

Mailings, 7
Mainline Protestants. *See* Protestantism, mainline
Mammon, 37–39, 53
Manipulation in fundraising, 7–8, 23, 25, 65, 67, 173
Mark: 2:23-27, 45; 6:8-11, 48; 7:9-13, 45; 10:17-22, 93; 12:41-44, 25
Marty, M., 154
Matthew: 5:40-42, 45; 6:2-3, 47; 6:21, 1; 6:24, 37–39; 6:25-33, 46; 10:5-15, 48; 10:8, 46; 19:16-21, 46; 19:30, 176, 183; 25:1-13, 108; 25:31-45, 46
McCarter, N. D., 96, 160
McClanen, D., 110
McKusick, A., 77, 97, 102
McManus, W. E., 151
Means to an end, treating donors as, 24, 25–26
Medieval church, 58–60
Megachurches, 174
Mendicant beggars, 48
Mennonite Central Committee (MCC), 104, 175
Mennonite Church, Giving Project, 97, 119
Mentors, 156–158
The Message, 72
Messiah Village, 121

Micah, 6:6-8, 28, 42, 178–179
Middle Eastern cultures, 41
Miller, L., 75
Ministry, concept of, 5, 12. *See also* Christian organizations; Fundraising as ministry
Ministry of Development, The (Frank), 105
Ministry of Money, 110
Mission instructions: in Gospels, 48–49; Paul's, 50–52
Mission statement, 110
Mission work, holistic/noncompetitive perspective on, 87–98
Mixer, J. R., 95, 142
Money: "chasing" the, 136–137; importance of people versus, 32–34; involvement with, Biblical teachings on, 37–39, 53; necessity of having, 37–39, 53; pastors' reluctance to talk about, 160; as root of all evil, 38, 160; tainted, 92–93
Money for Ministry (Willmer), 102, 137
Money Matters (Hoge et al.), 99–100
Moore, R. L., 30
Moral authority, 62–63, 66–67
Moreno, M., 118
Moses and the Judges, 166
Motivation, donor: categories of, 39–40; classical philanthropic tradition and, 58; confronting wrong, 92–93; contemporary perspectives of, in United States, 65–67; current fundraising approaches and, 7; historical perspectives on, in United States, 63–65; manipulation of, 65, 67; meaningful participation and, 114–116, 123–126; in middle ages, 58–60, 66; New Testament perspective on, 45–47, 49–50, 51, 53–54, 57; Old Testament perspective on, 41–42; psychological research on, 39–40. *See also* Community obligation; Fear; Gratitude or love; Guilt; Justice and fairness; Self-aggrandizement; Self-interest
Motivation, fundraiser/fundraising, 11; in Christian fundraising, 18; need for consciousness about, 38–39; New Testament perspectives on, 47–53
Motivation, volunteer, 39–40
Mouw, R., 89–90, 95, 116, 117–118

N

Namaan, 174
Naming opportunities, 26
Napoli, A., 27, 74, 96–97, 109
National Conference of Catholic Bishops, 5–6
National Society of Fund Raising Executives (NSFRE), 4
Neighborly love, 60, 64
Neill, S. C., 154
New Testament, 11, 38, 45–53; on calling and identity, 166–168; perspective of, key points of, 52–53; perspective of, on asking, 47–53; perspective of, on giving, 45–47, 49–50, 51, 52, 53–54, 57. *See also specific book headings*
Newtithing Group, 73, 74
Nietzsche, F., 132
Ninety-Five Theses, 55–56
Non-Profit Times, 77
Northwestern University, 139
Nouwen, H., 27, 147, 148
Numbers, 18:21, 18:25-29, 42

O

Oates, M. J., 61–62, 100
Obligation to community. *See* Community obligation
Obstacles to fundraising as ministry, 122–127

O'Connor, F., 145

Old Testament, 40–45; on calling and identity, 166; community obligation in, 40–42, 43, 44; on giving in faith, 28; perspectives of, on giving and receiving, 40–42; practices in, 42–45; prophetic ministry in, 180–184. *See also specific book headings*

Olford, S., 74, 108

Operating principles, 20–21, 116, 133, 146, 186–187

Opportunity: fundraising based on, 136–137; giving based on, 45–46

Ordination, calling to, 169

Organizational consistency, 134

Organizational culture, 80, 187

Organizational planning. *See* Integrated organizational planning

Orientation for development staff, 105–106

Oxford English Dictionary, 179, 180

P

Palmer, P. J., 97–98

Parachurch organizations: defined, 2–3, 3; focus on, rationale for, 3, 5; growth in, 35–36; holistic perspective of, 96–97

Participation. *See* Donor participation; Program staff

Paul, the apostle, 39; on calling and identity, 165, 166–168; on fundraising, 39, 49–52, 54, 57, 114, 129; on holistic perspective, 87, 97; on motives for giving, 49–50, 51, 52, 53, 57

Payton, R. W., 1

People versus money resources, 32–34

Permanence, cultural preference for, 174–176

Person-to-person communication, 121

Personal identity, calling and, 166–167. *See also* Calling or vocation

Personal relationships, professionalism and, 170–171

Peterson, E. H., 116

Pezzullo, T. R., 107

Pfiffner, H. A., 72, 88, 96, 102, 119–120, 135

Pharisees, 45

Philanthropy: in classical culture, 47–48, 58–59; in middle ages, 58–60; as underpinning of traditional fundraising, 22

Philippians: 2:1-2, 87, 97; 4:17-18, 114

Pious response to integrating faith and practice, 155, 156

Planned giving, 138–139

Planning: of donors, 140–142; goal setting and, 75–82; strategic versus following the Holy Spirit, 107–108; theological differences in, 107–108, 112. *See also* Goals; Integrated organizational planning

Plato, 47

Political context. *See* Cultural and political context

"The poor, the widows, and the orphans," 38, 44

Positive thinking, 84–86

Poverty: Greek/Roman view of, 48; voluntary, in Gospel mission instructions, 48–49

Power issues, organizational, 142–143

Prayer: with and for donors, 101–102, 127–128; fundraiser, 153

Premiums, 31, 118, 126

Principles of fundraising as ministry, 20–21, 185–187. *See also* Abundance; Donor participation; Holistic perspective; Integrated organizational planning; Leadership; Theological assumptions and differences

Privacy, donor, 24

Professionalism, 166; calling and, 168–176; conflicts between calling and, 170–176; exclusion of faith from, 154–156; ideals of, versus Christian ideals, 174–176; roots of, 168–170

Program evaluation, 139–140

Program staff, fundraising involvement of, 79–80, 121–122

Prophet and prophecy, defined, 179–180

Prophetic ministry, 178–184

Prophets, the, 41, 42, 44, 178–179

Prospecting, 7, 24

Protection money, 41

Protestant Reformation, 55–56; fundraising practices after, 61, 66, 100–101; state churches after, 61

Protestantism, mainline: concept of stewardship in, 6, 63; history of fundraising in, 61, 62, 63–65, 100–101

Proverbs 14:31, 42

Psalms: 1:2, 42; 16:2, 43; 24:1, 43; 27:13, 99; 146:9, 42

Public affirmation, 7. See also Self-aggrandizement

Public library fundraising, 143

Q

Quotas, 90

R

Ransom money, 41

Raschko, M. B., 29, 73, 104, 111

Reactionary response to integrating faith and practice, 155, 156

Reciprocity, in New Testament perspective, 45–46, 53

Recognition: differences in, according to gift size, 26; information gifts as, 117–118, 126–127

Redding, J. C., 139

Referral: of donors to appropriate organizations, 91, 92; of hurting donors, 128

Reflection: on fundraising as a calling, 165–166, 172–176; need for, 21, 23; of spiritually mature leaders, 156–158, 161, 186–187. See also Theological assumptions and differences

Reflective practitioners, 21, 186–187

Rejoicing in triumphs of other ministries, 95–96

Representative stories, 25

Research study. See Christian fundraising research study

Resources: confidence in God's abundance of, 71–86, 93; Jesus' view of, 46; necessity of material, 37–39; people as, 32–34; prophetic approach to, 180–184; scarcity of, reality of, 71–72, 73; sharing of, among organizations, 93–95

Respect for donors, 24, 90–92

Revelation, Book of, 179

Rita, M., 122, 141

Roman Catholic Church, medieval, 58–60

Roman Catholic Church, United States: concept of stewardship in, 5–6; concept of vocation in, 169–170; decline in giving to, 151; history of fundraising in, 61–62, 64–65

Roman Catholic Diocese of Tucson, 9; development work of, 33–34; donor participation in, 115, 118; donor relationships in, 109, 126; holistic/noncompetitive approach of, 89, 94–95; planning approach of, 135–136; staff development at, 106, 158–159

Roman Empire and culture, 47–48, 58–59